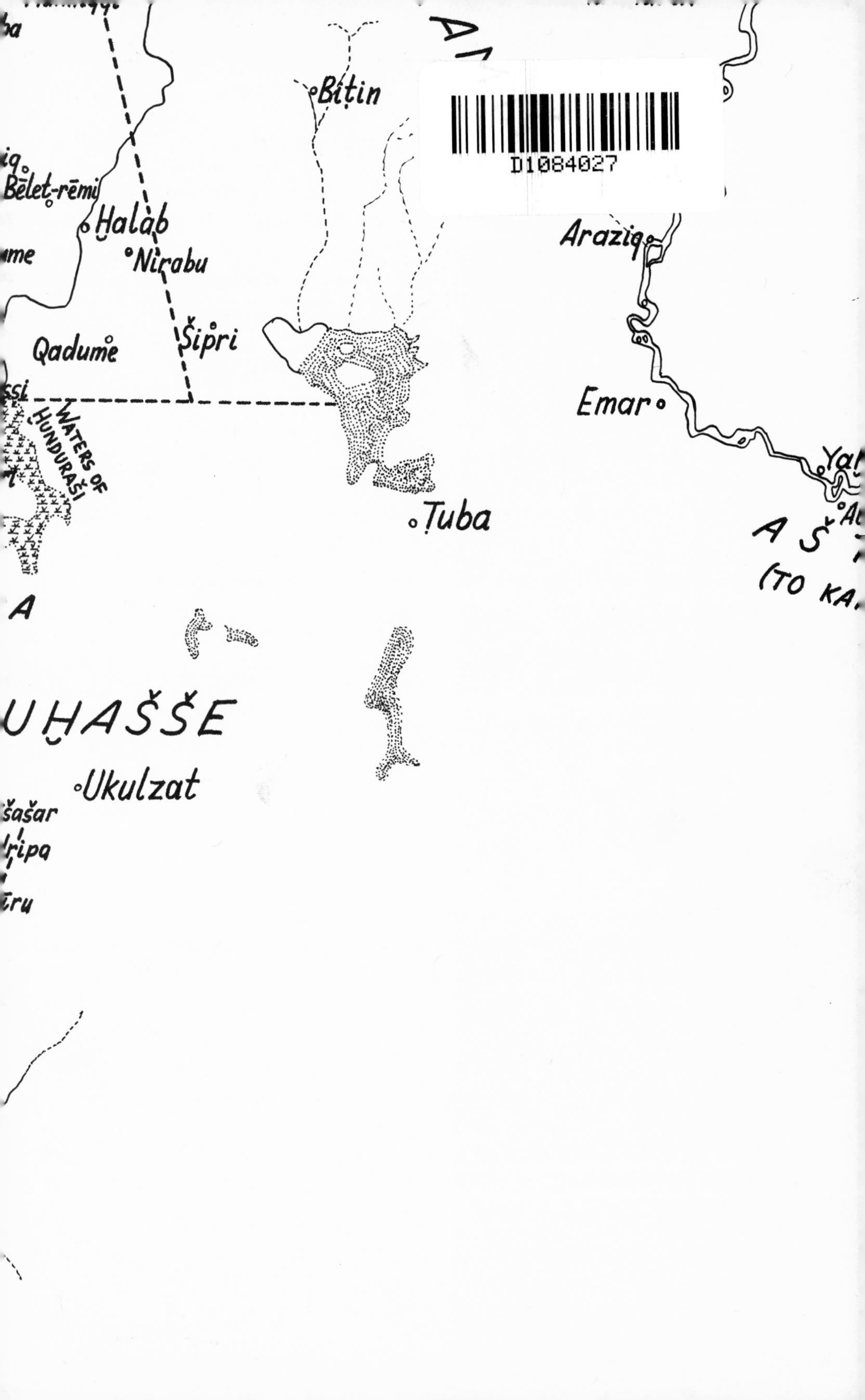
Biṭin
Bēlet-rēmi
Ḫalab
Nirabu
Šipri
Qadume
WATERS OF ḪUNDURAŠI
Araziq
Emar
Tuba
UḪAŠŠE
Ukulzat

UGARIT IN RETROSPECT

UGARIT IN RETROSPECT

Fifty Years of Ugarit and Ugaritic

Proceedings of the Symposium of the same title held at the University of Wisconsin at Madison, February 26, 1979, under the auspices of the Middle West Branch of the American Oriental Society and the Mid-West Region of the Society of Biblical Literature.

edited by GORDON DOUGLAS YOUNG

WINONA LAKE, INDIANA
EISENBRAUNS

Printed in the United States of America

Library of Congress Cataloging in Publication Data

Ugarit in retrospect.

Bibliography: p. 201.
Includes indexes.
1. Ugarit (Syria)—Congresses. 2. Ugaritic philology—Congresses. 3. Ugaritic literature—Relation to the Old Testament—Congresses. I. Young, Gordon D.
DS99.U35U35 939′.4 81-12664
ISBN 0-931464-07-2 AACR2

DEDICATION

We have assembled to honor you, Claude Schaeffer, on the jubilee of your discovery of the first Ugaritic tablets in 1929.

The alacrity with which you devoted your labors to Ugarit reflects the sound instinct of a great pioneer. You are gifted with that sixth sense known as "a nose" to sniff out what lies buried underground. Your persistence in continuing, decade after decade, to excavate an important site, when smaller spirits might have abandoned it, is eloquent testimony of your perseverance and boundless energy. When you extended your field work so productively to Enkomi because of the relationship between the two sites, you did so without abandoning Ugarit.

Many outstanding mounds have been unearthed during the half century of your campaigns, but none eclipses Ugarit. Your discovery of the earliest known form of the alphabet we still use, is of the greatest importance *per se*. But its significance is enhanced by the fact that it is the medium of myths and epics that bridge the gap between the earliest Greek and Hebrew literatures. Moreover, the Ugaritic tablets are couched in a language whose analysis has inaugurated a new era for Semitics in general, and for Hebrew philology in particular.

Ugaritica will continue to make a growing impact on our understanding of the synthesis that gave birth to classical Hebrew and Greek civilizations. But what has already been achieved through your published discoveries makes you the foremost archeological discoverer of our time.

This report of our symposium in your honor is our way of congratulating you on a tremendous task well done, and of wishing you and your gracious wife, Odile, many more happy years together in the enjoyment of health and further laurels.

Please accept the following papers and discussions as a token of our admiration and affection.

On behalf of all the participants in the symposium

Your devoted friend,

Cyrus Gordon

Cyrus Gordon

CONTENTS

ACKNOWLEDGMENTS

Several people deserve heartfelt thanks for assisting in the symposium and in the subsequent preparation of this volume: Conrad l'Heureux, my opposite number as secretary-treasurer of the Mid-West Region SBL, who helped in too many ways to mention; Keith Schoville, who as chairman of the Department of Hebrew and Semitic Languages at the University of Wisconsin chaired the local arrangements committee, and hosted the symposium; Mrs. Joan Gordon, who generously donated her picture of C. F. A. Schaeffer for the frontispiece; Mr. Brad Helms, a student at Purdue University, who helped in the huge task of indexing and proof-reading; Prof. Robert McDaniel, my colleague at Purdue, who devoted much time badly needed for his own work to problem-solving for my benefit; and Mrs. Joyce Good and her secretarial staff in Purdue's History Department.

A special word of thanks is offered to Prof. Cyrus Gordon, who composed the dedication of the volume and served as "capstone" chairman and presenter. His task—to organize a virtually extemporaneous commentary on the day's proceedings—was herculean, but carried off with the élan and grace for which he is famous.

Finally, a word of thanks also goes to Jim Eisenbraun and his staff in Winona Lake for the expeditious manner in which the manifold problems of preparing such a volume as this were solved.

PREFACE

This collection of essays grows out of a symposium entitled "Ugarit in Retrospect: Fifty Years of Ugarit and Ugaritic," held at the University of Wisconsin at Madison on February 26, 1979, as part of the annual joint meetings of the Middle West Branch of the American Oriental Society, and the Mid-West Region of the Society of Biblical Literature. As originally conceived by the editor and presented to the executive committees of both societies, the purpose of the symposium was to bring the disparate specialties of our members to bear on a single subject of interest to both societies. The approaching fiftieth anniversary of the opening of excavations at Ugarit offered an appropriate subject: a Ugaritic retrospective. This had the scholarly merit of offering something new and unprecedented in Ugaritic Studies—an opportunity to reflect upon the contributions of this most important site that has been enriching our various fields for quite some time. It also permitted a diversified group of scholars to blend their talents on a common theme, at an auspicious moment.

Although no special efforts at publicizing the event were undertaken beyond an announcement in Peter Craigie's *Newsletter for Ugaritic Studies*, it became apparent very quickly that we had tapped a reservoir of great interest. No one anticipated the immediate and enthusiastic response by specialists in Ugaritic studies and related fields or the rapidity with which the program was filled. What had begun with modest, regional expectations finished as an important international event, involving one Canadian, two French, three Israeli, and eight American scholars in major capacities. The enthusiasm of the program participants was shared by the audience, as attendance averaged over 150 people per session—record crowds for our meetings. It was, in short, an exciting day for Ugaritic Studies.

The symposium was organized into four sessions of papers, each emphasizing an area of major Ugaritic impact. Chairmen for the sessions came from the officers of the sponsoring societies, and their duties included the regulation of open discussion periods following the presentation of papers. A fifth session, which served as a capstone, featured an overview of the day's proceedings by Cyrus Gordon and shorter assessments and suggestions for future research by four of the panelists. The Program was as follows:

Session I: "Ugarit: History and Archaeology," Keith Schoville, University of Madison at Wisconsin, presiding.

1. "The Excavations at Ras Shamra and Their Place in the Current Archaeological Picture of Ancient Syria," Rudolph Dornemann, Milwaukee Public Museum.
2. "Ras Shamra: Nouvelles Perspectives des Fouilles," Jean-Claude Margueron, University of Strasbourg.
3. "Ugarit and the Great Powers," Michael Astour, Southern Illinois University at Edwardsville.

Session II: "Ugarit and the Bible," Conrad l'Heureux, University of Dayton, presiding.

1. "The Cult of the Dead at Ugarit," Marvin Pope, Yale University.
2. "Ugarit and the Bible: Progress and Regress in Fifty Years of Literary Study," Peter Craigie, University of Calgary.
3. "The Geographical Setting of the *Aqht* Story and Its Ramifications," Baruch Margalit, University of Haifa.

Session III: "Ugarit: Language and Literature," Gordon Young, Purdue University, presiding.

1. "Folklore Scholarship and Ugaritic Literature," Jack Sasson, University of North Carolina at Chapel Hill.
2. "A Formal Approach to Ugaritic Literature," Baruch Levine, New York University.
3. "Ugaritic and Hebrew Metrics," Dennis Pardee, Oriental Institute, University of Chicago.

Session IV: "The World of Ugarit," Gösta Ahlström, University of Chicago, presiding.

1. "Ugarit, Canaan, and Egypt: New Evidence from Aphek on the 13th Century B.C.E.," David Owen, Cornell University.
2. "Recent Epigraphic Discoveries at Ras Shamra from 1971 to 1974, and at Ras Ibn Hani in 1977 and 1978," Pierre Bordreuil, Institut d'Études Sémitiques, Collège de France.
3. "Egyptian Evidence for Ugarit," Rafael Giveon, Tel Aviv University.
4. "Ugarit: A Canaanite Thalassocracy," Elisha Linder, University of Haifa.

Session V: "Ugarit in Retrospect and Prospect," Cyrus Gordon, New York University, presiding and speaking. Additional commentary by Dennis Pardee, Michael Astour, Marvin Pope, and Rudolph Dornemann.

In organizing the symposium, we were constrained by the fact that other sessions of the meetings were in progress during the day, and we wished to have minimum subject conflicts between those sessions and the symposium. As a consequence, the order of papers in this volume does not follow the order of papers in the symposium. Here we group the papers dealing with History and Archaeology, and those dealing with Language and Literature, concluding with a slightly edited transcript of the tape recording of Session V.

We hoped from the start that the proceedings of the symposium merited publication, since nothing approaching such a collective examination of the current state of Ugaritic Studies had been done. All participants felt that such an effort was needed to help refocus scholarly attentions as Ugaritic Studies entered their second half-century. Unfortunately, it was necessary for Baruch Levine to withdraw his paper from the volume, since he felt his work was still too preliminary for a formal presentation. An abstract of his contribution is included, as are some of his pertinent remarks in Session V.

That two years have passed since the symposium took place is also unfortunate, but the positive result is the inclusion of some papers that were just preliminary studies in 1979. The subject, however, is no less timely that it was in 1979, and the publication of this volume is a happy conclusion to an extraordinary event.

GORDON D. YOUNG
Secretary-Treasurer
Middle West Branch
American Oriental Society

Purdue University
Department of History
West Lafayette, Indiana

May, 1981

Part One

HISTORY & ARCHAEOLOGY

UGARIT AND THE GREAT POWERS

MICHAEL C. ASTOUR

Southern Illinois University
at Edwardsville

The Geographical Location of Ugarit

Ugarit is a very old urban site. The beginnings of its settlement go back deep into the Neolithic Age. It was already a large city in the Early Bronze Age, and it kept growing until it became the principal commercial center of Late Bronze Northern Syria. This role was determined to a great extent by the geographical location of Ugarit. It was the terminal of one of the main highways of the region, which connected the interior of Northern Syria with the Mediterranean coast via the Bdāmā Pass in the long and steep Bargylus Range. It possessed, less than a mile away, a harbor on the shore of a small but convenient bight (now Minet el-Beiḍa),[1] and controlled a few secondary anchorages north and south of it. This made Ugarit a natural intermediary between Northern Syria and the islands and littorals of the Mediterranean. It also stood on the great coastal highway of Syria which led from Egypt to Anatolia via the Amanus and Taurus passes. The plain around Ugarit was, and still is, fertile and produced wheat and barley, while the foothills and slopes of Mt. Bargylus were covered with vineyards and olive groves. Higher elevations of the mountain provided timber for construction and shipbuilding. The sea was the source of murex snails for the production of valuable purple dye.

Though Ugarit never became a major power, neither was it a mere city-state of Phoenician and Canaanite type. Its territory, even before the great expansion by Šuppiluliumaš, was wide enough to consider it a medium-size state by Syrian standards. In addition to the capital, it contained open villages, and—as evidenced by the presence of several

[1]Its Ugaritic name was Maʾḫadu, cf. Astour (1970). No remains older than the fifteenth century have been found in the excavated segment of the port settlement, but cf. Astour (1973) 18.

sizable mounds and by statistical data of Ugaritian administrative texts—real towns with developed commerce and crafts.

The original territory of Ugarit, confined by the sea in the west, the crest of the Bargylus in the east, the uplands of Basīṭ and Baer in the north, and including the plain of Ǧablah in the south, measured approximately 2200 sq. km. Thus, the political history of Ugarit is that of a wealthy but second-rank state which had to adapt itself to the interplay of first-rank powers in the Syrian arena. Ugaritian records discovered to date do not go back beyond the fourteenth century,[2] but the rare mentions of Ugarit in extraneous sources, and certain indirect indications in local archaeological and epigraphic documentation, allow us to perceive the outlines of some earlier events and conditions.

Ugarit in the Age of the Ebla Archives

The earliest references to Ugarit are found in the amazing newly discovered archives of Ebla (Tell Mardīḫ). Their chronology is an object of controversy between P. Matthiae, the archaeologist, and G. Pettinato, the epigraphist, but both agree that they belong to the third millennium. To form a concrete image of Ebla's political role in the Early Bronze Age, one must await the publication of more reports, studies, and texts. But from what the discoverers and explorers of Ebla have already disclosed, one gains the impression that Ebla was the earliest great power in Western Asia, antedating the empire of Sargon of Akkad. It has long been known that, for Sargon, the land of Ebla extended "as far as the Cedar Forest and the Silver Mountains,"[3] but it is only now that it became clear that not only are the Silver Mountains identical with the Taurus, but the Cedar Forest is indeed the Lebanon.[4] We see now the real meaning of Gudea's attribution of Uršu, in northernmost Syria, to the "mountains of Ebla."[5] Whether Ebla was in the third millennium the capital of an actual empire,[6] or only of a loosely knit zone under its

[2]Hence the title of the first book on Ugaritian history—Liverani's *Storia di Ugarit nell'età degli archivi politici* (1962). An earlier palace (sixteenth-fifteenth century) was unearthed in Ras Shamra (cf. Schaeffer [1970], [1972]), but contained no written material.

[3]Hirsch (1963) 38.

[4]The identification of the Cedar Forest with the Lebanon (as distinct from the Cedar Mountain = Amanus) was advanced by Poebel (1914) 223-24, and more recently by Bottéro *ap*. Drower & Bottéro (1968) 324.

[5]Gudea's Statue B inscription, V:53-57, in Thureau-Dangin (1907) 70-71; transl. A. L. Oppenheim, *ANET*, 268-69. This, more than any other piece of evidence, made scholars think, prior to the discovery of the Tell Mardīḫ archives, that Ebla was located in the vicinity of Uršu (Gaziantep).

[6]Cf. the title of Matthiae's book *Ebla: Un impero ritrovato* (1977).

hegemony,[7] is a matter of terminology. A Syrian kingdom which concluded treaties with the distant Assur and Ḫamazi, claimed (with however much right) sovereignty over Kaniš,[8] and fought a war with Mari for the domination of the Euphrates valley,[9] must have been a truly important political entity.

In the recently published great Eblean tablet which Pettinato called "The Geographical Atlas of the Ancient Near East,"[10] but which, in English, should rather be defined as a "Gazetteer," *U*$_5$*-ga-ra-at*^{KI} appears as the fifth of its 279 entries. This early attestation is of great interest for historical as well as morphological toponymy,[11] but it tells us nothing about the political and economic relations between Ugarit and Ebla. Pending the publication of pertinent source material, we can only quote Pettinato's statement[12] that Syria in the age of the Ebla archives consisted, besides Ebla itself, of a few medium-size states, among which he named Uršu, Hamath, and Ugarit, and several small ones. We are already dealing with the pattern that will become familiar from Ugarit's subsequent history. In the meantime, we may guess that the copper from Alašiya, which is recorded in certain Tell Mardīḫ tablets,[13] was imported to Ebla by the way of Ugarit which, of all ports of the Syrian coast, is the closest to both Cyprus and Tell Mardīḫ.

The Beginning of Ugarit's Connection With Egypt

At the time of the Third Dynasty of Ur, Ebla, along with a few other states of Syria, maintained relations with the neo-Sumerian empire, but seems to have lost its preponderant role in Syria. Šu-Sin, the last but one king of the dynasty, claimed sovereignty over Ebla, Mari, Tuttul (on the Balīḫ), a place whose name started with *ma*, followed by Urgiš (in North Mesopotamia), Mugiš (the area of Alalaḫ on the lower Orontes), EZEN. NI-^{d}IM,[14] [Gub]la (Byblos), Abarnum (in northernmost Mesopotamia),

[7]As expounded by G. Pettinato in his report to the joint meeting of AAR-SBL—Midwest branch of AOS at St. Louis, October 30, 1976, and in (1977b) 235.

[8]Listed as No. 12 in TM 75.G.2136 (a list of 17 countries "in the hand of the king of Ebla"), in Pettinato (1978) 51-2. Cf. *idem* (1976) 48 on Kaniš in economic texts of Tell Mardīḫ. [A. Archi and P. Garelli deny that the locality in question corresponds to Kaniš in Cappadocia. Its very name may be read differently (July 1980).]

[9]TM 75.G.2367, summarized or excerpted by Pettinato (1977a).

[10]TM 75.G.2231, published by Pettinato (1978) with parallel entries in its Abū Ṣalabīḫ version.

[11]Cf. Albright (1961) 352 n. 9 on the origin of the toponym *Ugarit.*

[12]See n. 7 above, and Pettinato (1977b) 235.

[13]Pettinato (1976) 46 and report quoted in n. 7 above.

[14]Ideographic writing of "festival of the Storm-god"; unknown.

and "the mountain where they cut cedars" (Mt. Amanus).[15] Uršu, not mentioned in this list, regularly sent messengers to Ur. Ugarit is not attested in Ur III records, and this is strange in view of the frequent mentions of the much more distant Byblos.

In the period after the fall of Ur III, kings of the Twelfth Dynasty of Egypt became interested in Northern Syria. The names of the local cities are not found in the Execration Texts, they were too far to be feared, but Egypt evidently maintained with them some kind of diplomatic relations.[16] A sphinx with a dedication from Princess Ita, daughter of Amenemhat II (1929-1895), was found in the temple of Ninegal at Qaṭna;[17] another one, with an inscription of Amenemhat II (1842-1797), at Neirab near Aleppo.[18] The old temple of Dagan at Ugarit also received several ex-votos from Egypt: another sphinx of Amenemhat III, a figurine of the vizier Senusert-anḫ with his mother and sister, and a bust of an unidentified queen of the Twelfth Dynasty.[19] W. A. Ward saw in these monuments "tokens of Egyptian friendship to the local gods"; they "do not necessarily indicate an Egyptian military occupation nor a political domination over local affairs," but "the towns where these royal monuments were found were of no small importance. Ugarit, of course, was a great commercial center," and so were also Qaṭna and Aleppo, which made all three cities important to the Egyptians.[20]

The presence of gifts from Egyptian royalty or high officials at Ugarit indicates that the city was involved in commercial relations with Egypt of the Middle Kingdom.

Ugarit at the Time of the Hegemony of Yamḫad

Soon afterwards (how soon, depends on the chronology of Western Asia one chooses),[21] the abundant royal archives of Mari begin to throw light on the new political configuration in Northern Syria. After a gap of about a generation, the thread is picked up by the much more modest archive of Alalaḫ VII. Once again, as in the period of Eblean preponderance, all of Northern Syria was loosely united into a kind of a feudal monarchy under the scepter of a supreme ruler, and once again the central plain of the region formed its political nucleus. But this time the capital moved some 60 km to the northeast, to Ḫalab, a city which is

[15]Published by Civil (1967) 37-38.

[16]As early as the time of Amenemhat I and Senusert I, if one may rely on the story of Sinuhe.

[17]Du Mesnil du Buisson (1935) 17.

[18]Ward (1961) 132-33.

[19]Schaeffer (1933) pl. XV; (1939) 21.

[20]Ward (1961) 131, 134, 136.

[21]This author follows the "low" chronology.

never mentioned (at least under its historical name) in the Ebla records.[22] It was now the residence of the Great Kings of Yamhad (originally, in all likelihood, an Amorite tribal name). The history and political geography of Yamḫad cannot be expounded in detail within the framework of this paper, but our topic requires at least a short summary of what is known on its structure and its role as a great power.

An often quoted letter from Mari[23] expresses most clearly the power relation between five major states of the Fertile Crescent (not counting Mari itself). While the rulers of Babylon, Larsa, Ešnunna, and Qaṭna are followed by ten to fifteen kings each, Yarim-Lim, the ruler of Yamḫad, is followed by twenty kings. Another letter from Mari revealed as its "most surprising historical fact . . . the role played by the king of Aleppo in the Transtigridian regions of Dēr and Diniktum," and made it certain that "the kingdom of Aleppo has established itself as the first political power of that period in the Fertile Crescent."[24]

The territories under the overlordship of Yamḫad can be divided into three groups. There was the immediate domain of the Great King around the capital city, with exclaves in peripheral areas. It was surrounded by a ring of inner vassal states, most of which were appanages of the royal house. Their number and borders fluctuated, but in the latter part of Yamḫad's history the following states of this group are known by name: Alalaḫ, Niḫi(n), Ebla, Biṭin, Ṭuba, Naštarbi, and Emar. Then came the outer vassals, or peripheral client states, i.e. essentially independent political entities, some of them with a longer history than the upstart kingdom of Yamḫad, which were forced, or voluntarily chose, to accept the protection and leadership of the hegemonic power in control of their communication lines. To this group belonged Ḫaššum, Zarwar, Uršum, Carchemish, Ugarit, the tribal state of the Rabbeans, and Tunip. The total area under the suzerainty of Yamḫad can be estimated as approximately 43,000 sq. km.

The evidence for considering Ugarit a peripheral client state of Yamḫad is of circumstantial nature. A letter of Ḫammurapi, king of Yamḫad, to Zimri-Lim, king of Mari, sheds light on the international status of Ugarit: "The 'man' of Ugarit wrote to me as follows, 'Show me the house of Zimri-Lim: I desire to see (it).' Now, then, I am sending you his servant."[25] The fact that the king of Ugarit maintained relations with

[22] I owe this information to Prof. Pettinato. His suggestion that *Ì-li-bî*[KI], No. 270 of the "Gazetteer" (TM 75.G.2231 rev. I:17; *Il-íb*[KI] in the Abū Ṣalabīḫ version), may represent Ḫalab is not very probable because the etymological *ḫ* in that name (Ugar. *ḫlb* "hill," Akk. *ḫalbu* "forest") would not have been elided in cuneiform transcription. [There was an *Ilib* near Sippar.]

[23] Dossin (1938) 117.

[24] Dossin (1956) 67, 69.

[25] Dossin *ap*. Schaeffer (1939) 16.

Mari through the intermediary of the king of Yamḫad is an indication that (in the words of W. F. Albright) "Ugarit was tributary to Aleppo under Hammurabi."[26] The right of direct relations with foreign powers was indeed, in the ancient Near East, a prerogative of fully sovereign monarchs but not, in principle, of vassal and client states.[27]

Another letter to a king of Mari (almost certainly Zimri-Lim) recalls his trip to Ugarit.[28] At that time Mari and Yamḫad were closely allied with each other, and a diplomatic visit of Ugarit by a Mariote ruler implies that it belonged to the same political alignment. The "tin tablet" from Mari[29] mentions Ugarit twice: as the residence of two Mariote tin dealers and, more interestingly, as the place where tin from Mari is delivered "to the Caphtorian" and "to the interpreter," who was no doubt conversant in the Caphtorian (Cretan) language of the time. The objects defined in Mari texts as "Caphtorian" must have reached Mari via Ugarit.[30] Since two of the three land roads which connected Ugarit with the outer world passed through the territory of Yamḫad, it was in the best interests of the commercial port city to seek accommodation with the powerful neighbor in its hinterland; and this, according to the political conventions of the time, had to be formalized as a client-patron relationship.

Ugarit is mentioned only once in the texts of Alalaḫ VII: as the place of origin of one Puruqqa,[31] whom K. A. Kitchen raised to the dignity of a king of Ugarit,[32] but who was merely a purchaser of wool at Alalaḫ.[33]

Northern Syria Between Ḫatti, Mitanni, and Egypt

A profound change in the political situation of Northern Syria began in the second quarter of the sixteenth century. Two new powerful states arose on its borders: the Hittite kingdom to the North, and the kingdom of Mitanni/Ḫurri/Ḫanigalbat to the east. Ḫattušiliš I opened a series of destructive Hittite campaigns against Yamḫad and its client

[26]Albright (1940) II, 26.

[27]Cf. Finet (1964) 134 (on Talḫayum's relationship to Mari), and EA 9:31-35 (Babylonian protest to the Pharaoh for receiving diplomatic letters from Assur which Babylonia considered its vassal).

[28]Jean (1939a) 112; (139b) 67; quoted in *CAD*, B, 211, *s.v. bēru* B.

[29]A.1270, published by Dossin (1970), lines 8 and 31.

[30]Cf. Astour (1973) 18-21.

[31]AT 358:6.

[32]Kitchen (1977) *pass.*

[33]Kitchen (1977) 131 n. 6, refers, *i.e.*, to Klengel, *GS* II, 334, but all that is said there is that Puruqqa was "ein Lieferant von Wolle." It would seem from the context that he was a buyer rather than a deliverer of wool, but this changes nothing in his social position.

states; the Hurrians of North Mesopotamia immediately entered the fray on several fronts, fighting the Hittites on their own and as allies and protectors of Yamḫad. Confronted with the new extra-Syrian great powers, Yamḫad could not maintain for very long its status of "Great Kingship." It bravely fought in defense of its peripheral vassals and then for its own survival, but the protracted and terribly destructive war weakened it so much that it had to submit itself either to its Hittite enemies or to its Hurrian allies; it did both in turn, and a junior branch of the dynasty even tried briefly to restore the independence of Ḫalab after the death of its captor, Muršiliš I. At that time a third great power made its appearance on the North Syrian scene: the Egyptian king Thutmose I, about 1520, marched against "the land which is called Mitanni," reached the Euphrates, and returned via Nii, the southwestern area of Yamḫad. But at the end, the pretender to the throne of Ḫalab, Idrimi, had to return to Mittannian vassalage. He was confirmed as a king, but no longer a sovereign one; he was allowed to keep the historical capital, Ḫalab, but had to move his residence to the less prestigious Alalaḫ. The historic name *Yamḫad* was no longer used; Idrimi and his successors had to satisfy themselves with the title of "king of Alalaḫ" or "king of Mukiš."

The Great Kingdom of Yamḫad was now replaced by what may be called the Confederacy of Mukiš-Nuḫašše-Nii. Its territory no longer included the old peripheral client states, except, as we may assume from indirect geographical evidence, Ḫaššu. Hurrian influence, which had been very noticeable under the kings of Yamḫad, was now greatly strengthened by the political prestige of Mitanni. The submission, around 1500, of Alalaḫ and its confederates opened for Mitanni a road to central and southern Syria. Tunip, Qaṭna, Qidši, the areas of Amqi, Damascene, Bashan, Galilee, and most of the rest of Palestine rapidly became vassals of Mitanni, or were taken over by Mitannian governors and garrisons. When the Egyptians, under Thutmose III, returned to Palestine only twenty years later, they called the country *Ḫuru*, i.e., land ruled by Hurrians. Even a hundred years later, under Egyptian domination, Hurrian and Indo-Aryan names prevailed among the rulers of Palestine and of southern and central Syria. And it must be said that, in the triangular struggle for Syria between Ḫatti, Mitanni, and Egypt, it was Mitannian rule that was preferred by the majority of local princes.[34]

But no Hurrian influence can be discerned in the toponymy and anthroponymy of Phoenicia north of Achshaph, of the heartland of

[34]This historical outline is much too condensed to be provided with systematic references and substantiations of this particular point. See, in the near future, the proceedings of the XXIVe R.A.I. (Paris, July 1977), which was entirely devoted to the Hurrians, including our paper on Hurrians in Northern Syria. [Appeared as *RHA* 36.]

Amurru (the plains of ᶜAkkār and Buqeᶜiya and the southern Bargylus) in the Amarna Age, and very little of it is evident in the original territory of Ugarit and that of its southern neighbor Siyannu-Ušnatu. One cannot but conclude that the Mitannian expansion did not cross the ranges of Bargylus and Lebanon, and that Ugarit, freed by the stormy events of the sixteenth century from its allegiance to Yamḫad, remained independent from Mitanni as well.

Ugarit's First Alliance With Ḫatti

A letter of the Hittite conqueror Šuppiluliumaš to Niqmaddu, king of Ugarit, written ca. 1366, at the beginning of the "First Syrian War,"[35] contains a tantalizingly brief reference to events of an indefinite past: "As previously thy ancestors were friends and not foes of Ḫatti, now thou, Niqmandu, be in the same way a foe of my foes and a friend of my friends!"[36]

"But at what period [did it happen]?" asked Nougayrol, the publisher of Ugarit's diplomatic archives. "Could it go back to the activities in Syria of a prince Pitḫana[37] . . . or should we rather think of the times when Thutmose IV retreated from Northern Syria while Ḫattušil II showed his strength there? The insurrection of Ugarit against its Egyptian garrison, quickly suppressed by Amenophis II . . . could have been, in that case, a forerunner of a short-lasting political shift."[38]

Neither of the events mentioned by Nougayrol actually happened. The Pitḫanaš who was active in Syria was not the early Hittite king of that name[39] but an official of Šuppiluliumaš who, during the "Second Syrian Foray" (ca. 1368), was charged with the transfer of several cities from Alalaḫ to Tunip.[40] Thutmose IV did not retreat from Northern Syria. On the contrary, he gained some ground there. The presumed king Ḫattušiliš II never existed.[41] There was no Egyptian garrison at Ugarit at the time of Amenhotep II, nor did his reign coincide with a Hittite advance into Syria.[42]

[35]Thus according to the terminology of Kitchen (1962). It corresponds to the "Second Syrian War" of Goetze (1965) and the "Second Syrian Campaign" of Kitchen (1966).

[36]PRU IV 1:7-13. We follow the sequential numeration of the texts in PRU III and IV by Dietrich and Loretz (1972).

[37]With whom Nougayrol linked the origin of the *ḫarranāti ša* ᵐ*Pitḫana* on the border of the territory granted to Niqmaddu by Šuppiluliumaš.

[38]Nougayrol, *PRU IV*, 27 n. 2.

[39]The father of Anittaš of Kuššara, who was a contemporary of the Old Assyrian colonies in Cappadocia.

[40]KUB III 16 obv. 24 (= Weidner, *PDK*, 136, No. 10). Cf. Astour (1969) 392, 402.

[41]Otten (1968); cf. Astour (1972a).

[42]See the relevant sections below.

Two historically attested periods of Hittite military presence in Syria can be understood in the quoted passage: the Syrian wars of Ḫattušiliš I and Muršiliš I between ca. 1570 and 1530, and the incursion of Tudhaliyaš, the founder of the Hittite New Kingdom, who rose to the throne ca. 1415, and is credited by the preamble of the Talmi-Šarruma treaty with defeating Mittani and destroying Ḫalab.[43] Each of these three kings was responsible for a full or partial destruction of Alalaḫ: Ḫattušiliš put an end to Level VII of that city,[44] Muršiliš to its Level VI, and Tudḫaliyaš limited himself to burning the royal palace of Level IV.[45] Alalaḫ was so close to the northern borders of Ugarit that each appearance there of a Hittite army would be a cause of alarm for the prosperous maritime city, and would move it to seek accommodation with the powerful invader. At the time of Tudḫaliyaš's incursion, however, Ugarit probably belonged already to the zone of Egyptian supremacy. The Syrian wars of the sixteenth century seem a more likely time for Ugarit's pro-Hittite stand.

Ugarit in the Neutral Zone of Syria

The Hittite retreat from Syria under Ḫantiliš opened a century of Egypto-Mitannian contest for the control of the region. We have seen the first sweeping moves: ca. 1520, an Egyptian army on the Euphrates; ca. 1500, most of Syria and Palestine under Mitannian domination. In 1482, Thutmose III started the re-conquest and expansion of Egyptian possessions in Asia. By 1475, he controlled Palestine and the seacoast as far north as Ullaza and Ṣumer. From these bases he attacked Central Syria through the Eleutherus Valley. Thutmose III's greatest triumph came in 1472: the conquest of Qidši, Qaṭna, Sinzar, the area of Ḫalab, and for the second time in Egyptian history, he reached the Euphrates. In 1471 he captured cities in Nuḫašše. But the very next year all of Northern Syria was lost, and Thutmose's attempt to recover it was repelled by a Mitannian army as far south as Ariʾana, which we have reasons to locate at ᶜAšārneh on the Orontes south of Apamea (Nii).[46] The annals for 1469 and 1468 are lost, but in 1467 they record new battles in Nuḫašše, and tribute from Alalaḫ. The second Egyptian domination of Northern Syria

[43]KBo I 6 (and fragments of duplicates) = Weidner, *PDK* No. 6.

[44]He stated it himself in his *Res Gestae*, KBo X 2 obv. I 15 (Hittite version), KBo X 1 obv. 6 (Akkadian version).

[45]This is our inference from the chronological coincidence between the time of Tudḫaliyaš's activities in Syria and the end of the palace archives of Level IV, which encompassed the reigns of Niqmepa and Ilim-ilimma II—two generations beginning *ca.* 1460 (after the end of Thutmose III's brief domination in Northern Syria); cf. Astour (1972a) 108 and n. 58.

[46]See provisionally Astour (1977) 62, 64.

was almost as brief as the first: in 1463, the last recorded campaign in Thutmose III's annals, the Egyptians were again battling the Mitannians around Tunip and Qidši. Soon afterward, Tunip reverted to Mitannian overlordship.[47]

Curiously enough, Ugarit is never mentioned in Thutmose III's annals, not even among the foreign states which sent him diplomatic gifts. Nor does the city appear in that Pharaoh's other inscriptions, or in those of his subordinates. It is also missing in the great Naharina List of Thutmose III which enumerates not only places in Northern Syria within the reach of Egyptian advances into that region, but also several localities in other parts of the Mitannian Empire. Now the absence of Ugarit from the Naharina List would, in itself, be of little or no significance in view of the large number of destroyed entries in the only extant copy of it.[48] But along with it are missing—in the list as well as in the rest of Thutmose III's records—three other state capitals of the North Syrian coast: Arwad, Ušnatu, and Siyannu. Moreover, we know the names of at least 106 towns and villages which were located within the old borders of Ugarit, and in the kingdom of Siyannu-Ušnatu.[49] None of them can be detected in Thutmose III's annals or in the Naharina List.[50] We are dealing here with an obvious pattern. Such a persistent *silentium* is a strong *argumentum* in itself, but it is strengthened by what the documents *do* say. Once one crosses the northern border of Ugarit into the possessions of Alalaḫ, or the Bargylus into other lands of the Confederacy of Mukiš-Nuḫašše-Nii, names of local towns and villages show up in great numbers—too great to be listed here.[51]

If we recall that no Hurrian influence comparable to the powerful Hurrian impact upon Alalaḫ of Level IV is discernible at Ugarit, one must come to the conclusion that the whole territory north of Ṣumur, south of Alalaḫ, and west of the Bargylus, formed a neutral zone between Egypt and Mitanni during most of the fifteenth century—a situation that was recognized by Miss M. Drower.[52] We do not know how this

[47]According to the treaty between Niqmepa of Alalaḫ (ca. 1460-1430) and Ir-Tešub of Tunip, AT 2 (translation by E. Reiner, *ANET*, 531-32). On the location of Tunip see Astour (1977).

[48]Out of its original 270 entries, only 170, or 63%, have been preserved.

[49]See n. 73 below.

[50]There are two possible exceptions: No. 140, *Ḫa/Ḫu-ra-ka-ḫi*, which resembles the Ugaritian *Ḫurika* (syllabic form of alphabetic *Ḫrsbᶜ*, now Ḫraṣbō), and No. 190: *Ta-rə-b* , which resembles Ugaritian *Taribu* (now Tirbeh). However, the former may also correspond to modern Ḥarāki east of the Čebel Zāwiyeh, and the latter, to *Intarawe* (AT) = *Ellitarbi* (NAss), now el-Atārib.

[51]For the correspondences between the Naharina List and the Alalaḫ texts see Albright & Lambdin (1957); Helck (1962) 142-48. Astour (1963) is now obsolete in many details and should not be used for references.

[52]"It is significant that Arwad and Ugarit are not mentioned among the conquests of Thutmosis III and Amenophis II, and would appear to have played no role in Egyptian

came about, but the neutral status of the zone was evidently respected by both great powers.[53] We can understand why place names of the neutral zone were left out of the Naharina List: the towns in question were neither subjects nor enemies, and from the point of view of Egyptian imperial claims they were best to be ignored.

Is Ugarit Mentioned By Amenhotep II?

But what about the alleged mention of Ugarit as a city occupied by an Egyptian garrison in the Karnak stele of Thutmose III's successor Amenhotep II (1452-1426)? There is a virtual consensus that *ʾĀ-ku-tá-ṯɜ́*,[54] is just a misspelling of *ʾA-ku-ri-ta*, the normal Egyptian rendering of Ugarit.[55] Only two authors objected to this identification, in part for wrong reasons: S. Yeivin[56] and M. Drower.[57] We do not hesitate to join the minority in decisively rejecting the idea that the place mentioned in line 11 of the Karnak stele[58] has anything to do with Ugarit.

Let us see in what context it occurs there. During his first expedition to Syria, in the seventh year of his reign (1447), Amenhotep II forded the Orontes not far from the territory of hostile Qaṭna on the 26th of the first summer month.[59] The stele is silent about the following fourteen days: its next entry reports that on the 10th of the second summer month, the king and his troops came to the city of Niya "on the return of His Majesty southward to Egypt." Niya (also known as Niḫi and Nii) has been correctly identified, since A. Gardiner,[60] with Qalᶜat

---

history until the reign of Amenophis III; both cities appear to have enjoyed a special treaty relationship with Egypt during the early part of the fourteenth century, for the benefit of their mutual maritime trade," Drower (1968a) 475.

[53]A vase with the cartouche of Thutmose III was allegedly found at Ugarit: Nougayrol, *PRU IV*, 28; Liverani (1962) 62; but this does not necessarily point to Egyptian sovereignty over Ugarit at that time; neutrality would have been as favorable for trade as political dependence. [Moreover, R. Giveon, in his paper at the present Symposium, believes that this find, never published or listed in excavation reports, is apocryphic.]

[54]The last sign (Gardiner V 13) can be read either way in group writing. In the former reading, it renders the Semitic *taw*, in the latter, the Semitic *samek* or, less commonly, *zayin* or *ṣade*. Moreover, Egyptian *k*-holding signs transcribed both *gimmel* and *kaph*, and sometimes even *qoph*.

[55]It seems that this equation started with Brugsch, years before the cuneiform mention of Ugarit was first found in an Amarna letter. In more recent times, it was shared by, *i. a.*, Schaeffer (1939) 27; Gardiner (1947) I, 165*; (1961) 201; S. Smith (1949) 53; Edel (1953) 150-53; Nougayrol, *PRU IV*, 27 n. 2, 28; Helck (1962) 157; Drioton & Vandier (1962) 407; Garelli (1969) 153; Klengel, *GS* II, 336-37.

[56]Yeivin (1966) 25; (1967) 122.

[57]Drower (1968a) 460-61; (1968b) 133.

[58]The Memphis stele of Amenhotep II is an almost identical duplicate of the Karnak stele. A full, commented, comparative edition of both steles was presented by Edel (1953).

[59]The ford in question is no doubt that of Restan, 15 km southwest of Qaṭna.

[60]Gardiner (1947) I, 166*-68*.

el-Muḍīq (Apamea). The itinerary of Amenhotep II during the unreported fortnight can be hypothetically reconstructed on the basis of a short topographic list of his,[61] but here it will be enough to note that it carried him around the massif of Ǧebel Zāwiyeh. Now comes the essential part. Having arrived at Niya, "His Majesty heard that some Asians who were in the city of ʾ*Ā-ku-tá*/*ṯə̄* entered into a conspiracy to work out a plan to eject His Majesty's garrison from his city, and to turn about the face of the [prince of ʾ*Ā-ku-tá*/*ṯə̄*]: who was faithful to His Majesty." Amenhotep II came to ʾ*Ā-ku-tá*/*ṯə̄*, defeated the rebels, pacified it, and "returned from there in joy, because all this land was his subject." Then the 20th of the second summer month finds him already in a place called *Ṯə-rə-ḫə* on the road from Niya to Qidši, and on the way back to Egypt via the Biqaᶜ and Palestine.

Thus the stele provides us with very precise calendar dates: within ten days, from the 10th to the 20th of the second summer month, Amenhotep II and his army marched from Niya to ʾ*Ā-ku-tá*/*ṯə̄*, spent at least a day fighting the rebels, returned to Niya, and covered an additional day's march from there. So the question is not whether ʾ*Ā-ku-tá*/*ṯə̄* could or could not be a distortion of ʾ*A-ku-ri-ta* (*Ugarit*), but whether a round-trip Qalᶜat el-Muḍīq—Ras Shamra—Qalᶜat el-Muḍīq is feasible in nine days. Of all the authors who accepted the identification, only E. Edel asked himself this question. He "tentatively estimated the actual distance in the terrain between Niya and Ugarit as 80 km (instead of 60 km as the crow flies) by increasing the latter figure by one-third again"; this, he found, was compatible with the time schedule.[62] The truth, however, is that no direct communication between Niya and Ugarit was possible because of the impassable swamps of el-Ġāb, and the steep slopes of the Bargylus range. One has to take a long detour via Ǧisr eš-Šuġr and the Bdāmā Pass, which takes 130 km (one way) on the modern highways, and was probably even longer on the ancient, more winding roads.[63] A realistic figure of an average day's march of infantry through rugged terrain is 20 km. No army could cover 260 km, most of it through mountains, in eight, or even nine days. Thus Ugarit must be ruled out as the destination of Amenhotep II's side march from Niya. As for the actual location of ʾ*Ā-ku-tá*/*ṯə̄*, the extreme ambiguity of the Egyptian transcription makes any identification quite uncertain.

[61]Simons (1937), list No. VI.

[62]Edel (1953) 150-53.

[63]A trail from Ǧablah to Ḥama via Bikisraʾil and Tell Salḥab (18 km south of Qalᶜat el-Muḍīq) was used during the Crusades (Dussaud, *Top.*, 141-42) and, according to Riis (1960) 125, was still known at the turn of this century. This trail is described as very difficult by Arab historians of the Crusades. A journey Qalᶜat el-Muḍīq—Tell Salḥab—Ǧablah—Ras Shamra and back to Tell Salḥab would be no shorter than the easier road via the Bdāmā Pass.

Ugarit Passes Under Egyptian Overlordship

At the time of Thutmose IV (1426-1417) and his contemporary Artatama of Mitanni, a sudden change occurred in the relations between their countries. The century-old hostility was replaced by a real "entente cordiale." We know about it only from retrospective references in the Amarna correspondence, and from the observation of a totally changed international situation during the next fifty years or so which was now dominated by an Egypto-Mitannian alliance. One can only guess the reasons for this sharp turn. One of them may have been the growing certitude of the futility of further warfare—neither power could dislodge the other from its positions. Whether a renewed Hittite threat to Mitanni was also a motive for a rapprochement with Egypt is more questionable; it seems that the aggressive king Tudḫaliyaš came to power after the death of Thutmose IV. According to Artatama's grandson Tušratta, it was Thutmose IV who asked seven times for the hand of Artatama's daughter;[64] but we know from the new political configuration in Syria that it was Mitanni which made territorial concessions to Egypt. Not only Qidši and Qaṭna, but even Tunip further north, which a short time earlier had been a vassal of Mitanni, were ceded to the sovereignty of Egypt. True, the territory of Tunip was at that juncture divided: its northern part was detached and joined to the possessions of Ilim-ilimma, king of Alalaḫ,[65] who remained, along with the rest of the Confederacy of Mukiš-Nuḫašše-Nii, in the Mitannian zone of overlordship.

One may also assume that as a result of the Egypto-Mitannian agreement, Ugarit lost its neutral status. Mitanni seems to have given Egypt a free hand on the Syrian coast north of Amurru. The first signs of Ugarit's vassalage to Egypt appear during the reign of Thutmose IV's successor, Amenhotep III (1417-1379). It is under this Pharaoh that Ugarit (*ᵓA-ku-ri-ta*) is first mentioned in an Egyptian record.[66] An Egyptian monument from his, or his predecessor's, time presents an Asian goddess from Šuksi (*Šu-*[*k*]*a-ṯə*), a harbor town south of Ugarit.[67] This shows, at the least, that the Egyptians ceased to ignore that part of Syria, but there are also epistolary testimonies of a totally unambiguous nature. A letter in Ugaritic, unfortunately not fully preserved, is apparently a report to the king of Ugarit from the prefect of the harbor

[64]EA 29:16-20.

[65]As follows from the treaty of a Hittite king (no doubt Šuppiluliumaš) with Labᵓu and the people of Tunip, KUB III 16 (+ 21) = Weidner, *PDK* 136-47, No. 10. Ilim-ilimma, the successor of Niqmepa, reigned in the last third of the fifteenth century.

[66]List of Asian places in the temple of Soleb in Nubia, Col. B:4 according to the numeration of Giveon (1964) = Simons (1937), list No. IX:f:5. Also, in Simons (1937), list No. XII: 12 (ascribed by Simons to Haremheb, but actually of Amenhotep III).

[67]Helck (1971) 458; Weippert (1975) 14.

Maʾḫadu about his mission to Egypt. It speaks of *Nmry mlk ʿlm* "Nimmuriya, the eternal king," i.e. Amenhotep III, whose throne name, *Nb-mȝʿt-rʿ*, was transcribed in the same manner in the Amarna correspondence.[68]

A group of Amarna letters (EA 45-49) originated at Ugarit. One was sent by King Ammištamru,[69] and another by his successor Niqmaddu.[70] A third was sent by a Lady [. . .]-Ḫepa, almost certainly a Ugaritian queen.[71] In all of them, the senders declare themselves servants of Egyptian royalty. The earliest of these letters, EA 45 (to which we shall return in the next section), belongs to the reign of Amenhotep III, but according to EA 46 and 47, the "fathers" (plural) of the author were already vassals of Egypt. This indicates that the beginning of Ugarit's submission to Egypt came at least one or two generations before Ammištamru (whose reign can be dated, very roughly, 1390-1370).[72] In other words, Ugarit's submission to Egypt came in the time of Thutmose IV.

The concrete circumstances of Ugarit's passage under the sovereignty of Egypt are unknown, but it seems likely that they were peaceful. Ugarit had much to gain commercially from good relations with Egypt. From the point of view of Egyptian imperial policy, the accession of Ugarit was an important success. By that time, Ugarit had acquired suzerainty over its southern neighbor, the dual kingdom of Siyannu-Ušnatu,[73] and this relationship was respected by the Egyptian monarchs. The exact position of Ugarit within the system of Egyptian administration of Syria is not clear. It appears that the Asian domain of Egypt was subdivided into three provinces under Egyptian commissioners (Akk. *rabīṣu*) as supervisors of native rulers: Canaan (capital Gaza), Ube (capital Kumidi), and Amurru (capital Ṣumur).[74] Did Ugarit with its dependencies belong to the jurisdiction of the commissioner of Amurru, or was it a separate district of the empire, perhaps without an Egyptian resident?

The kings of Ugarit seemed to enjoy a privileged status among the vassals of Egypt. Niqmaddu not only sent gifts to the Pharaoh, but also asked him for two young Nubians as palace servants, and for a physician

[68]PRU II 18, a Ugaritic translation of a letter to an Egyptian king, mentions "Amon and all the gods of Egypt," and must therefore be dated earlier than Akhenaten's religious reform.

[69]EA 45. The name was restored as [ᵐ*Am*]-*mi-is-tam*-[*ru*] by Nougayrol, *PRU III*, xxxvii.

[70]EA 49. The name of the sender was correctly read and identified by Albright (1944).

[71]EA 48; cf. Albright (1944) and Liverani (1962) 51.

[72]As we shall see presently, Ammištamru was already on the throne around 1387, and was still alive at the beginning of Abdi-Aširta's activities, ca. 1371.

[73]On this kingdom see our article in the *Schaeffer-Festschrift* [*UF* 11 (1979) 13-28].

[74]Helck (1960); (1962) 256-67; Kitchen (1969) 80-82.

(EA 49). A broken alabaster vase of Egyptian workmanship, found in the royal palace of Ugarit, contains a representation of Niqmaddu's wedding with an Egyptian lady of high social standing—not a princess, to be sure (the rule of not giving daughters of the royal house in marriage to foreigners was never broken throughout the Egyptian history), but, to judge by her headdress, a lady in waiting.[75] Even this, no doubt, was regarded as an honor.

Ammištamru and the "First Hittite Foray"

Ammištamru's letter to the Pharaoh (EA 45) is significant for another reason besides being a piece of evidence on Ugarit's dependence on Egypt. Although very damaged, it is possible to make out that the king of a land (whose name is unfortunately broken off) twice sent messengers to Ammištamru, apparently blaming him for siding with Egypt, and threatening him with reprisals if he did not submit to him. This can be deduced from Ammištamru's protestation of loyalty to the Pharaoh, and fear that the king in question would begin hostilities, and invade the land of Ugarit.

Long ago Knudtzon completed LUGAL KUR [^{URU}*Ḫa-at-te*] in line 22, and restored [LUGAL KUR ^{URU}*Ḫa-at-te*] in line 30.[76] His guess must be accepted as correct, despite Liverani's attempt to see here a reference to hostile actions by Abdi-Aširta of Amurru which are mentioned in the treaty between Niqmaddu and Aziru.[77] Abdi-Aširta was never called "king,"[78] and the least appropriate place of calling him so would have been a letter to his Egyptian sovereign. Conversely, the Hittite interpretation permits us to link Ammištamru's letter to the Hittite foray into the dominion of Tušratta, king of Mitanni, who defeated it, and sent news of his victory to his ally, Amenhotep III, together with some gifts from the Hittite booty.[79] As K. Kitchen has demonstrated, Tušratta's letter in question, EA 17, could not have been written after year 34 of Amenhotep III, and might date back to year 30.[80] In absolute figures, following the system of chronology accepted in this paper, this would assign the "first Syrian foray" to one of the years between 1388 and 1385. Now who was the Hittite king who sent out, or led, the unsuccessful foray? Was it already Šuppiluliumaš?

[75]Schaeffer (1956) 164-68; Desroches-Noblecourt (1956) 179-220.

[76]Knudtzon, *EAT*, *ad loc.*; Weber, *ibid.*, 1098.

[77]Liverani (1962) 24, concerning PRU IV 122.

[78]Rib-Addi of Byblos, in his letters to the Pharaoh, had no other epithet for Abdi-Aširta but *ardu kalbu* "the slave, the dog." Aziru was the first of his family to have assumed the royal title.

[79]EA 17:30-38.

[80]Kitchen (1962) 24.

Šuppiluliumaš's accession date follows from a passage in his "Deeds As Told by His Son"[81] which states that he spent 20 years of his reign in reconquering lost Hittite possessions in Anatolia, and then invaded the Hurrian lands (Mitanni), and conquered Syria. Since the latter events (the "First Syrian War") took place, as we shall see, in 1366, Šuppiluliumaš must have ascended the throne in 1386.[82] Thus he could well have been king at the time of the foray. However, a fragment of the "Deeds" relating Šuppiluliumaš's earlier life[83] tells how he, while still only a prince, participated in a campaign under the leadership of his father,[84] and was sent by him to dislodge Sutu-troops (ERÍN.MEŠ *Sú-te-e*) from Mt. Nanni. The presence of Sutians—i.e., soldiers recruited from among Syrian tribesmen—as adversaries of the Hittites points to Syria as the theater of the campaign. The mention of Mt. Nanni helps to narrow down the locale. Nanni (or Namni) appears in Hittite ritual or mythological texts of Hurrian and Cannanite origin, usually coupled with Ḫazzi as the double mountain of the Storm-god.[85] In the list of mountains of the Hiššuwa festival description, *Na-an-ni Ḫa-az-zi* forms a single entry.[86] In the Edict of Šuppiluliumaš on the new boundaries of Ugarit, entry No. 47 is ^{URU}*Ḫal-bi* in one copy,[87] ^{URU}*Ḫal-bi* $^{\text{ḪUR.SAG}}$*Nana-a* in another one;[88] while in Ugaritian records this locality appears as ^{URU}*Ḫal-bi* $^{\text{ḪUR.SAG}}$*Ḫa-zi* (alph. *Ḫlb Ṣpn*). Therefore *Nanni* is simply another name for *Ḫazi*, classical Casius, now Ğebel ᶜAqra, on the Turkish-Syrian border where it reaches the Mediterranean Sea.[89]

The highway from Anatolia to Ugarit and Phoenicia, after crossing the Orontes at the site of Antioch, passed by the eastern foot of Mt.

[81]All extant parts of this work have been published by Güterbock (1956). The passage in question KUB XIX 9 I 6′-23′, is quoted in translation by Kitchen (1962) 3.

[82]Most works on Hittite and general ancient Near Eastern history date the beginning of Šuppiluliumaš's reign ca. 1380; but this cannot be reconciled with the plain language of the "Deeds." Goetze's (1957) 85 dates for Šuppiluliumaš's reign, 1385-1345, are very close to those assumed here, 1386-1346.

[83]Frg. 8, Güterbock (1956) 62. Cf. Gurney (1966) 683; Klengel, *GS* III, 35; Cornelius (1973) 137.

[84]The name of Šuppiluliumaš's father is unknown. Usually another Tudḫaliyaš is postulated to fill this role. Güterbock (1970) 75-77 thought of Ḫattušiliš II (whose very existence, however, is highly dubious); Otten (1968) 113, with greater plausibility, of Arnuwandaš I.

[85]For references, see Ertem (1973) 179, 184-85, *s. vv.* (add KUB XXXIII 108 19, 20); Gonnet (1968), *s. vv.*; additions Dinçol (1974) 32.

[86]Otten (1969) 250, No. 19.

[87]PRU IV 9:23′.

[88]PRU IV 5:rev.6′.

[89]That Nanni was located not far from Ḫazzi was seen by Otten (1969) 252 (who quotes Dr. Schrotthoff concerning the identity of Mt. *Na-na-a* and Mt. Nanni). See also Klengel, *GS* III, 134. But the correspondence *Ḫalbi-Nana // Ḫalbi-Ḫazi* speaks in favor of the identity of Nanni and Ḫazzi, and not just proximity.

Casius, as its modern successor still does for topographic reasons. Under Ammištamru, the northern border of Ugarit passed only a few miles south of that mountain. Hittite armed presence at the very door of his kingdom explains Ammištamru's anguish. The chronological and topographic circumstances of the quoted fragment of the "Deeds of Šuppiluliumaš" agree so well with the situation described in Ammištamru's letter (EA 45) that both documents can be safely assumed to refer to one and the same event—the Hittite foray defeated by Tušratta. Thus Ammištamru was saved from a Hittite intrusion not by his Egyptian sovereign, but by the latter's Mitannian ally. Incidentally, this military action—if our interpretation is correct—should not be called "Šuppiluliumaš's first Syrian foray:"[90] Šuppiluliumaš did participate in it, but in a subordinate, not in a leading role.

Niqmaddu and Šuppiluliumaš

Ammištamru died toward the middle of the reign of Akhenaten in Egypt; his last years coincided with the beginning of the unrest in Amurru stirred up by Abdi-Aširta.[91] His son and successor Niqmaddu initially continued the pro-Egyptian policy of his father, as we have seen, but soon the political situation in Syria began to change rapidly, bringing about Ugarit's transfer from the Egyptian sphere of influence to that of the Hittites. We must limit ourselves to the briefest possible outline of the events.[92]

In 1368, Šuppiluliumaš undertook the "Second Syrian foray." He came down from Melitene, marched south not far from the bank of the Euphrates, established a pro-Hittite ruler in Nuhašše, signed a treaty with Tunip, restored to it its lost northern cities, and tied up relations with Abdi-Aširta.

The very next year Tušratta crossed the Euphrates, re-established the status quo in Nuḫašše, and advanced into Amurru. Meanwhile, an Egyptian seaborn force landed in Amurru and recovered Ṣumur. Abdi-Aširta, caught in the middle, was killed by his own subjects. This success of Egyptian foreign policy, after years of inactivity, was publicized in the reliefs and texts of Year 12 of Akhenaten showing the presentation of tribute from Syria and Nubia.[93] Year 12 of Akhenaten was 1367; hence the "Second Syrian foray" occurred in 1368, and Šuppiluliumaš's "First

[90]According to the terminology of Kitchen (1962) 25, 40.

[91]See n. 72.

[92]These events are relatively well documented, and have been presented in consistent form many times in works on ancient Near Eastern history in general, and on Hittite history in particular.

[93]Aldred (1971) 60, with references; Helck (1969) 324.

Syrian War," which deprived Egypt of its dependencies in Northern and Central Syria, started in 1366.[94]

The "First Syrian War" began by Šuppiluliumaš's invasion of Mitanni from the north. While he was campaigning east of the Euphrates, the kings of Mukiš, Nuḫašše, and Nii prepared for resistance, and invited Niqmaddu to join their coalition. Since Egypt and Mitanni had acted together in the preceding year, and since a little later the remainder of the coalition was joined by states of Egyptian allegiance, and appealed to Egypt for help,[95] the anti-Hittite kings of the Mitannian zone had every reason to expect that Ugarit, an Egyptian vassal, would support them. But Šuppiluliumaš also appealed to Niqmaddu, invoking a former friendship between Ugarit and Ḫatti, promising help against the anti-Hittite kings, and guaranteeing that any prisoners of war, and border towns seized by Niqmaddu, would remain in his hands.[96] Niqmaddu decided to side with the Hittites.

The troops of the Confederacy of Mukiš-Nuḫašše-Nii invaded the territory of Ugarit and devastated it, but were robbed of their final victory over Niqmaddu by the arrival, from across the Euphrates, of Šuppiluliumaš with his army. He first occupied Ḫalab, then Alalaḫ. Mukiš was put out of action, but Nii, several principalities of Nuḫašše, Sinzar, Qaṭna, and Qidši continued the struggle for a while. As soon as Šuppiluliumaš entered Alalaḫ, Niqmaddu came there and made a formal submission to the Hittite king.[97] Thus began the Hittite era in the history of Ugarit.

Ugarit's Gains and Losses Under Hittite Supremacy

The annual tribute imposed upon Niqmaddu by Šuppiluliumaš[98] consisted, primarily, of 20 (Hittite) minas and 20 shekels (or 500 shekels in all) of gold, secondarily of a number of gold and silver vessels, pieces of clothing, and quantities of red and blue purple wool for the king, queen, heir apparent, and a few Hittite high officials. Not knowing the

[94]These are, coincidentally, the same dates as those calculated by Kitchen (1962) from somewhat different premises, and within the framework of a chronology which puts Akhenaten's Year 1 at 1377 rather than 1379 according to the chronology of W. C. Hayes adopted in *CAH*^{3} and followed here. In Kitchen (1966) all dates have been lowered by further two years.

[95]This follows especially from EA 51, 53, 54, 55, 57, 59.

[96]PRU IV 1. The tablet is very well preserved, but the lack of a seal is puzzling. Could it be a later copy?

[97]These events are known from the preamble to the treaty imposed on Niqmaddu by Šuppiluliumaš, PRU IV 2, and the latter's edict on the territorial accretion of Ugarit.

[98]The tribute list has been preserved in two Akkadian and one Ugaritic version, PRU IV 2, 3, 4, investigated by Nougayrol, *PRU IV*, 37-40; Dietrich & Loretz (1966).

amount of tribute previously paid to Egypt, we cannot tell whether the new obligation was heavier or lighter than the old one. Amurru, upon becoming a vassal of Ḫatti, paid only 300 shekels of gold as principal tribute.[99] Ugarit was thus considered far richer than Amurru. It does not seem that the tribute weighed heavily upon the economy of Ugarit.[100]

If there was an increase in tribute, it was no doubt compensated by the vast accretion of territory at the expense of the vanquished Mukiš and its allies. An edict of Šuppiluliumaš, later confirmed by Muršiliš II, describes in detail the new borders of Ugarit.[101] The territorial gains of Ugarit can be summarized as follows. Toward the north, the boundary was moved from the latitude of Bdāmā to that of Mt. Casius. This added an area of ca. 1000 sq. km, much of it valuable forest land. In the east, Ugarit received a long stretch of the Orontes valley, the plain of Rūğ, the massif of Ğebel Zāwiyeh, and a segment of the plain of Chalcis with a salient to the marshy lagoon of Maṭḫ. This amounted to ca. 2225 sq. km, mostly cereal cultures, vineyards, and olive groves. Altogether the new territories of Ugarit measured ca. 3225 sq. km, or half as much again as the old domain of the kingdom (not counting the vassal state of Siyannu-Ušnatu).[102]

On the negative side must be inscribed the loss by Ugarit of its traditional overlordship over Siyannu-Ušnatu. During the reign of Niqmepa, Niqmaddu's son and second successor, that vassal state seceded from Ugarit, and put itself under the suzerainty of the newly established Hittite appanage kingdom of Carchemish. Muršiliš II confirmed the new situation, decreed a delimitation between the two states (which did not work and had to be radically changed), and only conceded to Niqmepa's request of lowering Ugarit's tribute by one-third in view of the reduction of its resources.[103] But, in J. Nougayrol's words, "the

[99]Treaty of Muršiliš II with Duppi-Tešub of Amurru, Akkadian version, KUB III 14 (=Weidner, *PDK*, 76-79, No. 5) obv. 9; English transl. Goetze, *ANET*, 203-25.

[100]The Akkadian Ras Shamra tablet published by Thureau-Dangin (1934), registers the remittance of quantities of purple wool by 29 producers, each of them contributing from 100 to 400 shekels, the total collection amounting to 2 talents 600 shekels. The total weight of purple wool delivered as tribute to Ḫatti (not counting ready clothing) equaled one talent.

[101]See Astour (1969) 398-405 and map. The reconstruction of Ugarit's new borders given there must be corrected as follows: (a) Ḫenzuriwa should be identified with Ḥazzārīn in the southwestern part of Ğebel Zāwiyeh rather than with Tell Ḫanzīr; (b) the identification of Tell Mardīḫ with Ebla, which was still inhabited in the thirteenth century (it is mentioned in a tablet from Emar, Msk 74.39:1) but did not belong to the Ugaritian zone, necessitates a shift of the eastern border of Ugarit south of Apsuna a few km to the west; (c) Magdala should be located at Mağdalīya northeast of Erīḥa rather than at Mġeydleh on the Orontes. See our map of Hittite Syria appended to this article.

[102]This is a reduction from our earlier estimate of at least 4000 sq. km.

[103]See n. 73 above.

relations between Siyannu and Ugarit caused much clay to be kneaded in the fourteenth and thirteenth centuries B.C."[104]

Another disadvantage for Ugarit was the disruption of its trade with Egypt and Egyptian possessions in Asia in periods of tense relations, or open conflicts, between Egypt and Ḫatti. This was, to an extent, compensated by Ugarit's access to Anatolian markets. A veritable "bank" or "central clearing house" (*bīt ṭuppašši*) with a considerable capital was established at Ḫattušaš by Ugaritian "caravans" (*ḫarranāti*) or commercial companies.[105] A letter to one of the biggest merchants of Ugarit from his associate tells about lucrative trade possibilities in Hittite country.[106] Ugarit, too, was visited by merchants from Anatolia, some of which came by sea—namely the men of Ura, a harbor in western Cilicia, who enjoyed a special protection from the Hittite king, and whose activities in Ugarit were regarded by local businessmen and administration with mixed feelings.[107] Ugaritian contracts, and other documents, testify to the presence at Ugarit of men (sometimes specifically designated as *tamkāru*) from the following cities and areas of Anatolia: KUR*Ḫat-ti* at large;[108] KUR*Tar-ḫu-da-aš-ši* in south central Anatolia;[109] KUR*Pa-a-li/Pa-li*, probably the land of Palā;[110] U[RU]*Ḫa-ba-al-la*, a land in west central Anatolia;[111] URU*U-da-a*, classical Hyde in Lycaonia;[112] and URU*Ta-ga-ri-ma*!, same as Tagarama in Militene.[113]

An additional burden for Ugarit was the obligation to participate with its soldiers, chariots, and no doubt ships in Hittite wars. However, with the exception of the final desperate struggle against the invasion of the Peoples of the Sea, Ugaritian armed forces were called up only for service in Syria: to quell the revolt of Tette of Nuḫašše against Muršiliš II;[114] to fight under Qidši, in the ranks of the great imperial army of Muwatalliš, against the Egyptian army of Ramesses II;[115] and, in the final stage of the Hittite-Egyptian war, to defend the freshly reconquered

[104]Nougayrol, *PRU IV*, 290.

[105]Its existence is known from PRU IV 53:17-19 (about 1244); cf. Nougayrol, *PRU IV*, 22.

[106]Urḫaʾe to Yabninu, PRU VI 14; cf. n. 132 below.

[107]PRU III 26:rev. 6′; PRU IV 29, 74, 78, 88; U 5 N 100; in addition, *ibid.* 33 and 171 on transportation of grain from Mukiš to Ura on Ugaritian ships.

[108]PRU IV 70:5; U 5 N 41:38; PRU II 90:4-5 ("a jar of wine for Hittites at Maʾḫadu").

[109]PRU IV 63 and 64.

[110]U 5 N 41:16, 21.

[111]U 5 N 45:1′.

[112]PRU III 26: obv.3′.

[113]*Ibid.* rev.3′. Nougayrol transliterated the last sign *la*(?); actually it is a *ma* with an elongated middle horizontal wedge. The same form of Hittite *Tagarama/Tegarama* is found in an inscription of Shalmaneser III (Laessøe [1959]) frgm. F:5, as URU*Ta-ga-ri-*[*ma*!].

[114]PRU IV 7.

[115]*ʾA-ku-ri-ta* is listed among the contingents of the Hittite forces in Egyptian reports on the battle of Qidši; see Helck (1962) 206.

coastland of Amurru from an expected Egyptian counter-offensive.[116] But it had to contribute heavy sums of money to at least certain wars on other fronts.[117]

Ugarit remained loyal to Ḫatti to their common bitter end, but it is worth noting that not one single tablet in Hittite has so far been found at Ras Shamra. The intellectuals of Ugarit, who were deeply fascinated by Sumerian, Akkadian, and Hurrian languages, literatures, and religions, displayed an absolute lack of interest in Hittite culture. The use of seals with hieroglyphic Hittite inscriptions, which appeared among native Syrians in the thirteenth century,[118] did not spread to Ugarit.

The Position of Ugarit in the Hittite Empire

During the "Second Syrian War"[119] (1353-1347), Šuppiluliumaš completed the organization of Hittite Syria, and it remained essentially the same to the end of the imperial era.

The mainstay of Hittite power in Syria was the appanage kingdom of Carchemish, which, in addition to the old state of Carchemish, included the northeastern part of the former Confederacy of Mukiš-Nuḫašše-Nii, and both banks of the Euphrates from Emar to the confluence of the Balīḫ.[120] Its kings served as viceroys over all of Hittite Syria. Ugarit, as the rest of the Hittite vassal states in Syria, found itself under a dual control: it communicated with, and received orders from, the Great King of Ḫatti, but many decisions were transmitted or initiated by the king of Carchemish. Ugarit maintained very close and intense political, juridical, and economic ties with Carchemish.

Another Hittite appanage was created out of the remaining part of Mukiš. It carried the name of the kingdom of Ḫalab, which had historical connotations for the Hittites, but its capital was in Alalaḫ.[121]

[116] The vivid and colorful "letter of the general" U 5 N 20. See Rainey (1971) for its historical and geographical interpretation.

[117] See below, "Ugarit, Assyria, and Babylonia."

[118] Seals of Šaušgamuwa, king of Amurru, on tablets PRU IV 48, 49, 51; seal of Kiliya, priest of Sinzaru, PRU IV 87.

[119] We follow the original terminology of Kitchen (1962). In his (1966), he adopted instead the appellation "Hurrian War," used by Goetze (1965) 16. As noted by Garelli (1969) 314, that war was "in fact, neither more nor less Hurrian than the preceding ones."

[120] Astour (1969) 405-8. Much new information has been disclosed by the tablets from Old Meskeneh-Emar, see Arnaud (1975). Forrer (1929) 47 attributed Commagene to the kingdom of Carchemish, but for wrong reasons. It is known from Hittite sources that identifiable towns in Commagene belonged directly to the kingdom of Ḫatti since the time of Šuppiluliumaš's treaty with Šunaššura of Kizzuwadna.

[121] This follows from the presence of a Hittite tablet, a stele of King Tudḫaliyaš (second half of the thirteenth century), and a hieroglyphic seal of a Hittite governor in Level II-I of Alalaḫ, see Woolley (1953) 160-1, and especially from the letter U 5 N 26, addressed to Ammištamru by a Hittite prince who resided at Alalaḫ, but also had the town of Bēlet-rēmi (now Belleramūn) near Ḫalab under his jurisdiction.

Ugarit shared its entire northern border with this new creation, and maintained friendly relations with it, though its ruler, as a Hittite royal prince, was considered of higher rank than the king of Ugarit.[122]

The largest states of Hittite Syria under the rule of native dynasties were Ugarit and Amurru. There were frictions between them in the troubled years of Abdi-Aširta and the "First Syrian War," but after Aziru's return from Egypt and formal submission to Hittite overlordship, he and Niqmaddu concluded a treaty of friendship and cooperation.[123] A characteristic feature of the treaty is the unilateral commitment of Aziru to defend Ugarit from aggression by a third party. Niqmaddu, in lieu of a reciprocal obligation, remitted the sum of 5000 shekels of silver to Aziru. In the following century, when Amurru returned to the Hittite fold, Ammištamru married an Amurrian princess, daughter of King Bentešina. The scandalous end of this marriage greatly strained the relations between Ugarit and Amurru, and it is significant that the affair was settled by a series of arbitrations by Ini-Tešub, king of Carchemish, and Tudḫaliyaš, the Great King of Ḫatti.[124]

To judge from Hittite royal arbitrations of territorial disputes between vassal states (Ugarit and Siyan̆nu-Ušnatu, Barga and Nuḫašše[125]), the Hittite government took good care to maintain internal peace in its zone of Syria. This was beneficial for Ugaritian trade within this zone, in particular with Kinza (Qidši), where it sent large amounts of bronze and tin.[126]

The Renewal of Ugarit's Trade With the Egyptian Empire

The traditional economic links between Ugarit and Egypt were interrupted by the recurring Egypto-Hittite wars. A possible resumption of Ugarit's relations with Egypt took place during the brief reign of Ar-Ḫalba (ca. 1340-1335), and may have cost him his throne.[127] The conclusion of the peace treaty between Ramesses II and Ḫattušiliš III in 1284 inaugurated an unprecedented era of peace in Syria which was to last almost ninety years, and which enabled Ugarit to re-establish its commercial ties with Egypt, and its possessions in Phoenicia and Palestine.

[122]Cf. U 5 N 26 and the letters of Ammištamru, *ibid.* 27 and 28, which, in our opinion, were also addressed to a Hittite prince in charge of Alalaḫ-Ḫalab.

[123]PRU IV 122. The date of the treaty is in dispute; we agree with Kitchen (1962) 32, 46; cf. Astour (1969) 397-98.

[124]The story of Ammištamru's tragic marriage is very complicated and contradictory, and has no direct relationship to the topic of this article.

[125]KBo III 3 I 3 - II 38; see Klengel (1963).

[126]U 5 N 39. Other letters from Kinza are *ibid.* 38 and 40.

[127]The evidence is circumstantial; see Nougayrol, *PRU IV*, 57-58; Liverani (1962) 31, 57-66.

In fact, Ugarit was the principal stage on the great north-south artery from Anatolia to Egypt. The importance of the traffic on that route is illustrated by the privilege granted by Tudḫaliyaš to Ammištamru to exercise some sort of control over the movement of horses from Ḫatti to Egypt and vice versa.[128] The same Ugaritian merchants who conducted large-scale operations in Ḫatti were eager to participate in "caravans" to Egypt.[129] There are mentions of a Ugaritian, backed by four guarantors, who is about to "voyage to Egypt for trading";[130] of a Ugaritian ship which sailed to Egypt and was forced by a tempest to stop at Accho;[131] and of a joint business voyage to Egypt by citizens of Ugarit and Ušnatu.[132]

On the other hand, Egyptians (some with Egyptian, some with Semitic names) visited Ugarit, entered into money deals,[133] received hereditary land grants from the king,[134] bought large quantities of oil,[135] participated in purchases of produce from a royal estate,[136] and formed a distinct corporate group.[137] Persons designated as "Egyptians" were distinguished from "Canaanites" (Ug. *kn*ᶜ*ny*, Akk. DUMU.MEŠ ^{KUR}*Ki-na-ḫi*),[138] i.e., inhabitants of the Egyptian province of Canaan (Phoenicia and Palestine). These, too, were recognized at Ugarit as a corporation with a juridical personality and collective responsibility, whose interests were protected by their sovereign, the Pharaoh.[139] They also appear in Ugaritian records under the ethnics of their particular cities. The most important of them was the community of Ashdodians,[140] who were so well integrated into the business world of Ugarit that one may safely assume that Ugaritians enjoyed reciprocal rights at Ashdod. Indeed, the letter from Ugarit recently found at Apheq in the State of Israel, on which we shall hear from Dr. David Owen, testifies to the importance of

[128]PRU VI 179.

[129]PRU VI 14: 19-29; cf. n. 109 above; PRU III 179, a royal grant of trading concessions (*ḫarranāti* "caravans") to Ḫatti *and* Egypt. On Ugaritian merchants and their companies see Astour (1972b).

[130]PRU V 116.

[131]PRU V 59.

[132]U 5 N 42.

[133]PRU III 21.

[134]PRU III 149.

[135]PRU V 95:4.

[136]CTA 91 (UT 311):6.

[137]*Mṣrym* and *bn mṣrym* among groups of Ugaritians and foreigners who received wine, PRU II 89:7, 10.

[138]CTA 91 (UT 311):7 *Y*ᶜ*l kn*ᶜ*ny* immediately following *N*ᶜ*mn mṣry*; U 5 N 36:6′, 8′.

[139]U 5 N 36 is a letter from a king or a high official of Ugarit to a king of Egypt concerning the settlement of a litigation in the amount of one talent and 500 shekels of silver between "Ugaritians" and "Canaanites."

[140]Cf. Astour (1970) 123-26.

Ugaritian commercial activities in southern Canaan.[141] Ugarit also traded with Byblos, Berytus, Sidon, Tyre, Accho, and Ashkelon.[142]

Ugarit's desire for good relations with Egypt found its expression in the beautiful bronze sword engraved with the cartouche of Pharaoh Merneptah which was found at Ras Shamra.[143] It was probably intended as a diplomatic gift, but was never delivered—perhaps because of Merneptah's death.

Ugarit, Assyria, and Babylonia

Compared with Ugarit's thriving commercial activities along the north-south axis of the East Mediterranean world, its connections with the East were quite insignificant. There was a group of Assyrians (*ašr*[*y*]*m*) at Ugarit,[144] and one letter found at Ras Shamra was sent from Assyria, by an official named Bēlubur to his representative in Ugarit, concerning something of interest to the Ugaritian queen.[145] In one document, however, Assyria appears in a very different aspect: as being at war with Ugarit's Hittite overlord.[146] Since much has been written on the alleged repercussions of this particular war upon Northern Syria in general and Ugarit in particular, a short clarification will not be out of place.

The message from Tudḫaliyaš to Ammištamru, transmitted by Ini-Tešub, king of Carchemish, about a state of war between Ḫatti and Assyria, has been correectly correlated with the commercial blockade of Assyria imposed by the same Tudḫaliyaš upon Šaušgamuwa of Amurru,[147] and with the mention in a late version of Tukulti-Ninurta I's annals[148] that in his first regnal year (1244) he crossed the Euphrates and carried off eight sar (28,800) Hittites. This was understood by certain authors as a full-fledged Assyrian invasion of Hittite Syria. Helck suspected that Tukulti-Ninurta's advance may have ended the dynasty of

[141]See D. I. Owen, "Ugarit, Canaan, and Egypt" at the present Symposium.

[142]PRU II 110:4; PRU III 12; PRU IV 58; PRU V 106; PRU VI 79, 81, 126; U 5 N 41.

[143]Schaeffer (1956) 169-77.

[144]PRU II 89:3 (cf. n. 140 above).

[145]RS 6.198, published by Thureau-Dangin (1935). Cf. Liverani (1962) 101; Klengel, *GS* II, 376. Ugaritian queens had their own estates and merchants.

[146]PRU IV 53.

[147]Treaty of Tudḫaliyaš with Šaušgamuwa, IUB XXIII 1 + 1a, b + KUB XXXI 43; last edition and study: Kühne & Otten (1971). The clause in question appears in col. IV 14ss., quoted in Klengel, *GS* II, 222-23, 320-22.

[148]All relevant inscriptions can be found in Weidner (1959). The passage in question is translated in Grayson, *ARI* I, § 773, as follows: "In the year of my accession to the throne, at the beginning of my reign, I uprooted 28,800 Hittite people from Syria (lit. "Beyond the Euphrates") and led (them) into my land." The introduction of "Syria" in the translation is an unwarranted license; the Euphrates is a long river and flows for hundreds of miles before it forms the border of historical Syria.

Amurru;[149] Klengel thought that he invaded Northern Syria for booty rather than for annexation;[150] and Albright, disregarding clear chronological and geographical data of documents from the last days of Ugarit on the joint Hittite-Ugaritian struggle against the Peoples of the Sea around 1200-1194, reinterpreted them as referring to Tukulti-Ninurta's invasion of Commagene in 1234.[151]

However, all that Tukulti-Ninurta repeatedly claimed in his inscriptions to have accomplished in his first year on the throne was a march across several small districts along the upper Tigris, and up to the upper Euphrates in the area of its confluence with the Arsanias. One of them, Tepurzi, is listed in the preamble to the Šattiwaza treaty[152] as a Hittite border territory in eastern Anatolia. It was thus located west of the upper Euphrates, and its encroachment by Tukulti-Ninurta was regarded as a violation of Hittite sovereignty and a *casus belli*. As a matter of fact, this border incident did not lead to a real war, and it did not affect the security of Northern Syria in the least.[153] The message of Ini-Tešub to Ammištamru is very illuminating in this respect: Ammištamru was freed from the normal obligation of a vassal to furnish troops and chariots against Assyria, and was assessed instead with an extra contribution of 50 minas of gold.[154] It is interesting that Tudḫaliyaš, without waiting for the arrival of the gold from Ugarit, simply took this amount from the Ugaritian "bank" (*bīt ṭuppašši*) at Ḫattušaš.

As for Kassite Babylonia, Ugarit was well known there. It is mentioned in a quotation from a letter of Kadašman-Enlil I to Amenhotep III concerning the Babylonian king's sister in the Pharaoh's harem.[155] Then, over a hundred years later, Ḫattušiliš III, in a letter to Kadašman-Enlil II, quotes the latter's complaint that Babylonian merchants had been murdered in the lands of Amurru and Ugarit.[156] In the sequence of the letter, however, Ugarit is not mentioned again, and all attention is given to Bentešina, king of Amurru, who had his own claims to "men of

[149]Helck (1962) 239 n. 3.

[150]Klengel, *GS* II, 322.

[151]Albright (1968) 235-36. 1234 is his date for the first year of Tukulti-Ninurta I. He put the final destruction of Ugarit at the same time, but ascribed it to an otherwise unknown first attack of the Peoples of the Sea on Syria; see also his remarks on that topic in (1966) 514-15.

[152]KBo I 1 obv. I 13, 22 (= Weidner, *PDK*, 4-7).

[153]This episode is very lucidly treated by Munn-Rankin (1967) 290-92.

[154]Four times the annual tribute in gold as imposed upon Niqmaddu, as noted by Nougayrol, *PRU IV*, 149; or six times the annual tribute payed by Niqmepa after it was cut by one-third.

[155]EA 1:37-40: "Perhaps she is the daughter of a *muškênu*, or of a Gagean, or the daughter of a Ḫanigalbatian, or perhaps from the land of Ugarit, she whom my messengers have seen."

[156]KBo I 10 + KUB III 72; summarized by Klengel, *GS* II, 218-19, with bibliography.

Akkad" who owed him, in his words, three talents of silver. Not one single Babylonian is mentioned in Ras Shamra texts, nor do they ever refer to Babylonia under any of its names, be it Babili, Akkad, Karduniaš, Kaššu, or Šanḫara.[157] Visits of Ugarit by Babylonian traders must have been few and far between, while they were considerably more frequent farther south, in Amurru. Klengel supposed that "Amurru lay on the important commercial route which led from Mesopotamia via Tadmir/Palmyra to the Mediterranean coast,"[158] and this is a plausible idea, especially in view of the appearance of *Tadmir* in a thirteenth century tablet from Emar.[159] The road from Babylonia to Ḫatti went along the Euphrates, via Tuttul, Emar, and Carchemish,[160] and also bypassed Ugarit.

Ugarit, Cyprus, and the Aegean

Alašiya, whose identity with Cyprus can be considered as certain, was not a great power of the caliber of Egypt, Ḫatti, Assyria, or Babylonia, but during the fourteenth and most of the thirteenth century it was an independent kingdom,[161] with an international policy of its own.[162] It was a close neighbor of Ugarit—only 105 km from the harbor at Minet el-Beiḍa—and one of its most active commercial partners. References to Alašiya, Alašiotes and their ships at Ugarit, to Ugaritians dealing with Alašiya are too numerous in the Ras Shamra texts to be listed here. Alašiya provided Ugarit with copper and was its intermediary in acquiring Mycenaean ceramics; Ugarit, in turn, exported food to Alašiya. Four Akkadian letters, exchanged between the kings and high officials of Ugarit and Alašiya on the eve of Ugarit's destruction,[163] testify to close and very cordial relations between the two kingdoms.

Farther west lay another great island, Crete, known in Mesopotamia as Kaptara and at Ugarit as *Kptr/Kapturi* (biblical Caphtor).[164] We have

[157]Except in standard enumerations of foreign countries in the treaty of Muršiliš II with Niqmepa.

[158]Klengel, *GS* II, 316; similarly Kühne (1973) 80 n. 406.

[159]Msk 21:16, 18 (courtesy of D. Arnaud).

[160]On the economic ties between Babylonia and Emar (a sub-kingdom of Carchemish) see Arnaud (1975) 88.

[161]On the time of the Hittite conquest of Cyprus, see Güterbock (1967). He, and other authors cited by him, attribute this event to Tudḫaliyaš "IV" (the successor of Ḫattušiliš III).

[162]As is apparent from the letters EA 33-40, and in particular from the Alašiote king's advice to the Pharaoh: "With the king of Ḫatte and the king of Šanḫar (Babylonia), do not make a treaty," EA 34:49-50.

[163]U 5 N 21-24. It is possible that PRU V 61 is a Ugaritic translation of a letter from the king of Alašiya, as suggested in Astour (1965) 255.

[164]I have summarized the available evidence on Ugarit's contacts with the Aegean in my (1973) article.

seen that, around 1700, Caphtorian and Mariote traders came together at Ugarit. In the thirteenth century Crete formed part of Mycenaean Greece. In our opinion, the controversial land of Aḫḫiyawa of Hittite records, which Tudḫaliyaš, in a well-known passage, almost included among the great powers equal in status to Ḫatti,[165] can represent nothing else but the Achaean kingdom, or kingdoms, centered around Mycenae. We know from the Šaušgamuwa treaty that merchants from Aḫḫiyawa visited harbors of Amurru and even established links with Assyria. One would expect to find them, all the more, at Ugarit, which was located much closer than Amurru to both Assyria and the Aegean. But, strangely enough, there is no trace in the Ras Shamra texts of anything resembling Aḫḫiyawa, nor can there be discerned any personal name or ethnic pointing to Mycenaean Greece as its place of origin. The only mention of Crete (Caphtor) at Ras Shamra outside mythological poems tells about a ship of one of the richest men in Ugarit returning from a voyage to Kapturi (KURDUGUD-*ri*) at the time of Ammištamru.[166] So there were, after all, cases of direct sailings from Ugarit to Crete—and yet so little of these ventures found its way into written records.

It was from those quarters, however, that the destruction of Ugarit came. The same mysterious forces that dealt a crushing blow to the Mycenaean civilization around 1200, the so-called Peoples of the Sea, continued to roll eastward, and, in a storm of devastation, put a simultaneous end to the existence of both Ḫattušaš and Ugarit, the overlord and the vassal, so thoroughly that the former emerged from oblivion only in 1906, and the latter in 1929, fifty years ago—an event which we celebrate at our present Symposium in the jubilee year of Ugarit and Ugaritic studies.[167]

165. Treaty with Šaušgamuwa (see n. 150), KUB XXIII 1 IV 1-3.
166. PRU III 112:9-15.
167. The Ugaritian evidence on the last days of Ugarit is collected in Astour (1965).

UGARIT: A CANAANITE THALASSOCRACY

ELISHA LINDER

Center for Maritime Studies
University of Haifa

Over ten years have passed since I first took up the study of Ugarit's maritime texts under Professor Cyrus Gordon.[1] I found before me the pioneering work of J. Sasson on Canaanite Maritime involvement in the second millennium[2] which remains a valuable source of information to this day; M. Astour's publication on Maʾhadu;[3] and several other short essays related to various aspects of Ugarit and the sea.[4] Little has been added since then in the form of new "raw material" directly related to the subject. Consequently, no major work on the kingdom's maritime history has as yet been published. Ugarit's maritime heritage, however, should neither be ignored, nor merely mentioned casually in other contexts.

When defining Ugarit as a "Canaanite Thalassocracy," there are a number of basic components to be considered, of which two are of cardinal importance: a sea-oriented economy, and a significant naval power, both reflected in the social stratification, and in the legal statutes of the kingdom.

Studies in the social and economic history of Ugarit are at an advanced stage. With Heltzer's latest monograph on trade in Ugarit, a classified catalogue of the published texts dealing with raw materials, finished goods, food products, livestock, etc., is at last available.[5] These items are compared with materials from neighboring countries, and summed up in a synthesis on the organization of trade, and problems of transportation. This work, and other studies on trade and merchants,[6]

[1]Linder (1970).

[2]Sasson (1966).

[3]Astour (1970).

[4]For detailed bibliography, see Linder (1970) 228ff.

[5]Heltzer (1978a).

[6]Cf. Astour (1972b); Rainey (1967). For comprehensive background on trade in the second millennium B.C.E., see studies presented at the XXIII Rencontre Assyriologique Internationale (Birmingham, July, 1976), and published in *Iraq* 39 (1977).

has proven most helpful in our examination of Ugarit's sea-oriented economy. We shall confine our observations herein to those aspects of the socioeconomic life of the kingdom which relate *directly* to *maritime* commercial activities. We must be wary of drawing final conclusions from records published to date, however, since we feel that these are still incomplete.[7]

As a "Port of Trade," Ugarit is not confined to an intermediate status engaged in export and import only. With its face to the sea, Ugarit developed several industries and crafts which were of purely marine character, such as purple dye manufacture, and shipbuilding. Other industries and crafts developed as a result of the kingdom's intensive commercial transactions in raw materials such as copper, and agricultural products such as grain.[8]

When turning to the merchant class which evolved with these industries and crafts, the relatively rich documentation provides an ever-clearer picture of their role in Ugarit's society.[9] The seafaring merchants, however, and the guilds engaged in the marine industries, are still subject to close examination nevertheless.

As to naval power, direct information regarding its strength and operational capacities comes mainly from the last days of Ugarit. As we shall see further on, our understanding of its role in earlier periods of the kingdom's history evolves by comparison with the overall development of naval warfare in the Late Bronze Age.[10]

In the so-called "International Age" (15th-13th centuries B.C.E.), a certain equilibrium was reached between the conflicting interests of Egypt, the Hittites, Mitanni, Kassite Babylonia, and Assyria. These were the "Great Powers" then dominating the Western Asiatic scene, with commercial interests largely serving as the basis of the relationship between them.[11] Ugarit, whose economic prosperity has already been enhanced in the Old Babylonian period, found itself well fitted into the ecumene of an international organization of trade. The kingdom skillfully exploited every advantage offered by its unique geographical position and rich natural resources.

[7]Almost every new publication of Ugaritic texts adds to the knowledge and understanding of this specific field of our interest. In PRU VI, for example, several fragmentary cuneiform texts relate to ships or organization of shipping. *Cf.* RS 19.115; RS 19.107a; RS 19.26; RS 19.71; RS 19.28; RS 19.46; RS 19.112; RS 18.101a.

[8]See our discussion on the major export-import items in maritime trade, below.

[9]See note 6, above.

[10]See Linder (1972b).

[11]For a recent discussion on the historical background of this period, see H. Tadmor, "The Decline of Empires in Western Asia ca. 1200 B.C.E.," in F. M. Cross, ed., *Symposia Celebrating the Seventy-fifth Anniversary of the Founding of the American Schools of Oriental Research (1900-1975),* American Schools of Oriental Research, 1979.

Those engaged in maritime trade in Ugarit, both citizens and foreigners, were acting within the framework of a central government, whether Ugaritic or Hittite. They were subject to taxes and customs duties, their interests being guarded by law, and they enjoyed naval protection. We suggest that four categories of commercial shipping existed: (a) royal; (b) private; (c) joint royal-private; and (d) foreign.

A. *Royal Shipping*. The king of Ugarit had his ships and business agents who traded with Alašia (UT 2008), Egypt (UT 2059), and Cilicia (RS 20.212). These shipping activities were not of a purely mercantile character. Merchants trading in foreign lands were always regarded, as well, as ambassadors: diplomacy and trade being closely interwoven in the Ancient Near East.[12] Such involvement of merchants and officials in a commercial transaction between Egypt, the Ugaritic royal family, and Alašia is echoed in UT 2008, in which the ships mentioned belong to the king.[13]

In another text (UT 2059), we learn of a ship belonging to the king of Ugarit which was stranded. In this instance, the merchantman in the king's fleet was legally protected, while a political agreement between the concerned coastal states was implemented.[14]

Is there any connection between the type of cargo transported, and the category of shipping discussed here? We know that the king's fleet was engaged in grain shipments to Alašia (UT 2061) and Ura (RS 20.212; RS 20.158). Because of the primary importance of grain in the economy of all countries, and the special position of Ugarit as supplier and agent for this essential commodity, its transport was monopolized by the king, and shipped by his fleet.

Copper was handled in a similar manner. This metal was of paramount importance to the economy of Ugarit, especially in the transit trade. Its shipment from Alašia must have been a royal monopoly involving political agreements. Its distribution to various merchants for further shipment (UT 90) was carried out in the harbours on its arrival from the island (UT 2110; UT 2056).

A third prominent item in the economy, oil, was also subjected to royal handling. It was a major product of export under the direct

[12]See Zaccagnini (1973), and Holmes (1975).

[13]We do not accept the reading and interpretation of this text in Lipinsky (1977). The commercial transaction of ships relates to Ugarit and Alašia, as will be shown in a forthcoming paper on the subject.

[14]Such an international code regulating sea traffic is spelled out in one section of the treaty between Asarhaddon, King of Assyria, and Ba^{c}al of Tyre. This document of the 7th century B.C.E. mentions both the "ship of Ba^{c}al" and the "people of your land." Here the agreement covers both royal and private shipping, which may not have been the usual practice under the political circumstances of that time. See Weidner (1932-33) 29-34, and Borger (1967) 107-9.

supervision of the king (RS 20.168), and special levies were imposed when purchased by foreign traders (RS 17.424c+). Its distribution for export was supervised by the *akîl kâri*, "harbor master" (UT 2095).

The same category included those cases where large-scale building projects were undertaken by the king, and his ships went out to bring the necessary stones which had been quarried along the coast (UT 2067).

B. *Private Enterprises.* The outstanding example of a private shipowner at Ugarit is Sinaranu.[15] He enjoyed special privileges (RS 16.238), and rated among the wealthiest merchants of Ugarit in his time.[16] When Sinaranu was trading with $^{m\hat{a}t}$*kabtu-ri*, "Crete," the king enforced certain rules which may be interpreted as more direct involvement, and tighter supervision on his own behalf, in cases of international commerce (RS 16.238: 10-13).

In the law suit between Šukku and the "man of Ugarit" (RS 17.133), Šukku served as the *malaḫḫu*, "seaman," and his opponent appears to have been a private shipowner. In the economic structure of the Ur III and Old Babylonian periods, a third party was usually involved, the "capitalist-investor."[17] It is most likely that a similar economic system existed in Ugarit, and that the investor, though not mentioned, was either a wealthy merchant, or the palace itself. In the case cited, the investor would not have been from Ugarit, but from the Hittite kingdom.

C. *Joint Ventures: Royal and Private.* We have just mentioned the possibility of an investing party being the palace, while the owner of the ship or ships, or travelling merchant, might have been a private person. Such is probably the case in UT 2123, where *prkl* is the *b*^{c}*l any*, "fleet master," or simply the owner of several ships. Since *prkl* in this text is under the supervision of Abiramu, whom we identify as "harbor master," a joint commercial operation with the palace seems to have taken place. There is, however, another aspect to the text which points to the existence of a trading corporation—a *ḫubur* in Ugarit—representing a trading fleet long before such a mercantile organization is mentioned in the Wen-Amon story.[18]

[15]He appears in several texts. Cf. PRU III 101-8.

[16]These privileges indicate the exemption from certain customs duties, and special immunity given to merchants engaged in maritime trade. The practice of forbidding regular inspection of the officials in charge is echoed in the request made by the king of Alašia to the king of Egypt mentioned in the El-Amarna correspondence (EA 39-40).

[17]Oppenheim (1954) 14.

[18]Its use in the mercantile organization of shipping was recognized by W. F. Albright [Albright (1965) 482 n. 80], and B. Mazar (Maisler) calls our attention to the biblical use of *ḥbr* in the same sense, as mentioned in II Chron. 20:35-37, and Job 40:30. See Mazar (1946) 10.

D. *Foreign Traders.* Foreigners in Ugarit must have comprised a substantial portion of the population.[19] In using the term "Foreign Sea-Traders," we refer to those whose permanent port of embarcation was in a foreign land, but who sailed regularly to the Ugaritic realm, and sometimes spent part of the year on Ugaritic soil, as temporary residents of the harbor district. These seafaring merchants came directly under the jurisdiction of the *akîl kâri*, the "harbor master," who represented the economic interests of Ugarit. The major commercial transactions were carried out in the harbor district, where the marketplace and stores were close to the quays. Thus, whenever the *akîl kâri* of Ugarit exercised his authority over the merchants, he was most likely dealing with an issue concerning maritime trade involving seafaring merchants.

The most clearly defined group of foreign merchants in Ugarit were the "merchants of Ura,"[20] who are taken to be maritime traders. It is known that they originated from a coastal city with a harbor, and that grain from Mukiš for the Hittite Empire was transported by ship to Ura—the port of entry (RS 20.212; RS 20.158).[21]

Our principal source of information concerning these merchants is a text (RS 17.130) which regulates their commercial activities in Ugarit.[22] Herein, we learn of their privileges and restrictions.[23] The privileges seem to indicate a protected status under the aegis of the Hittites, for whom their harbor served as a principal outlet to the sea, closest to their inland routes. The restrictions forbade the purchase of land, and prevented any permanent settlement in Ugarit by these foreign merchants. One of the stipulations confines their trading to the summer (*i-na e-bu-ri*, lit. "the harvest"), and orders their return to their own land during the winter. An economic explanation has been offered suggesting that in the summer, after the harvest, the people were able to pay for their purchases in cash, making trade profitable.[24]

[19]Astour (1969a) 70-76.

[20]Principally mentioned in RS 17.130, RS 17.316, RS 17.319, and RS 18.20.

[21]The place of Mukiš in the geographical setting of the period, and its relations with the Hittite empire is fully documented in Astour (1969b). [See also his contribution to this volume, ed.] Al-Mina, at the mouth of the Orontes, served as the principal harbour of Alalakh in its heyday, and was probably used as port of departure for the Ura merchants carrying grain from Mukiš to Cilicia, while the ships and sailors were supplied by Ugarit, (RS 20.212; 19-26). Whether Ugarit was in control of this important harbour after annexing large areas of the kingdom of Mukiš following the "First Syrian War" of Suppiluliuma [Astour (1969b) 398] is not clear. The only harbour town explicitly mentioned in his edict is "Ḫimuli in the west of the sea." See Nougayrol in PRU IV 13.

[22]This text has been touched upon by C. H. Gordon in Gordon (1958).

[23]The legal aspects of this text were profoundly analysed in Yaron (1969). The author failed to recognize, however, the specific nature of the merchants, whose privileges and duties were conditioned by their maritime involvement.

[24]Gordon (1958) 28.

In accordance with our understanding that the merchants of Ura were seafaring traders, we suggest the following explanation of such restrictions: summer (in the broad sense, from April to October) is the most suitable sailing season in the eastern Mediterranean. The merchants of Ura arrived in their ships from Cilicia, bringing Anatolian products to Ugarit where they traded for local goods. It is because of the limitations dictated by nature that special privileges were accorded to merchants engaged in maritime trade. They must have also included a certain priority status in legal procedures. Whether or not special maritime courts already existed in Ugarit, as are known of later Athenian institutions, is still open to further investigation.[25]

There are signs that other seafaring merchants may have established temporary residence in the harbour areas of Ugarit. The kingdom's economic policy must have encouraged foreign traders to use its port facilities and marketplaces. The existence of such an international "family" of sea merchants is indicated in at least one text where, in a single document (UT 2095), oil shipments to ports of Egypt, Alašia, Ashdod, Riš, and others are enumerated.

What Were the Export and Import Items of Maritime Trade?

In the economic-administrative texts, over 350 diverse items of raw materials, finished goods, utensils, food products, livestock, and others are listed.[26] When analyzing these lists closely, it can be seen that a number of items occur, often in large quantities, and for diverse uses. The most prominent are copper (*ṯlṯ*) and bronze utensils, fabrics and garments, grain and oil.

In addition, there is a whole assortment of luxury items, some of which are listed quite frequently, and include ointments, herbs, precious stones, precious metals, and rare woods. Only a small proportion of the commodities mentioned could have been absorbed by the local market in Ugarit—the bulk being used in the extensive commercial enterprises which characterized the Ugaritic economy.

What Part of This Trade Involved Shipping?

The scope and diversity of the maritime trade in Ugarit should not be judged merely by the handful of available texts which deal *explicitly* with cargoes. Nevertheless, few and sporadic as they are, they include important information which can serve as guidelines for our knowledge and understanding of the principles of maritime trade in Ugarit, and its importance for the kingdom's prosperous existence.

[25]Cf. Cohen (1973).

[26]For full references, see Heltzer (1978a) 17-52.

An examination of the role played by copper may give us a key to the overall development of Ugarit's maritime commerce. Copper was shipped from Alašia. Its large quantities in Ugarit are known from both the written records, and archaeological finds.[27] The regular transport of this metal by sea must have had an enormous impact on the development of a merchant marine in Ugarit, even if use was also made of the Alašian fleet for transport purposes.[28]

Of the two texts which deal directly with copper shipments, one (UT 2110) is unfortunately badly damaged. The ship carried over one hundred units (presumably talents) of copper to be distributed to various customer-merchants or craftsmen. The other text (UT 2056) yields additional information: both the ship's origin (Alašia), and its port of entry in Ugarit (Atalligu). This "bill of lading" lists crude copper and finished products—mainly weapons and agricultural tools. The cargo of a Late Bronze Age wreck discovered at Cape Gelidonya consisted of similar items.[29] This ship may serve as an example of a specific phenomenon in ancient shipping, representing a complex social and economic development, whereby a seafaring merchant joined forces with a coppersmith in a maritime venture.[30]

Our knowledge of the copper industry and trading in Ugarit is supplemented by indirect evidence. Larger quantities of *t̲lt̲* are mentioned in the economic texts.[31] Some refer directly to the *nskm birtym* "smith from Beirut," who came to Ugarit, probably by ship, to get the supplies mentioned. The numerous bronze tools and weapons listed in the texts, together with those found in excavation, serve as conclusive evidence of the highly developed copper industry.[32]

Increasingly, the economy of Ugarit became based on the sea and shipping. As it grew, the balance of trade became more complex, demanding countershipments for the imported copper, in the form of products available in Ugarit. Hence, oil and grain were used to maintain the balance of payment.

[27]See, for example, the archaeological report on the hoard of bronzes discovered during the excavations of the home of the High Priest (*Ugaritica* III 249-79).

[28]Although the direct evidence for Alašian shipping is still scanty, the references in the El Amarna correspondence and the Ugaritic texts point to the existence of a sizeable fleet operating out of the island's harbours. This is well understood in the light of Alašia's complete dependence on ships for maintaining its "lifeline." Fortunately, the island was rich in timber, which served not only its shipbuilding industry, but became a major export item into Egypt (cf. EA 40:15; 35:27-28; 36:13).

[29]See Bass (1967).

[30]See Linder (1972a) 1:63-164.

[31]Cf. Heltzer (1978a) 30-33.

[32]On the copper trade and industry, see most recently Heltzer (1977), with documentation and commentary, and Muhly (1977), with emphasis on the metallurgical aspects of the copper trade.

Large oil shipments are the issue in dispute between Alašia and Ugarit (RS 20.168). In UT 2061, *Pgn* requested grain from Ugarit in additional quantities. Both cases serve as examples of this economic trend.

There is much evidence of Ugarit's specialization in the purple dye industry, and the production of dye materials and finished garments. A plant for purple dye manufacture has been excavated.[33] The list of textiles is the largest among the groups of goods recorded. At least 35 types of garments and cloth are mentioned in the texts, with over a thousand items, and point to great specialization in this industry.[34] It is reasonable to assume that these famous Phoenician products were included among the major export items, and were handled by the *akîl kâri* (RS 17.465).

Timber and wooden artifacts are mentioned frequently in the texts.[35] We know of the *ḥršdanyt,* "shipwrights," who were employed in the ship industry. Two texts (RS 14.28 and UT 2008) are definitely concerned with commercial transactions relating to shipping, involving Byblos and Alašia.[36] Other texts mention wooden ship parts such as *ta-ar-ni,* "mast" (RS 19.115), and *ma-sa-wa-tu-ma,* "oars" (RS 19.26; RS 19.71).

Ugarit's merchant marine was undoubtedly well established by the time the Hittite Empire expanded into northern Syria. The increasing maritime trade due to the relative political stability must have developed new distant markets. These, in turn, required larger ships in greater numbers, as well as more and better qualified seamen, to make the commercial transactions profitable.

Peace at sea is essential to any political entity whose economy is based on maritime trade and communications. Such peace can be achieved by diplomatic agreement between the major political powers in the area, and is realized through treaties ensuring free and safe passage of ships and their content. Another factor must be considered, however. The seas must be free of the pirates who have plagued the sea routes since the earliest maritime commercial ventures, looking for the easy prey of isolated and unprotected merchantmen. Hence, Ugarit's advantages—growing wealth, geographical position, and favorable relationship with the Hittites—turned against her, once outside forces, attracted by potentially rich prey, entered the scene.

These outsiders who endangered the peaceful mercantile ventures were the seafaring people from the western and south-western coasts of

[33]Schaeffer (1952) 38.
[34]Heltzer (1978a) 38-50.
[35]Heltzer (1978a) 36-38.
[36]See note 13, above.

Anatolia. Whether belonging originally to the *Lukka*,[37] the *Mi-ši* people of the El Amarna correspondence,[38] or the *Aḫḫiyawa*, whose early contacts with the Hittites have now been reestablished,[39] they became a menace, and endangered even the largest fleet of merchantmen. Their attacks must have increased in frequency, until the "hit-and-run" tactics gave way to large-scale assaults against major maritime centers. In order to create conditions necessary for a relative state of *pacem in maribus* in the north-eastern Mediterranean basin during the second millennium B.C.E., the possession of a strong navy was preconditional for Ugarit. It must be admitted that the textual data on the initial growth of its naval power is still very scarce. We must therefore rely mostly on indirect evidence relating primarily to the organization of shipping, and the stratification of the kingdom's naval power. Let us first bear in mind, however, the last days of Ugarit, when its war fleet gained full expression, and played a decisive role in this dramatic chapter of ancient history, involving the Hittites, Alašia, Amurru, and Ugarit itself. Full-scale naval battles were conducted, with Ugarit providing the core of the sea power both in ships (in numbers exceeding 150 according to UT 2062), and in serving as the leading force resisting the invaders at sea. Considering the political background, and the Hittites' dependence on Ugarit's previous "good services" in maritime matters, there is all the more reason to believe that the offensive naval operation taken by the Hittites against the enemy fleet near Alašia was *an Ugaritic display of its sea power*. All important elements constituting a naval battle are well represented here. There was initial planning. The encounter took place at sea between two contingents of ships. The goal was to destroy the enemy's power. Tactical use of fire for sinking the vessels was introduced. An effective intelligence information network served the attackers. Finally, we witness the coordination of a naval offensive at sea, and the attack on land. Although describing an event dating to the end of the 13th century B.C.E., this text from the Hittite archives (KBo XII, 38)[40]

[37]The militant character of the people of the land of Lukka is well demonstrated in EA 38:9-12, where their raid on the Alašian coast is described. In his letter to the king of Alašia, the king of Ugarit complains that his ships were in the land of Lukka, where they were engaged in protecting Hittite interests during the final assault of the "Sea People" (RS 29.38:22-24).

[38]We do not accept Lambdin's identification of *mi-ši* in the EA letters with "Egyptian troops." See Lambdin (1953) 75-77. We believe, rather, that these are a new type of naval mercenary. *Mi-ši* defines a *nomen-professionale* derived from the Egyptian loan word *mš*[c], normally meaning "army," but also referring to "warship," and should not be seen as defining an ethnic group. See Linder (1972b) 319-20.

[39]See the discussion in Houwink ten Cate (1973).

[40]This important text was discussed recently in Otten (1976) 27-29. The following excerpt from the text (col. III, 5-10), contains the essential data: "The ships of Alašiya met me in the sea three times for battle and I smote them; and I seized the ships and set fire to

reflects a long history of naval warfare to which Ugarit must have contributed a major portion in its development.

Let us now turn to the internal evidence bearing on Ugarit's fleet, and the manpower in its service. Ships appear under different names in Ugarit: some in the construct state with *any* (such as *anyt-mlk, any-alṯy, anyt yam*), others in Akkadian as *elippe-rabâ*. Two ship terms, *br* and *tkt* are also known from the Egyptian New Kingdom records. Until marine archaeology supplies us with the hard-core material evidence of the different ship types used in the Late Bronze Age, we must accept the principle of multi-purpose use of ships, which was a characteristic of ancient shipping. Ships of the same type, with certain modifications in construction and composition of crew, could serve as merchantmen, troopers, cavalry carriers, and warships engaged in combat. As late as the medieval period, we know of this multi-purpose principle in the Mediterranean, although the distinction between the *longship* and the *round ship* is known as early as the first millennium B.C.E.

In numbers, Ugarit possessed a remarkable fleet. In the so-called "Catalogues of Ships" (UT 319; UT 2085), we count sixteen entries in one text, and fifteen in another. These must have represented only a fraction of Ugarit's fleet, if we bear in mind the reference to the demand for 150 ships, equipped and ready for action, which was mentioned earlier (UT 2062), or the hundred ships to carry the grain mentioned in a Hittite text (Bo 2810), which must have referred to the Ugaritic fleet.

The ships' crews were divided into two major categories: (a) professional, skilled seafarers and artisans who were permanently engaged in shipping; and (b) unskilled manpower in temporary service. To the first category belong the captains, or commanders, of the ships, the sailors (*malaḫḫe* or *māre malaḫḫe*) in their various capacities, and shipwrights [*ḥrš any*(*t*)]. The second category includes rowers and warriors on auxiliary duties [*sbn ellepi*, or *sbn any*(*t*)].

We believe that the emergence of a new breed of aristocratic citizenry developed with the growing importance of the Ugaritic navy. These were the captain-commanders of the ships, a counterpart of the *maryannu*, "elite chariot warriors," who represented the highest of the military guilds. For them to be able to engage permanently in shipping, privileges must have been bestowed on the captains in the way of economic grants and hereditary rights.[41]

---

them in the sea. But when I arrived on dry land (?) the enemies from Alašiya came in multitudes against me for battle. I fought them...." [Güterbock (1967) 78].

[41]Astour suggested that "the merchants served in the élite corps of the army as *mariannu*, "charioteers" [Astour (1972b) 26]. This idea, if applied to seafaring merchants, suits our assumption well, with the difference that instead of rendering their services to the king on land as charioteers, they were required to serve on board ship.

As for the professional crews, we assume that they were called in for limited periods (during the sailing season) to serve as rowers and/or "marines" as part of their *corvée* duties. These are the *ṣbu any*(*t*), "personnel of the ship," a term which indicates not only the wider meaning of *ṣbu*, but also, more specifically, the type and character of the service rendered by the conscripted men listed in the text. They were sailors and warriors who served on ships, while their *ṣbu* counterparts served on land.

The principal of mobilization, and the system of manning the ships, as they appear in the administrative texts (UT 83, UT 319, and UT 2085), find their exact parallels in the so-called "Homeric Catalogue of Ships,"[42] and in some of the Linear B tablets.[43] Here, as well as in Ugarit, the military character of this system of mobilization points to the existence of a well-organized war fleet in the heyday of Ugarit's history.

The Aegean example in the organization of the war fleet, and the influence on the development of combat tactics at sea, must have evolved from direct contact between Ugarit and its western neighbors. Can we see in this an historical repetition in an opposed direction—when Canaanite seafarers in the third millennium B.C.E. may have transmitted the skills of building large *kfty* ships to the Cretans?

Peaceful relationships alone, however, could not have brought about the growth of Ugarit's navy to the necessary proportions for defending its merchant marine. It must also have been the continuous conflict of piratical nature, forced upon Ugarit by the early sea people from the north-west, which shaped its "sea power."[44] Is it possible that the *šardanu* mentioned in the texts served in the capacity of naval mercenaries, and thus contributed to Ugarit's skills in naval warfare?

Finally, the question of regulating the activities of the merchants and seamen in a specific framework of legal procedures must be raised. Is there any indication of the existence of commercial maritime laws, or anything even vaguely resembling Athens' *"dikai emporikai,"* so typical of a thalassocracy?[45]

The closest we come to finding any parallel is the case of the merchants of Ura, with regard to whom a clear distinction is made between their rights in the summer, and those in the winter. Such

[42]See Gaster (1938). He has drawn attention to the striking analogy between the Ugaritic texts under discussion, and the list of ships which appears in the second book of the *Iliad* (lines 494-827).

[43]Tablet no. 53 (=Ahl2 from Pylos), for example, mentions 30 rowers recruited from five different localities to serve as the crew of a single Mycenaean ship. See Ventris and Chadwick (1959).

[44]See notes 37-39, above.

[45]See Cohen (1973) chapter 1.

distinctions, we find, served as a basis for the treatment of foreign merchants in the maritime courts of Athens.[46]

We are just at the beginning of our efforts to unfold the leaves of Ugarit's maritime heritage. What is very much needed is a wide and penetrating, comparative study with other sea powers—be it Tyre, Athens, Carthage, or Venice. We believe that Ugarit holds the basis, both in concept and in detail, of the makings of a true thalassocracy.

[46]Cohen (1973) 52-53.

LES RECENTES DECOUVERTES EPIGRAPHIQUES A RAS SHAMRA ET A RAS IBN HANI

PIERRE BORDREUIL

Chargé de recherche au C.N.R.S.
Institut d'études sémitiques
Collège de France

I. *Ras Shamra:*

La Tablette akkadienne RS 32.204, découverte fortuitement en surface au début de 1971,[1] a fait l'objet d'une communication à l'Académie des Inscriptions et Belles Lettres le 7 janvier 1972 par le regretté Jean Nougayrol, mais son décès prématuré a empêché la publication de ce document. Il m'a été possible d'avoir connaissance du texte de cette communication,[2] d'aprés laquelle la tablette est une double lettre; une face contient une requête au roi, qui est formulée par un homme du nom de Kilaʾe. Informé du voyage entrepris par le roi à Neirab, il demande au monarque de provoquer à cette occasion et en sa présence, une confrontation entre lui Kilaʾe et un habitant de Neirab, dont le nom est Bin Kabkamma.

L'autre face contient la copie d'une lettre envoyée précédement par le même expéditeur Kilaʾe, à la reine d'Ougarit, au sujet du voyage du roi et de la reine à Neirab.

La découverte accidentelle de cette tablette dans un tas de déblais non archéologiques fut à l'origine de la fouille de ces déblais pendant la 34e campagne de 1973 qui mit au jour un grand nombre de fragments inscrits. Les textes alphabétiques ont fait l'objet d'une publication préliminaire,[3] et la publication des textes syllabiques est en préparation.

On doit encore ajouter un fragment de tablette alphabétique trouvé en 1974 par un ouvrier en dehors de la campagne de fouilles. Ce fragment, que nous appellerons 34.356 est la copie d'une lettre du roi

[1]Sur les circonstances exactes de la découverte, voir Bordreuil (1975) esp. p. 19.
[2]Mes remerciements vont à Madame Jean Nougayrol qui m'a autorisé à en faire etat.
[3]Voir Caquot (1975) 427-31, et Bordreuil (1975).

ᶜAmmourapi à un autre souverain qu'il appelle "le Soleil, le grand Roi, mon Seigneur," et dont il se considère comme le serviteur. Seules ont été conservées les formules épistolaires introductives, mais, bien que fragmentaire, cette tablette nous permet de restituer à la ligne 9 le titre *mlk mlk*[*m*], "Roi des rois," maintenant attesté sans aucun doute sur une tablette de Ras Ibn Hani dont nous reparlerons. De plus, la présence du nom ᶜAmmourapi nous permet d'établir une concordance chronologique entre la tablette 34.356 et la tablette 34.126, mise au jour l'année précédente. En effet, ce dernier texte, consacré aux Rephaim, mentionne également le roi ᶜAmmourapi.[4] Ces deux textes seraient donc à dater des dernières années de la ville d'Ougarit.

II. *Ras Ibn Hani:*

Depuis 1975, une mission conjointe franco-syrienne a entrepris de fouiller le site de Ras Ibn Hani, situé à 5 km environ au sud-ouest de Ras Shamra. La direction de cette entreprise a été confiée à MM. Adnan Bounni, Directeur des fouilles à la Direction Générale des Antiquités et des Musées de la République Arabe Syrienne, et Jacques Lagarce, Chargé de recherche au Centre National de la Recherche Scientifique.

Le site s'étend sur un promontoire qui s'avance dans la mer, sur une longueur de 2.500 m et une largeur de 500 m. On y distingue encore les vestiges d'une ville hellenistique, mais le tell lui-même, d'une hauteur de 10 m environ a été occupé depuis le Bronze Ancien jusqu'à l'époque byzantine.

A la fin de quatre campagnes de fouilles, l'installation du Bronze Récent est connue dans trois secteurs du tell:

1) Dans la partie sud-ouest qui est la plus élevée, un important batiment a été découvert et partiellement dégagé. Considéré comme le Palais Sud, il couvre une surface environ 5.000 m^2. La technique de construction est comparable à celle du Palais Royal d'Ougarit qui date de la même époque. Bati sur une éminence artificielle formée de plusieurs terrasses, il domine la mer alentour.
2) Un sondage entrepris à 600 m au nord-ouest de ce palais a permis de dégager des murs d'une maison du Bronze Récent, dont l'orientation coincide avec celle du palais.
3) A plus de 200 m du palais sud, le long de la côte nord de la péninsule, avait été découvert, il y a quelques années, un caveau funéraire analogue à ceux d'Ougarit, dont le dégagement fut

[4]Voir Caquot (1975) 428ff.

confié à M. Kassem Toueir de la Direction Générale des Antiquités et des Musées de la République Arabe Syrienne.[5] Comme à Ougarit, cette tombe formait en réalité le sous sol d'une habitation importante que les fouilleurs considèrent comme un palais. Une cour s'ouvre vers l'est sur une série de pièces. Dans l'une d'entre elles, à l'angle sud-ouest de la cour, quelques marches conduisent à une chambre édifiée au dessus du caveau funéraire. Notons en passant que les murs de ce batiment sont orientés nord-ouest—sud-est, comme dans les deux secteurs déjà mentionnés en 1) et en 2).

Comme le palais sud, le palais nord fut détruit par un violent incendie qui a laissé une épaisse couche de cendres et de matériaux calcinés. C'est dans le palais nord que furent découvertes plusieurs dizaines de tablettes écrites en ougaritique et en akkadien, dont il va être question plus loin. Leur état, souvent fragmentaire est du probablement à l'ecroulement de leur lieu de stockage, situé au premier étage.

Une partie du palais sud fut bientôt réaménagée en habitations privées qui ont livré du matériel daté du 12e siècle av. J.C., parmi lequel des tessons de style mycénien tardif, qui sont des imitations de Mycénien III C 1. Cela pourrait signifier que ce site a connu une réoccupation rapide par des populations apparentées aux Peuples de la Mer, ce qui ne fut pas le cas à Ougarit. Sur la côte de Méditerranée orientale, une telle séquence d'occupation ne paraît attestée jusqu'à présent que dans quelques sites, parmi lesquels la plaine d'Antioche et Sarafand.

Les textes découverts en 1977 par la mission conjointe franco-syrienne sont trés variés.[6] En voici un rapide inventaire, accompagné de quelques extraits.

77/26 Texte

. . . .

3) *id . ydbḥ . mlk . lilib*
4) *bdb . ap . wnpš . ksp*
5) *wḫrṣ . kmm . alp . wš*
6) *šrp . lilib . wšlm*

. . . .

[5]Parmi les découvertes, figure un beau cratère mycénien III B. Voir Toueir (1975) 66-70.

[6]Les principaux textes alphabétiques de 1977 ont fait l'objet d'une publication préliminaire comprenant la transcription, la traduction et un bref commentaire par A. Caquot in Caquot (1977-78) 570-77. L'ensemble des textes, accompagnés de planches photographiques, est publié par P. Bordreuil et A. Caquot sous le titre, "Les textes cunéiformes alphabétiques de Ras Ibn Hani 1977," *Syria* 56, 1979, 295-315.

Traduction

3) Quand le roi sacrifie à Ilib (=Dieu Père)
4) dans le *db*, un nez et une gorge, de l'argent
5) et de l'or, de même un taureau et un mouton
6) en holocauste au Dieu Père et un sacrifice *šlm*

On notera la mention de Ilib, déjà connu par trois listes de divinités.[7]

77/10b

Double rituel de quatorze lignes dont le vocabulaire est identique à celui de PRU V, 5, mais ici, les sept premières lignes sont consacrées à Rashap et la suite du texte, séparée du début par un double trait horizontal, concerne le culte de ᶜAnat.

Texte

1) *i]d . yph . mlk . ršp*
2) *ḥgb . a[p] . wnpš*
3) *ksp . wḫ[rṣ] . kmm*

. . . .

8) *id . yph . mlk . ᶜnt*
9) *slḫ . ap . wnpš . ksp*
10) *w]ḫrṣ . kmm*

Traduction

1) Qu]and le roi voit Rašap
2) *ḥgb*, un ne[z] et une gorge,
3) argent et o[r] de même

. . . .

8) Quand le roi voit ᶜAnat
9) de *slḫ*, un nez et une gorge, argent
10) et] or, de même . . .

Les lignes 4-7 sont incomplètes. Le terme *ḥgb* associé à Rashap reste encore inexpliqué; *slḫ*, au contraire, est un toponyme déjà connu par les textes d'Ougarit.

77/21

Bien qu'endommagé, ce fragment est important en raison de la mention de Baal et de Dagan à la ligne 10 et de *lšd . qdš*, "au *šd* saint," à la ligne 13. La mention de *rpi . yqr* à la ligne 14 pourrait favoriser l'interpretation des Rephaim comme les anciens rois d'Ougarit divinisés.[8]

[7]La dernière est publiée dans Ugaritica VII, p. 1-3 (1.1). Le nom propre *ᶜbdʾlʾb̊* est peut-être connu par un sceau; cf. Vattioni (1969) 368, no. 73.

[8]Voir Kitchen (1977) 131-42.

En l'occurence, le *rpi* pourrait être Yaqarou, le premier roi de la dynastie d'Ougarit.

77/1, 77/23, et 77/21b sont de petits fragments de lettres royales. Dans 77/21b, la lacune empêche de connaître l'identité de l'auteur du message, dont le nom commençant par ^{c}*ayn* pourrait être celui de ^{c}Ammiṯtamrou ou de ^{c}Ammourapi.

77/14 est une liste de 71 lignes. Les noms propres lisibles sont souvent des patronymes suivis du nombre 10 ou 20.

Au cours de cette même campagne, plusieurs tablettes accadiennes furent découvertes, parmi lesquelles figure un colophon signé par le "scribe de la reine d'Ougarit."[9]

La campagne de 1978 fut encore plus riche. Le principal texte, 78/20, compte actuellement 21 lignes dont 16 sont facilement lisibles. Il s'agit d'un formulaire magique demandant à Ḥoron d'expulser d'un individu les êtres malfaisants. Par le pouvoir du sacrifice, la malédiction disparaîtra . . .

kqṭr . urbtm . kbṯn . ^{c}*mdm*
ky^{c}*lm . ẓrh . klbim . skh*

"Comme une fumée par le trou, comme un
serpent par l'assise (du mur),
Comme des bouquetins vers le sommet, comme
des lions vers le fourré. . . . "[10]

Le fragment mythologique 78/9+17 presente un nouveau titre divin qui pourrait être l'apanage de Baal, *mšmṭr* (*mušamṭir*), participe *shaph*^{c}*el* signifiant "celui qui fait pleuvoir."

Parmi quelques rituels incomplets, le texte 78/11, qui mentionne les noms de Dagan, Pidray et Baal Sapon, atteste une activité sacrificielle de la reine.

Les textes épistolaires sont représentés par 78/12, qui est une lettre adressée "à la reine ma mère" (*lmlkt . umy*) et 78/3, qui relève de la correspondance internationale et mentionne les ougaritains (*ugrtym*) et le roi d'Egypte (*mlk mṣrm*), qui pourrait être qualifié de roi des rois (*mlk mlkm*) et de roi juste (*mlk ṣdq*).

On peut d'ores et déjà tirer de l'ensemble de ces textes quelques conclusions concernant l'histoire du site:

1) Le *rpi yqr,* que l'on peut identifier à Yaqarou, évoque la dynastie d'Ougarit, ce qui permet de supposer l'existence de liens entre les deux villes.

[9]Nous renvoyons à ce sujet à la publication de ces textes par D. Arnaud et D. Kennedy *Syria* 56, 1979.

[10]Traduction des lignes 3-4 par A. Caquot, *Annuaire du Collège de France* 79 (1978-9).

2) Les rituels découverts à Ras Ibn Hani sont rédigés dans les mêmes termes que ceux d'Ougarit.
3) Les anthroponymes nous révèlent un groupe ethnique apparenté à celui d'Ougarit; sur un peu plus de cinquante noms propres, une dizaine seulement sont nouveaux dans l'onomastique ougaritienne.

Les fouilles ont aussi révélé des différences entre Ougarit et la ville du Bronze Récent découverte à Ras Ibn Hani. Dans cette dernière, et contrairement à Ougarit, on distingue un tracé orthogonal des rues et les murs mis au jour sont perpendiculaires et orientés nord-ouest — sud-est. L'ensemble du site, tel qu'il est connu jusqu'à maintenant, donne l'impression d'avoir été conçu comme un tout et d'avoir été édifié pour servir les desseins de la métropole. La présence même de deux palais permet de se demander si la ville ancienne de Ras Ibn Hani n'aurait pas servi de résidence secondaire (estivale?) à la famille royale d'Ougarit. En tous cas, ce site constitue un exemple remarquable d'agglomération provinciale du Bronze Récent à quelques kilomètres d'Ougarit.

La réoccupation du site aprés une destruction probablement contemporaine de celle d'Ougarit, aux environs de 1200 av. J.C., contraste avec l'abandon définitif d'Ougarit. A Ras Ibn Hani, on constate l'existence d'un niveau d'occupation comprenant plusieurs exemples de poterie de style local, copiant le Mycénien III C 1, datée des premières décennies du 12e siècle. L'existence d'une telle séquence stratigraphique dans d'autre sites du Levant n'est pas sans importance pour essayer de comprendre les causes de la destruction finale d'Ougarit.

Une dernière question s'est posée aux membres de la mission: quel est le nom de la ville du Bronze Récent qui occupe le Ras Ibn Hani? Nous allons apporter un essai de réponse.

Une ville du nom de Appou (*ap* en écriture alphabétique) est citée quatre fois dans les archives du palais royal d'Ougarit.[11] Notre hypothèse est qu' Appou, pourrait correspondre à la position géographique du Ras Ibn Hani, étroite péninsule s'enfonçant dans la mer comme un nez (en ougaritique, *ap*). A l'appui de cette idée, rappelons que le terme géographique arabe pour ce type de promontoire est parfois *anf*, littéralement, "nez," ce qui est le cas pour Enfé, cap situé au sud de Tripoli du Liban, à un peu plus de cent kilomètres d'Ougarit.[12]

[11]PRU V, nos. 40:1, 42:2, et 74:1. KTU 4.693, 11.

[12]M. H. Cazelles me signale un cap, situé peut-être en Palestine, que le texte égyptien de l'expedition d'Ouni appelle Sheret-Tep-Géhès, "Nez de la gazelle;" cf. J. A. Wilson dans ANET 228, n. 10, et Helck (1962) 18, nn. 51 et 52.

UGARIT, CANAAN AND EGYPT

SOME NEW EPIGRAPHIC EVIDENCE FROM TEL APHEK IN ISRAEL*

DAVID I. OWEN

Cornell University

During the seventh season of excavation (1978) at the site of Tel Aphek (Tell Ras el-ᶜAin) in Israel, two cuneiform tablets—one nearly complete (Reg. No. 52055/1) and a second mostly fragmentary (Reg. No. 52060/1)—were discovered.[1] They had been found during the removal of a large, partially eroded, balk (Locus 5218) which had been standing over part of building 1104, a structure now designated as the "government house."[2] The removal of the balk was made necessary to allow for the restoration of this remarkably well preserved Late Bronze Age structure.[3] Five cuneiform text fragments of various types had been discovered in earlier seasons in this building, and all are now published.[4] A sixth fragment, previously identified as a Sumero-Akkadian bilingual literary text, was found in the alley (Locus 2725) adjacent to the "government house."[5] However, W. W. Hallo has now more convincingly

*Summary of paper delivered at the Ugarit Symposium. A full edition of the cuneiform text described in this summary is in press and will appear in *Tel Aviv* 7 (1980). I would like to thank Professor Moshe Kochavi, director of the Tel Aphek-Antipatris excavations, for the permission to discuss this important discovery in advance of its final publication. I would also like to thank Cornell University, College of Arts and Sciences for the Humanities Faculty Research Grant which partly supported my research on the Aphek inscriptions.

[1]The seventh season of excavation at Aphek was directed by Professor Moshe Kochavi and sponsored by Tel Aviv University Institute of Archaeology, the Petah Tiqva Municipality, Allegheny College, Cornell University and Rice University. See Owen (1980), forthcoming.

[2]See Kochavi (1978a) 14-15 for a description, plan, and photos of the building.

[3]The restoration of this building was completed during the ninth season of excavation (1980) and is open to the general public.

[4]Rainey (1975) and (1976), reprinted in Kochavi (1978c) 8-16, and summarized in Kochavi (1978a) 15-17.

[5]Kochavi (1978a) 17 *sub* no. 4, and (1978b) 5.

explained the text as a fragment of an Akkadian letter.[6] Two other inscriptions—one a Hittite hieroglyphic bulla,[7] and a second, an Egyptian hieroglyphic inscription on a faience ring[8]—were also found in the same locus. Thus, to date, eight cuneiform texts and fragments have been excavated from the debris of the "government house" along with the other inscriptions noted above.[9]

The "government house" was destroyed sometime during the second half of the thirteenth century B.C.E. probably towards the middle of the century according to the latest estimate.[10] On the basis of a wide variety of local and imported pottery found in the destruction level (collared-rim pithoi, Cypriote milkbowls and Mycenaean IIIb stirrup vases, among others), Prof. Kochavi now dates the destruction to between 1250-1240,[11] and not to the end of the century as had been previously suggested.[12] The building was engulfed in a huge conflagration whose remains, nearly two meters of red, burned brick debris and charred wooden beams, cover the site. Bronze arrowheads removed from the southern facade of the "government house" attest to the battle which probably raged around the building before its final destruction.[13]

Aphek sits at a strategic point on the Via Maris controlling the relatively narrow pass between the swamps at the source of the River Yarkon and the rocky Hills of Samaria. The city had been subjugated by the Egyptians as early as the reign of Thutmoses III when he took the city in ca. 1475 B.C., and again under his son, Amehotep II during his second Asiatic campaign.[14] No additional information is forthcoming from Egyptian or other sources until the end of the Late Bronze Age when it is listed as among the Canaanite cities conquered by Joshua (Joshua 12:18).[15] The archaeological materials from the site strongly suggest that it was under Egyptian control at least in the first half of the

[6]See Hallo (1980), forthcoming. I would like to thank Prof. Hallo for providing me with a copy of his article in advance of its publication.

[7]Singer (1977), reprinted in Kochavi (1978c) 17-29.

[8]Giveon (1978), reprinted in Kochavi (1978c) 5.

[9]The Egyptian faience foundation tablet (Reg. No. 33400/80) found during the sixth season (1977) did not actually come from the level of the "government house" but from a pit in stratum X8, about one meter above the level of the courtyard. See Kochavi (1978c) 6 for a discussion of the circumstances of the find.

[10]Kochavi (1978a) 14.

[11]Verbal communication from Prof. Kochavi.

[12]See Rainey (1975) 125. The stratum representing most of the thirteenth century B.C.E. has been assigned the number X12 (M. Kochavi 1978c: 3).

[13]Kochavi (1978a) 15.

[14]Kochavi (1975) 18-19, reprinted in Kochavi and Beck (1976). See also Kochavi (1977) 7-8.

[15]A comprehensive history of the site by R. Frankel will appear as a chapter in volume one of the final excavation report now in preparation. For the present cf. Kochavi (1975) 17-20.

thirteenth century B.C.E. until the destruction described above when it, perhaps, reverted to Canaanite control. In any case caravans, diplomatic messengers, and officials traveling to and from Syria and Egypt would surely have stopped at this site, particularly during the period of relaxed and cordial relations that existed between Egypt and Ḫatti in the reigns of Ḫattušiliš III, Tudḫaliyaš IV and Ramses II.[16] The fortress-like construction of the "government house" at Aphek suggests some military presence, perhaps an Egyptian garrison. The discovery of a diplomatic letter from Ugarit addressed to Ḫaya, a high Egyptian official, is, of course, no proof that the official resided in Aphek any more so than the previously discovered Hittite hieroglyphic bulla was proof that a Hittite prince had passed through the site. The new text does not provide any direct evidence that it was destined for Aphek since it does not indicate where Ḫaya was located. However, if the restoration of the city name in line 17 is correct (written URU [*ia-p*]*u-ú*) then Jaffa might have been its destination.[17] The city of Jaffa is known to have been an important center of Egyptian power at this time and the seat of the Egyptian governor. But the substantial evidence from Aphek indicates that it too was part of the Egyptian sphere of influence with very strong Egyptian presence at the site, including the possibility that an Egyptian temple to Isis was situated there.[18] Thus there is no reason to exclude the likelihood that the letter was destined for Ḫaya at Aphek.

The letter was found lying on a collapsed plastered floor which had fallen onto the ground floor from an upper story. It was found in association with another, albeit larger, cuneiform tablet which, unfortunately, contained only a few legible signs.[19] In addition to the tablets, two bead necklaces, a bone hairpin and a substantial amount of pottery were recovered from the same locus. The well preserved tablet (cf. photo of obverse below) is forty-one lines long.

The text consists of a letter written by Takuḫlina, prefect of Ugarit (LÚ.ŠA.KI KUR URU *ú-ga-ri-it*), to Ḫaya, the great man (*a-na* ^{m}*ḫa-a-ia* LÚ.GAL). We have tentatively identified the writer with Takḫulina and Takuḫlu of Ugarit, both active in the first half of the thirteenth century B.C.E. at Ugarit, Ḫattušaš and Karkemiš,[20] although this remains to be worked out in detail. As for Ḫaya, he is likely to be identified with the Egyptian *ḥy*, an ambassador active in the reign of Ramses II,[21] although

[16]Singer (1977) 186-87, reprinted in Kochavi (1978c) 25-26.

[17]The restoration was suggested to me by both Prof. H. Tadmor and Prof. W. W. Hallo.

[18]Giveon (1978) 188-90, reprinted in Kochavi (1978c) 32-33.

[19]Owen (1980), forthcoming.

[20]Nougayrol (1968) 99 n.2. I am grateful to Prof. I. Singer of Tel Aviv University for sharing his insights into the Hittite and Ugarit sources for Takḫulina and Takuḫlu and discussing the problems associated with the ordering of events in the dossiers.

[21]Vallogia (1976) 128-30 nos. 74-76, with bibliography.

Aphek 7:52055/1, obverse of Akkadian letter from Ugarit, found at Tel Aphek. Photo: M. Weinberg.

here too the equation requires further study. On the basis of what is known about the careers of these two officials, a date for the letter around the middle of the thirteenth century, ca. 1250, can be suggested. This would agree with and support the conclusions of the excavator of Aphek who arrived at a similar date for the destruction.

After twelve lines of introduction and greetings, the substance of the letter begins. It concerns a request by Takuḫlina for Ḫaya to return a quantity of wheat which a certain Adduya had given to an individual named Turšimati in Jaffa. The letter continues with another request by Takuḫlina that Ḫaya adjudicate the taking of some silver from Takuḫlina's courier, Adduya, by some unnamed enemy. The text concludes with a note concerning a gift of a quantity of blue and red wool sent by Takuḫlina to Ḫaya. The letter is written in the scribal dialect of Ugarit and contains a number of innovations to the otherwise well-known address and greeting formulae from Ugarit.[22]

Thus, for the first time, we have a contemporary historical inscription from Canaan proper in the thirteenth century B.C.E. directly relating to the relationship between Ugarit and Egypt via Canaan. The find of the royal Hittite bulla can now be placed more accurately in this period, allaying whatever doubts its publisher may have had concerning its date.[23] These finds, added to the other cuneiform and hieroglyphic texts and fragments from Aphek, attest to the importance of this site for our understanding of the Late Bronze Age in Canaan. The discovery of lexical texts among the inscriptions has suggested the possibility that a local scribal school existed at Aphek.[24] At this stage, the excavations at Aphek have already produced the most varied inscriptional finds of any Late Bronze Age site in Israel. Furthermore, the close dating of a large corpus of pottery from the "government house" may provide an invaluable aid for the absolute dating of similar materials from related sites. While the full study of the Aphek finds has yet to be completed,[25] the implications of these finds are clear. No longer can we doubt the literacy of the Canaanites in the South, nor can we dismiss the possibility that continued excavations at Aphek or elsewhere will one day soon produce a long sought Canaanite archive.

[22]Finley (1979) 50-51, and Owen (1980), forthcoming.

[23]Singer (1977) 187, reprinted in Kochavi (1978c) 26.

[24]Kochavi (1978a) 17.

[25]Volume one of the final report has just been completed (1980) and will shortly go to press.

SOME EGYPTOLOGICAL CONSIDERATIONS CONCERNING UGARIT

RAPHAEL GIVEON

Institute of Archeology, Tel Aviv University

I. *The Name of Ugarit in Hieroglyphic Writing.*

The oldest known mention of Ugarit is of the time of Amenophis II.[1] The writing there is 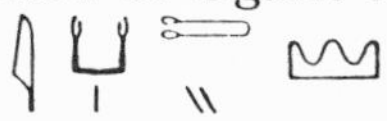 . Yeivin (1967) 122 denies the identity with Ugarit. The problem is the transcription of the biliteral hieroglyph *kꜣ* (Gardiner's Sign List: D.28) after the Middle Kingdom, when there is no doubt concerning the transcription as *kr* and *kl.* This writing of Ugarit, as we shall see, is not normal; it has its parallel in a series of scarabs which have the inscription *mn-ḫpr-r*^{c} *nb hkꜣim nṯr nfr* $^{\supset}$*Imn-R*^{c} "Thutmosis III, Lord of Hekalim, the good god, Amon-Re."[2] These inscriptions, to be dated to the time of Thutmosis III and later, have clearly *hkꜣỉm,* with the same *kꜣ* (Gardiner's D.28) which has to be read *hkrỉm-hklỉm* (= temples); this is a parallel case to the reading of Ugarit in the Karnak-and Memphis Stelae of Amenophis II. It is an archaic use of the biliteral hieroglyph *kꜣ*, the normal writing has the same *kꜣ* and the *r* written in addition, perhaps to avoid mistakes in reading at a time when the Middle Kingdom method of writing went out of use. In the Nubian temple of Amenophis III at Soleb, Ugarit is written 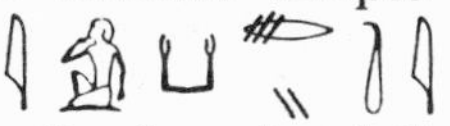 .[3]

In the related lists, also from Nubia, of the time of Rameses II, at Aksha and Amarah West the writing is  (Aksha),[4] and  (Amarah).[5] List XII of the work by Simons,[6]

[1]Helck (1955) 1303,9; Edel (1953) 149.
[2]Edel (1966) 21, Giveon (1979) 138-41.
[3]Simons (1937) 132 N. a5; Giveon (1964) 246 No. V B 4.
[4]Kitchen (1979) 211,9.
[5]Kitchen (1979) 215,9.
[6]Simons (1937) 135.

again has as No. 12 Ugarit. Only the first part of the word is preserved, and this is written exactly as in the lists in Nubia. Simons dated this list to Haremhab, but the right date is Amenophis III, as is the list of Soleb.[7] In practically the same form we have the writing of the name of the city in the account of the Battle of Qadesh, when Ugarit was allied with the Hittites.[8] Recently Edel has published another occurrence of the name of the city from the representation of the prisoners taken at the battle of Qadesh.[9] It seems that we have here (*mariannu* soldiers of) . . . Ugarit. This is written: 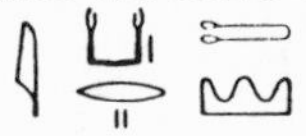 .

II. *The Egyptian Middle Kingdom in Ugarit.*

A series of objects of the XII Dynasty have been found in Ugarit. We list these in chronological order.

1) Sesostris I

a) carnelian bead with private name of the king *ḫpr-kȝ-rꜥ*. The name is preceded by "the good god" and followed by "Beloved of Hathor, the Lady of Dendera."[10]

b) cylinder seal, light brown jasper. It has the private name of the king *ḫpr-kȝ-rꜥ* only. It was bought in Lataqia, and said to come from Ugarit. It is now in the Chabachoff Collection, Paris.[11]

2) Amenemhet II

A partly destroyed statuette of the princess *Khenemet-nefer-khedjet* has been discovered at Ugarit.[12] The text has twice repeated, "The daughter of the king, of his body—*Khenemet-nefer-khedjet*, may she live." A princess of the same name appears on a cylinder seal of the Timmins Collection together with the prenomen of Amenemhet II.[13] This does not mean that father and daughter appear together on this seal: she may be the daughter of another king, associated with Amenemhet II. However, the seal of the Timmins Collection points to a date for the princess, so does her dress.[14] In Qatna there was found a statuette of another princess of Amenemhet II, *ʾIta*. Helck[15] claims that both princesses were buried in a common grave near the pyramid of Amenemhet at Dashur, and that both statuettes had been robbed from the tomb during the Hyksos period and exported to Western Asia.

[7]Edel (1966) 51.
[8]Kuentz (1928) 214, 227, 241, 342.
[9]Edel (1979) 84.
[10]Schaeffer (1962) 215 & fig. 20.
[11]Giveon (1967) 35-36 & fig. 2.
[12]Schaeffer (1962) 212 & fig. 19.
[13]Newberry (1907) 11, No. 9.
[14]For this problem see Perdu (1977) 68-70, 80-82.
[15]Helck (1976) 107.

3) Amenemhet III

a) Two Sphinxes of Amenemhet III[16]

The literature always mentions two objects. They were found in many fragments, and Helck suspects that they represent only one piece, and were wrongly reconstructed as two. The object which is listed as belonging to the Louvre could not be found there.[17]

b) Cylinder Seal of Amenemhet III[18]

This seal, in the Chabachoff Collection, was bought in Lataqia and comes most probably from Ugarit. It has the prenomen of the king twice.

c) Statue of Sesostris—ᶜankh[19]

This vizier is generally identified with the official of the same name in an inscription in Florence.[20] Vallogia[21] points out the likelihood that this important official, who has been given the title "vizier," had an essential function as regards messengers coming from Egypt to Ugarit, just as Sinuhet had in another context.

The listing of these XIIth Dynasty objects makes it necessary to refer to Helck's position.[22] He maintains that these objects—the bead, the royal sculpture, and the statuette of the official—had come to Ugarit during a later period than the Middle Kingdom. He thinks that the Hyksos, being strangers to Egypt, had no scruples to export the objects (after robbing royal and private tombs). It seems to us that the Hyksos, despite their Asiatic background, did not regard themselves strangers to Egypt; they identified with Egypt, some of their names were Egyptian, nor was their religion restricted to Baal (or Seth). Nearly all of their officials had Egyptian names. It is true that we lack Middle Bronze IIA contexts for the Middle Kingdom objects found in Canaan; but it is equally true that we lack Hyksos contexts for the same objects almost everywhere. We do not agree with Helck that the Middle Kingdom objects were the result of "antiquities trade" in Hyksos or New Kingdom times. We should rather think that the Egyptians sent sculpture of royalty to Ugarit, and other important cities in the northern part of Western Asia, as diplomatic presents. The sculpture of officials found in Ugarit and in Palestine seems to indicate that Egyptian officials were sent there who took these statuettes with them for an eventual burial should death overcome them

[16]Schaeffer (1962) 223 & fig. 25.
[17]Helck (1976) 104.
[18]Giveon (1967) 36.
[19]Schaeffer (1962) 217 & figs. 22-23.
[20]S. Bostico (1965) 44, No. 39, Pl. 39.
[21]Vallogia (1976) 223.
[22]Helck (1976) 104-14.

at their outpost abroad. We have to regard the famous statuette of *Ḏḥwty-ḥtp* at Megiddo[23] in just this manner.

We think in this context not of Egyptian "imperialism" in the style of the New Kingdom, but of firm control by the Egyptians of the important trade routes from Egypt to Asia, and the existence of Egyptian strongholds in some Canaanite cities.[24] The Stelae of Nesmont (Louvre C 1)[25] (which, by the way, is *not* of Asiatic origin) and of *Ḫw-sbk*[26] show that there was military activity in Palestine to establish or maintain control. We imagine the relations with the great northern cities like Ugarit to have been more of a diplomatic kind. Presents of royal sculpture on the one hand, and the presence of pharaonic emissaries, as in Ugarit, are evidence for this.

The treasure of Tod—of the time of Amenemhet II—is an additional indication of the mutual relations between Egypt and Northern Canaan. The finds in Tod include Mesopotamian seals and Aegean silverware. Great commercial centres like Ugarit could well be the source of this treasure.

[23]Wilson (1941) 225.
[24]Giveon (1967) 29-32.
[25]Porter-Moss (1962) 382.
[26]Mentioned in Helck (1976) 110.

THE EXCAVATIONS AT RAS SHAMRA

AND THEIR PLACE IN THE CURRENT ARCHAEOLOGICAL PICTURE OF ANCIENT SYRIA

RUDOLPH H. DORNEMANN

Milwaukee Public Museum

It is my pleasure this morning to present the first paper in the Ugaritic Symposium which your officers have organized with so much diligence and hard work. I must begin by paying tribute to the 50 years of dedicated French effort which has been expended at Ugarit and its environs under the guidance of Professor Claude Schaeffer. It is scarcely worthwhile for me, here, to review this extremely significant and extensive effort, except in the broadest of terms. The emphasis in the earliest decades of excavation was placed on broad exposures of the final Late Bronze Age occupation at Ugarit as well as exposures at Minet el Beidah and the tombs in its vicinity.[1] Much remains to be published of the details of this work, and recent efforts have been directed toward tightening the archaeological controls. Such control is needed particularly for the separation of Late and Middle Bronze Age materials in the vast exposures surrounding the temples in the northeastern section of the site. After the second World War, excavations concentrated on exposure of the palaces and surrounding building complexes in the northwestern portion of the site.[2] The main administrative palace, with its five basic phases of development, was outlined for the period from the mid-15th through early 12th centuries B.C.[3] The massive textual and artifactual remains provide a gold mine of information on the wealth of the rulers at Ugarit, their international activities and the strength of the local artistic tradition, to mention only a few areas of study. We do not have the time to go into great detail on the palace finds, as we similarly do not have time to discuss the contexts in which the mythological texts and the temple-related artifacts were found in the northeastern area of

[1]Schaeffer (1948) 8-39.
[2]Schaeffer (1962) 1-150.
[3]Schaeffer (1962) 9-15.

the site. Studies have appeared on many details of the Mycenaean and Cypriote imported vessels, the art style of the extensive collection of carved ivories, and on the many categories of metal and other objects; much more, however, needs to be done. The gradual publication of the vast body of inscriptional materials in local or Babylonian cuneiform scripts, Cypriote scripts, Egyptian or Hittite scripts has proceeded with almost greater diligence in detailed presentation than the artifactual materials. In the past two decades, greater effort has been expended on understanding and documenting the earlier history of Ugarit. In addition to the deep soundings made initially by Schaeffer in 1934 and 1935,[4] other soundings have been made (between 1953-60,[5] 1962-68[6] and again in the 1970s[7]) which reveal the roughly 6000 years of accumulated layers built up from bedrock. Areas of Late Bronze Age I and Middle Bronze Age II buildings have more recently been exposed, between the years 1968 and 1976.[8] The basic sequence of Early Bronze Age, Chalcolithic and Neolithic materials is valuable for comparative purposes with the still limited materials available elsewhere. The strength of each tradition at Ugarit indicates that this site continually played a significant role in history.

Certainly the 50 years of excavation at Ugarit have shown without doubt the critical importance of the site, but the excavations have reached a critical point with a shift of the supervision of work to a new generation exemplified by Professor Margueron and his colleagues. Many challenges face both the new and the previous generation of excavators in the area of publication. The new generation is faced with setting priorities on where to dig, and on refining the methods of excavation, a concern which Professor Margueron has already shown through his work in 1975 and 1976.[9]

The massive body of written materials at Ugarit has of course attracted tremendous interest from Near Eastern and Biblical scholars. We must remember, however, that Ugarit was not the only city in Syria. It has, *a priori,* no greater claim to being the point of origin of certain traditions, myths, customs, styles, assemblages, and so forth, that Hama, Aleppo, Qatna, Kadesh, Emar, Ebla, Damascus, Kumidi, Sumur, Hazor, or any other major city throughout the area, or the capital cities of some of the major states like Ni'i, Nuhashe, or Mukish. We do not know where specific myths or pantheons originated in Syria, or how long a

[4]Schaeffer (1935) 160-68; (1936) 130-37; (1962) 153-249.

[5]Schaeffer (1962) 251-519.

[6]de Contenson (1970) 1-23; (1973) 13-33.

[7]de Contenson, *et al* (1973) 308-9.

[8]de Contenson, *et al* (1972) 15-21; (1973) 287-308; de Contenson (1974) 30; (1977) 1-23; and Schaeffer (1972) 27-33.

[9]Margueron (1977) 153-56.

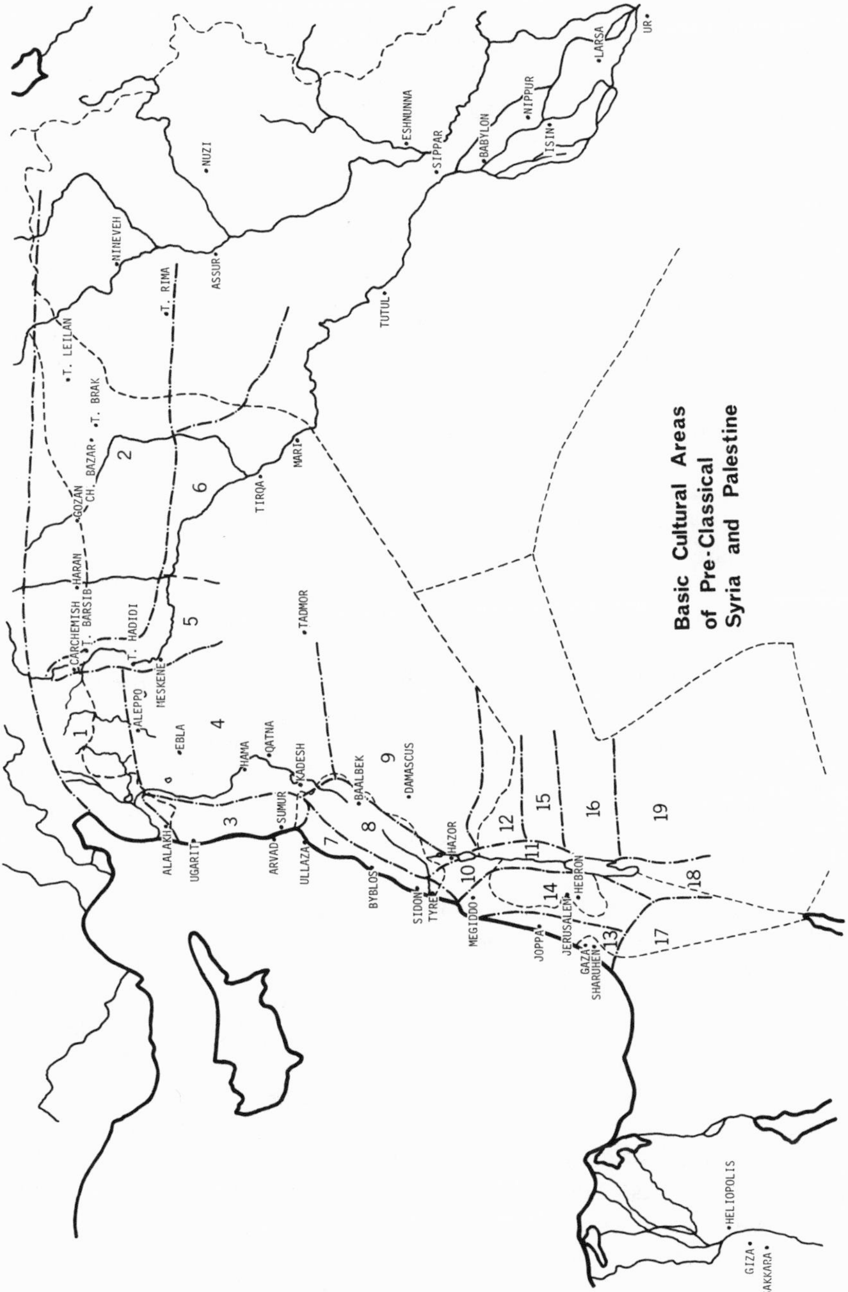
Basic Cultural Areas
of Pre-Classical
Syria and Palestine
UR
LARSA
NIPPUR
ISIN
BABYLON
SIPPAR
ESHNUNNA
NUZI
NINEVEH
ASSUR
T. RIMA
TUTUL
T. LEILAN
T. BRAK
CH. BAZAR
GOZAN
MARI
TIRQA
HARAN
CARCHEMISH
T. BARSIB
T. HADIDI
TADMOR
MESKENE
ALEPPO
EBLA
QATNA
HAMA
KADESH
BAALBEK
DAMASCUS
ALALAKH
UGARIT
SUMUR
ARVAD
ULLAZA
BYBLOS
SIDON
TYRE
HAZOR
MEGIDDO
JOPPA
JERUSALEM
HEBRON
GAZA
SHARUHEN
HELIOPOLIS
GIZA
SAKKARA
1
2
3
4
5
6
7
8
9
10
11
12
13
14
15
16
17
18
19

Figure 1

tradition existed behind any one of them. Are we able to generalize from the Ugaritic material to what is to be expected of Alalakh, or Emar, or Aleppo, or Damascus, or any other major city? We must be concerned in the future with defining the local manifestations of all aspects of cultures and traditions within the many distinct political and geographical areas of Syria.

It is unfortunate that the problematic stratigraphy of the temple area at Ugarit impedes, on the basis of currently published materials, a clear understanding of the temple plans, and the development of those plans through the three centuries or longer of the buildings' use. Since we have such a wealth of religious texts from this temple area, it is unfortunate that we cannot tie the architectural evidence securely into a broader context. Temple buildings conforming to several distinct types have now been excavated primarily at Megiddo, Shechem, Hazor, Mardikh, Alalakh, Mumbaqat, Meskene, and Mari. The thick-walled temples of Megiddo VIII, Shechem, Hazor acropolis, Mardikh in Area B, Alalakh VII, and the Dagon temple at Mari provide a distinct variation of the temples with normal wall thicknesses.

All share the general feature of a basically isolated rectangular structure, usually organized quite symmetrically on a central axis. The focal point of activities in all temples is centered directly at the rear on the long axis. Only at Ugarit, Meskene, and Mari does specific evidence exist for a linkage between a specific deity or deities, and a specific temple.[10] Certainly the great similarities in temple plans between temples in Palestine and those in northern Syria illustrate a basic and underlying continuity of religious practice throughout the area. But how are these temple plans to be connected directly to city gods, local gods, and local pantheons? The temple sequence at Alalakh is extremely interesting in its conservative practice of maintaining the same location for the sacred area through a long sequence of temples, while palace buildings are destroyed and rebuilt in different locations on the site.[11] The typical temple plans, with the parallels previously mentioned, represent only a few of the temple types present in the sequence at Alalakh. A local style of temple building illustrated in the buildings from levels XVI thru VIII, and reappearing in III, seems to provide the best parallel for some phases of the temples at Ugarit. Do the changes in temple plan mean a radical change in the religion of the area, or are they merely a reflection of cultural influences from period to period on those religious traditions? The situation is clearly complicated, and my point here is that if caution must be exercised in distinguishing traditions and

[10]Schaeffer (1931) 22, fig. 16; Dussaud (1935); Margueron (1974) 89; and Parrot (1940) 4-8, 20-24.

[11]Woolley (1955) 33-131.

influences in temple building, should not similar caution be exercised in making conclusions on the basis of traditions and influences drawn from the written materials?

The exciting potential of Ugarit, with its voluminous written materials, is the possibility of studying the mute artifactual remains within the context defined historically and chronologically by the written materials. General guidelines have been established by Schaeffer,[12] but so much more needs to be published, before Ugarit can take its rightful place among the archaeological sequences excavated in Syria. At Ugarit and Alalakh, the Aegean, Cypriote[13] and Nuzi[14] wares have received considerable attention, but in areas farther removed from the coast, most of these materials are much rarer, and we are dependent upon the sequence of local wares. At Ugarit, we have available a very basic corpus through careful study of *Ugaritica* II,[15] and the few selected illustrations in more recent reports.[16] At Alalakh, the published pottery and other artifacts can in some way be placed in their proper stratigraphic sequence. Our recent work at Hadidi, and on the Amuq materials from the Oriental Institute Excavations, has given us more confidence in the basic Alalakh sequence than we had hitherto expected. We will turn to the evidence from Hadidi shortly in a brief duscussion of the 15th and 16th century materials. A comparative review of Ugaritic and Amuq materials substantiates Schaeffer's dating of Alalakh III to I as contemporary with *Ugarit Récent* 2,[17] but leaves very little local pottery illustrated for *Ugarit Récent* 3, or pottery present in the Alalakh corpus representing contemporary level 0. The other Amuq sites provide a scanty collection of material for the 13th century B.C. Despite the tremendous finds at Ugarit, then, and the vast Late Bronze Age II exposures, we have very little with which to illustrate the basic pottery types and the simple, non-artistic, small finds of the Hittite Empire. The publication of the pottery from Meskene in the Euphrates Valley will be critical in filling this void,[18] as will the publication of more of the materials excavated in Ugarit.

Study of the painted wares of *Ugarit Récent* 2, and the contemporary Syrian painted wares provides a number of interesting insights. The Nuzi and Alalakh painted wares begin in level IV at Alalakh, and are

[12]Schaeffer (1962).

[13]Schaeffer (1939) 53-106; and Merrillees (1968) 187-202.

[14]Mallowan (1939) 887-94; Woolley (1955) 347-50; and Hrouda (1957) 10-21.

[15]Schaeffer (1949).

[16]Schaeffer (1962) Chapter II, figs. 6, 8, 9, 10, 11, 14, 16, 17, 27, 31, pls. I-V; Chapter III, Taf. I-XII, XVI; Chapter V, figs. 3, 5, 7, 9, 13, 17-19, 21-27, 31-42; Chapter VI, figs. 1, 2 16-20, 22-26, 29-31, 33-38, 40-47; and Chapter VII, figs. 1-7, 22-27.

[17]Schaeffer (1948) 98-99.

[18]Margueron (1975).

most common in levels III and II, especially II.[19] Level IV, of course, is fixed securely near the beginning of the Mitannian hegemony in north Syria,[20] and level II predates the Hittite conquests, if we follow Schaeffer,[21] or at least is to be dated to the very beginning of this period. Nuzi ware is not illustrated in the earlier publications from Ugarit, nor are the other vessels found which are decorated with light paint designs on dark paint, usually on heavier wares,[22] nor are the beakers painted with broad bands.[23] The light paint on dark bands is found at Ugarit in *Ugarit Récent* 3, but on the inside of imported Aegean bowls.[24] The Amuq painted wares find parallels at Hadidi, Tell Braq, Chaghar Bazar,[25] and Nuzi[26] to the east. Other painted types which derive from an earlier Syrian painted tradition are also present at Ugarit.[27] The numbers seem somewhat less than in the Amuq, but this may be an accident of excavation, recording, and publication. Polychrome variations are clearly more common at Ugarit than elsewhere.[28] Amuq Late Bronze Age bichrome is usually found in earlier contexts comparable to *Ugarit Récent* 1.[29]

A number of straight-sided plates with squared rims are attributed to *Ugarit Récent* 2.[30] Several examples are decorated with a red slip,[31] and are burnished; the same is true in the Amuq, and also at Tell Braq,[32] though the pedestal bases on these plates at Ugarit are not as common elsewhere.[33] The red-burnish decoration also occurs on bowls and jugs,[34] and it is difficult, in the Amuq, to distinguish it from that on the early (roughly 1000 B.C.) Iron Age, red hand-burnished bowls.[35] In the most common L.B. examples, the red slip does not cover the entire bowl; the inside center, and the base and lower outside of the vessel are usually not covered with red slip. The Late Bronze Age antecedents for the common

[19]Woolley (1955) 347.

[20]Smith (1940) 46-47.

[21]Schaeffer (1949).

[22]Mallowan (1947) pl. LXXXI: 6, 7; and Moortgat (1957) Abb. 11.

[23]Woolley (1955) pl. CXIX:112 and CXXII:114B; and Mallowan (1947) pls. LXXVI: 1, 2, 4, 8, 10, 26; LXXVII: 3; and LXXVIII: 4, 10, 13.

[24]Schaeffer (1949) figs. 58: 3, 6; 59:3, 40; 63: 2; and 64: 10.

[25]Mallowan (1947) pl. LXXXI: 6, 7.

[26]Starr (1937-39) 69:A^2.

[27]Schaeffer (1949) figs. 50: 7; 73: 24; 84: 7; 99: 28; 100: 30; 101: 25; and pl. XXVIII: 1.

[28]Schaeffer (1949) figs. 50: 8-10, 13, 14, 16-19, 21, 24, and 25; 62:12; 67: 2; 74: 18; 75: 19; 78; 104: 11; 106: 11; 107: 2; 108: 22; and Schaeffer (1962) 269, pl. III: 19; 416, fig. 1:19.

[29]Woolley (1955) figs. XCIV: b; XCV: ATP: 48/64 and XCVI: d.

[30]Schaeffer (1949) figs. 54: 3; 115: 3, 7-11, 13, 14; 116: 1, 3, 4, 6-9, 11, 12; and 117: 26.

[31]Schaeffer (1949) fig. 115: 8.

[32]Mallowan (1947) pl. XLIII: 5.

[33]Schaeffer (1949) figs. 115: 1, 3-5, 7-11, 13-15, and 116: 1, 3, 6-9, 11, 12.

[34]Woolley (1955) pl. XCIX h, j.

[35]Amiran (1970) 195-212.

Iron Age bowls, and their characteristic decoration, are extremely important because of the ethnic designations which have been attributed to the Iron Age wares,[36] and because of the sudden appearance of the red-burnished wares in Syria and Palestine around 1000 B.C.[37] The Amuq sequence clearly shows an absence of red-burnished forms in phase N (the first two centuries of the Iron Age), at which point monochrome, sub-Mycenaean wares dominate the painted pottery repertoire.

To date the architectural and stratigraphic context of the published Ugarit Late Bronze Age materials is very limited. Once again, the distribution of painted wares is interesting. The local painted wares are present apparently in equal strength at Ugarit, and in the Amuq. Ajjul ware seems slightly more common at Ugarit than in the Amuq.[38] In the Amuq, there is a development in the stratified forms from levels VI and V at Alalakh which contain Ajjul ware, to level IV in which the Nuzi ware is said to begin.[39]

Our excavations at Hadidi provide little painted pottery for the discussion since the Euphrates Valley Bronze Age traditions consistently have only rare pieces of painted vessels. The plain ware forms fit best with levels V and IV at Alalakh, particularly level V, though our work is still in progress and much vessel reconstruction is still needed.[40] A percentage of the corpus has no exact parallels in the more elaborate rim profiles of larger jugs and jars, and in the large storage jars and cooking pots. Several exact parallels do exist with level V,[41] and the general proportions of many vessels clearly fall in the time range mentioned.

The level immediately beneath the tablet building at Hadidi still belongs to the Late Bronze Age,[42] but must be placed at its very beginning, primarily in the 16th century. The pottery forms, for the most part, are closer to the Middle Bronze IIC tradition, and the parallels with Alalakh are less noticeable. There are several striking components to the pottery assemblage, however, which have clear parallels elsewhere. There is a very high proportion of gray-burnished sherds which come primarily from medium to small ring-based jars and jugs. Only a few of the rims are more complicated than the simple out-curved, rounded rims, and only a few bowls and larger jar sherds seem to be present. Few similar jugs exist at Alalakh, but a good selection of grey wares is present in the Amuq. Many similar grey jugs are found in *Ugarit Moyen*

[36]Hrouda (1962) 76-81.

[37]Amiran (1970) 191, 192, 195-212, and James (1966) 149-53.

[38]Schaeffer (1949) fig. 50: 2, 4, 11, 12, 15, 22, 23; 62: 18, 19; 74: 8; and 83: 8; and Woolley (1955) pl. XCIV: b, XCV: ATP/48/64; and XCVI: d.

[39]Woolley (1955) 347.

[40]Dornemann (1979) fig. 24.

[41]Woolley (1955) corpus types 62a, 91b, 93a & b, 99a, 103b, 104b, and 165a.

[42]Dornemann (1978) 23-24, and Dornemann (1979) figs. 19: 8-24, and 20: 1-37.

2 and 3, primarily in tomb contexts.[43] The other striking component is a rare collection, for Hadidi, of painted sherds. There are varieties of "chocolate-on-cream" sherds which are in color range of red to red-orange paint on orange to orange-cream slip, and most are burnished. Present are painted jug rims, jar shoulder sherds, and small jar body sherds. Similar sherds are not illustrated at Alalakh but are present at Ugarit in 16th century context where Cypriote wares have begun to appear.[44] In the case of both the gray-burnished and "chocolate-on-cream" sherds, we seem to have better parallels with materials from south Syria and Palestine than at any other time in the history of the sequence at Hadidi. This may well represent a specific cultural orientation at the very beginning of the Late Bronze Age. This orientation seems to be very short-lived, and gives way in time to the more normal similarities to ceramic materials from the north-central Syrian area, and from farther south on the Euphrates.

At Ugarit, contemporary Late Bronze, and also Middle Bronze, architecture exposed since 1968 has been mentioned earlier. The architectural plan of one Middle Bronze Age building, designated the north palace at Ugarit, has been compared with Alalakh level IV. Though the use of orthostats already occurs in level VII at Alalakh, the north palace plan is closer in its organization to that of Alalakh IV.[45] Orthostats had also been used in the M.B. II palace of Tell Mardikh.[46] Only the highlights of these Middle Bronze Age materials have been presented in preliminary reports, so little can now be done in the way of comparisons of pottery and small finds. Written materials are scarce, but we can hope that continued concentration on the *Ugarit Moyen* 3 levels will provide the kind of written records which will answer some of the crucial problems of the 17th and 16th centuries B.C. in connections with Egypt and the Mesopotamian powers.

Since 1975, additional light on the Late Bronze Age state at Ugarit has come to light, not from Ugarit itself, but from the salvage excavation at Ras Ibn Hani on the coast, 5 kilometers southwest of Ugarit.[47] The dramatic linkage of the destruction of the Late Bronze city at Ugarit, and the destruction of the Hittite state are documented by the finds in the south archive of the royal palace. We look forward to Mr. Bordreuil's paper this afternoon for additional information on the exciting building remains and tablets which are contemporary with Ugarit's Late Bronze Age palace. The destruction of the Late Bronze Age buildings at Ras Ibn

[43]Schaeffer (1949) 80: 13, 14; 100: 6-8, 22; 102: 1, 2, 11; 103: A (2); 105: 7, 8, 22-24; and 108: 8-10, 13.

[44]Schaeffer (1962) 265, pl. I: 8; 269; pl. III: 4, 7, 13, and 16.

[45]Schaeffer (1972) 29.

[46]Matthiae (1970) 66-68.

[47]Bounni, *et al* (1976), and (1978).

Hani is followed by several levels of 12th and 11th century materials.[48] The typical painted wares related to the sub-Mycenean materials present in the Amuq, Tarsus, and Tyre illustrate a chronological period which is still sparsely documented. Similar painted wares have recently been found in surface collections from northern Syria, and Middle Assyrian tablets have appeared in excavation at Tell Sheikh Hammad on the southern Habur.[49] The Ibn Hani materials show that selective excavation can yield the materials necessary to bring light into this dark age.

The Late Bronze Age remains at Ras Ibn Hani provide a greater insight into the structure of the Ugaritic state by emphasizing what was illustrated many years ago at Minet el Beidah. Ras Shamra is the capital city, and many surrounding towns and settlements were clearly dependent on it, and played a vital part in the administration, culture, and economic activity of the state. Professor Astour's, and other's, efforts to pinpoint the coastal towns mentioned in the Ugarit texts[50] can hopefully be reviewed soon in light of the Ibn Hani evidence, and hopefully we will gain a greater insight into settlement patterns in the area of Ugarit.

The final matter we would like to discuss today is the common practice of lumping the geographical areas of Palestine and Syria into one cultural unit. At Ugarit, more than at many sites, materials of far-flung, international origins have been found in abundance, and the presence of a large body of unique mythological texts has drawn considerable comment which attributes to them extended chronological and geographical importance. In this respect, I must urge caution on reading too much into arguments from silence, since some of these materials are unique, and so many large ancient sites dot the Syrian horizons.

Jean Nougayrol estimated in 1956 that the area dominated by Ugarit stretched for 60 kilometers along the Syrian coast, from the borders of the territory of Mukish in the north to the territories of Siyannu in the South.[51] He also estimated that it extended inland about 60 kilometers, into the Orontes Valley. This 60 kilometer stretch of coast compares with 300 plus kilometers of coastline from just north of Iskanderun to the Lebanese border, 200-plus kilometers of Lebanese coast, and over 200 kilometers of Palestinian coast down to Gaza. The state of Ugarit thus controlled about 1/5th of the Syrian coast, and less than 1/10th of the total coastal areas of Syria and Palestine. Direct cultural influence, and specific cultural traditions may not have extended far beyond the political boundaries of the state, and we do not

[48]Bounni, *et al* (1978) 280-82.
[49]Kühne (1978).
[50]Astour (1970) 113-27.
[51]Nougayrol (1956) 14.

know at this point how much and what specifics were shared by neighboring states, much less by distant geographical areas. Our work on the pottery traditions in Syria and the Transjordan indicates that if the general term Syria-Palestine can be used at all, it should be confined to Palestine and South Syria, certainly no farther north than the Homs area. The coastal area is more complicated since sea connections spread influence over a wider area, but these influences do not necessarily penetrate far inland. From period to period, there seems to be some variation or change in the extent of distinct cultural spheres, depending upon political realities; while at the same time, each specific physical area maintains an internal consistency and cohesion which seems to be established by set geographical determinants.

Briefly, we would note that several sub-units must be distinguished within the area of Palestine and Transjordan.[52] The coastal materials of the area north of Haifa are usually consistent with the coastal areas of Lebanon up to Tripoli; but in the central area of Syria, that is the area of Homs, Qadesh, Qatna, Arqa, Symirian, Kazel, Sukas, and Amrit in particular, we are not yet certain that a distinct cultural district can be defined. Certainly this area forms the border between larger general units to the north and south. The Lebanese Beqa provides a natural conduit for connections from central Syria (the Homs area) to Palestine, primarily via the Jordan rift. The Damascus area and the Golan seem to be related to the Beqa materials in the same way the Transjordan material relates to that in the Jordan Valley. In north-central Syria, the Orontes Valley and the Aleppo Plateau usually form a general group. The area along the Syrian-Turkish border, basically the plateau areas adjacent to the Turkish foothills, from the coast to the heartland of ancient Assyria forms another. The Euphrates Valley provides another unit with the presence of Mesopotamian influence throughout, but with the area south of Raqqa having the strongest Mesopotamian orientation,[53] and the area upstream from Raqqa being distinct from, but closely related to, the north-central Syrian area. Ugarit shows its special position on the coast with its basic ceramic inventory oriented primarily to the south, and with lesser connections to the Amuq Valley to the north. Basic pottery forms and decorative features which provide a link between Ugarit and the inland areas are primarily the same forms that are shared with the Amuq. The Amuq has a distinct component of materials which link it to the Aegean, Cyprus, and southern coastal areas, but these, on the whole, are less important here than they are at Ugarit.

In conclusion, I hope we have been able to review some of the significant archaeological information which has resulted from the

[52]Dornemann (1970) 17-23.

[53]Kelly-Buccellati and Shelby (1977) 11-12.

excavations at Ugarit. The finds, of course, have far-reaching implications, and we have tried to concentrate on a few generalizations and comparisons using the Ugaritic materials as a starting point. Certainly, as is the case everywhere in Syria, much needs to be done in the specific publication of older excavations, and in seeking the answers to the many outstanding problems of historical, chronological, and cultural importance by clearly defining the objectives for new excavations. It will take many centuries to exhaust the possibilities of the rich site of Ugarit, and the rich finds of the past can only accentuate the importance of what still lies buried. The generations of scholars who take up the work of Professor Claude Schaeffer have much for which to look forward, and much work still to do.

RAS-SHAMRA: NOUVELLES PERSPECTIVES DES FOUILLES

JEAN MARGUERON

Université des Sciences Humaines
de Strasbourg

Convient-il de dresser un bilan de l'action archéologique conduite depuis 1929 sur le tell de Ras-Shamra par Monsieur le Professeur Schaeffer, alors que les conclusions de 50 années d'exploration sont loin d'être tirées? Le risque est grand, et ce risque je n'ose le courir seul, mais par chance les savantes communications qui sont données en ce moment même dans cette Université de Madison et les différentes manifestations prévues prochainement en Allemagne, en Syrie et en France pour commémorer sous des formes diverses le cinquantenaire de l'entreprise, sont autant de témoignages qui se passent de longs commentaires. Aussi bien vouloir dresser un bilan alors que sur le terrain les travaux n'ont jamais été réellement arrêtés, n'est-ce pas fausser le sens d'une action qui, tout en s'enraçinant dans un passé récent, cherche à répondre à une interrogation toujours en devenir de la recherche historique et qui réoriente continuellement la fouille en fonction de ce qui est acquis et des problèmes nouveaux? C'est pourquoi il ne me paraît pas nécessaire d'évoquer maintenant les extraordinaires découvertes qui ont entièrement renouvelé nos connaissances du monde proche-oriental et qui ont été réalisées au cours des 31 campagnes dirigées par M. Schaeffer. En revanche, il me semble que la communauté scientifique sera intéressée par l'annonce des travaux de publication en cours, par les résultats des dernières fouilles et par l'exposé des nouveaux programmes de recherche. C'est donc dans cette voie que je voudrais m'engager devant vous, très modestement et sans prétendre à l'exhaustivité.

* * *

Il convient tout d'abord de marquer que, si de nombreux travaux sont engagés, je ne veux mentionner ici que ceux qui, à ma connaissance, sont destinés à voir le jour dans un proche avenir.

M. Schaeffer et son équipe, qui viennent de faire paraître le septième volume des *Ugaritica*, riche de nombreux textes et d'articles archéologiques dont un important corpus céramique, continuent de travailler sur les découvertes réalisées jusqu'en 1969. Du vaste programme de publication on retiendra tout d'abord l'étude que l'inventeur du site prépare sur la glyptique d'Ugarit. Il n'est pas besoin de rappeler que la cité d'Ugarit a été féconde en sceaux-cylindres et en empreintes de sceaux retrouvées sur les tablettes. Certains de ces documents ont déjà été publiés soit dans des rapports préliminaires, soit dans divers articles parus dans les *Ugaritica*; on rappellera pour mémoire l'intérêt du sceau dynastique et de celui d'Ini-teshub. On peut beaucoup attendre de cette étude pour notre connaissance de l'iconographie de la Syrie côtière du second millénaire.

M. J.Cl. Courtois pour sa part a rédigé une importante mise au point des fouilles de Ras-Shamra pour le Supplément du Dictionnaire de la Bible. De la part de cet excellent connaisseur du site une telle étude ne peut que favoriser l'éclosion d'études nouvelles.

M. et Mme Lagarce devraient publier dans un proche avenir un volume consacré à la Maison aux Albâtres, bâtiment installé à l'est du Palais Royal et qui a été fouillé en 1966, 1968, 1973 et 1974. On aura alors une étude précise d'une belle maison de la cité avec son évolution et son contenu situé exactement dans le contexte du moment de la découverte.

Quant à M. H. de Contenson, qui a assumé la direction des fouilles de 1969 à 1973, il s'attache maintenant à la publication du grand sondage qu'il a conduit des années durant sur le versant occidental de l'Acropole et qui lui a permis d'atteindre au rocher vierge les débuts de l'installation au Néolithique. On aura ainsi une séquence complète de l'occupation du site, les caractéristiques de chacune des phases et les possibilités d'établir les relations spatiales synchrones.

Enfin M. R. Stucky, qui a fouillé de 1969 à 1972 le niveau héllénistique qui s'étendait au sud de l'Acropole, en a préparé et achevé la publication avec une célérité remarquable puisque le manuscrit est actuellement à l'impression.

Nul doute que ces divers travaux, prémices d'oeuvres non moins importantes à venir, n'apportent un grand enrichissement à la documentation archéologique actuellement connue de l'ancienne cité de la côte syrienne.

* * *

En 1974 la Commission des Recherches Archéologiques du Ministère des Affaires Etrangères, en accord avec la Direction Générale des Antiquités de Syrie me confiait la charge de poursuivre l'exploration du site de Ras-Shamra. J'élaborais alors un programme qui donnait la priorité à l'étude de l'architecture et de l'urbanisme de la cité du Bronze Récent, mais qui ne négligeait pour autant aucun des objectifs traditionnels de la recherche archéologique; en particulier il me paraissait nécessaire, mais en seconde urgence seulement, d'étudier, grâce à un dégagement de vaste dimensions, la ville du Bronze Moyen.

J'ai conduit sur le site deux campagnes d'automne en 1975 et 1976. A ce moment une nouvelle orientation de mon activité de fouilleur m'a conduit à demander à être relevé de cette direction qui fut dès lors confiée à Mme Yon, Maître de Recherches au Centre National de la Recherche Scientifique.

Ces deux seules campagnes n'ont pas permis de remplir le programme initialement prévu, en particulier en ce qui concerne l'étude de l'urbanisme ou celle du niveau du Bronze Moyen. Elles ont cependant mis en lumière des faits nouveaux, donné le jour à des découvertes qui précisent certaines données antérieures, et orienté dans une certaine mesure les recherches à venir. Les résultats les plus importants peuvent être regroupés sous trois grandes rubriques.

1° / *Architecture civile*

Sur ce point l'objectif a été partiellement réalisé. En effet, un grand édifice a été repéré en 1975 et dégagé en 1976; il se trouve installé sur le rebord septentrional du tell, emplacement qui a malheureusement entraîné sa disparition partielle dans l'érosion de la pente. Ce qui a été retrouvé fait regretter cette lacune, car avec des murs conservés sur une hauteur supérieure à 2,50 m, on se trouve en présence d'une architecture tout à fait suggestive et particulièrement féconde en enseignements de tous ordres.

Pourvu d'un étage accessible grâce à un escalier installé en son coeur, cet édifice, organisé autour de deux cours équipées chacune sur son côté nord d'un porche à double colonne du même modèle que ceux retrouvés dans le Palais Royal par exemple, n'a malheureusement pas laissé deviner sa destination; en effet, en dehors de quelques jarres retrouvées écrasées sur le sol en des endroits assez peu significatifs (derrière les porches à colonnes par exemple), on n'a retrouvé que des pointes de flèche et des éléments d'armure en bronze; ces vestiges sont insuffisants pour y voir en toute certitude un édifice à vocation militaire, mais il reste que sa conception même, les caractères techniques de sa réalisation et la hauteur des murs retrouvés en font dans l'état présent de nos connaissances un monument de grande importance.

2° / *Architecture funéraire*

Il n'est pas nécessaire de rappeler les anciennes découvertes en ce domaine pour marquer la nouveauté du matériel dégagé en 1976. Deux tombes ont en effet été retrouvées. La première en 1975, de petites dimensions, n'est pas sans intérêt, mais elle n'offre guère de caractères inédits. En revanche la seconde est de qualité exceptionnelle. Elle se trouvait dans le sous-sol de l'édifice monumental qui avait vu la concentration des efforts de fouille de 1976. C'est peut-être l'une des plus belles de toutes celles que le site a fournies jusqu'à maintenant, tant par les dimensions que par le soin apporté à sa construction. Toutefois ces caractéristiques se retrouvent à l'occasion ailleurs et elles ne suffisent pas à en faire un cas d'exception.

Comme à l'habitude on trouve un *dromos* qui conduit à la chambre funéraire entièrement voûtée en encorbellement; mais cette fois une chambre supplémentaire est associée à cet ensemble: située à l'opposé du *dromos*, elle a pour particularité d'être absolument inaccessible et de n'avoir de relations avec la chambre funéraire que par des lucarnes qui ne peuvent laisser passer un corps humain. Ces caractéristiques que l'on ne connaît qu'une seule autre fois semble-t-il, dans une tombe d'Ibn Hani, sont déjà d'un grand intérêt.

En second lieu on a pu constater lors du dégagement de la chambre funéraire que la masse de terre d'infiltration était pleine des débris d'un grand coffre en pierre curieusement incomplet et qui pourrait être une sorte de sarcophage dépourvu de couvercle.

Enfin, et en dépit des violeurs de tombes qui étaient venus à deux reprises la visiter, le fond du puits funéraire recélait encore deux très beaux vases d'albâtre; or, le diamètre de l'orifice du puits ne permettait pas le passage de ces vases: il faut donc conclure qu'ils avaient été vraisemblablement placés au fond du puits avant l'installation du dallage de la chambre funéraire. C'est là une indication tout à fait nouvelle sur l'usage de ce puits.

Ces trois faits sont particulièrement remarquables et font de cette tombe un monument unique en son genre, qui remet en question son mode d'utilisation.

3° / *Stratigraphie*

C'est la question des derniers moments de la cité d'Ugarit qui est posée à la suite d'une série d'observations faites en cours de fouille. En effet, alors que l'histoire du Bâtiment étudié ci-dessus pourrait avoir connu une certaine durée si l'on en croit les multiples signes de transformation et l'existence vraisemblable de deux sols dans la majeure partie de l'édifice, à l'extérieur plusieurs niveaux d'occupation, trois en certains endroits, sont jonchés par de grands blocs de pierre taillée qui ne peuvent provenir que des murs du Grand Bâtiment. Comme ces blocs n'ont pu franchir plusieurs mètres de terrain stratifié pour atteindre la base des fondations, cela signifie que plusieurs destructions se sont succédé jusqu'à l'incendie final: il ne paraît pas déraisonnable d'y voir les traces de plusieurs tremblements de terre qui auraient rythmé la vie de l'édifice jusqu'à sa destruction définitive.

Comme on le voit ces trois chapitres ouvrent des horizons nouveaux pour les études à venir et montrent que la poursuite de la fouille est un impératif plein de promesses.

La publication concernant ces deux campagnes est en cours d'élaboration; elle ne pourra toutefois être achevée qu'à l'issue d'une petite campagne complémentaire qui pourrait avoir lieu en 1980. Il s'agit d'achever le dégagement du Grand Bâtiment de façon à ne laisser aucune des parties subsistantes dans l'ombre et de chercher à préciser au niveau des fondations la situation stratigraphique. Un soin particulier sera consacré à des catégories de matériel qui n'ont pas attiré l'attention comme les silex taillés trouvés en abondance dans ces niveaux du Bronze Récent alors que la ville est riche en outils de bronze; en outre, la belle collection de vases d'albâtre trouvés tant dans la tombe du Grand Bâtiment que dans un niveau de réoccupation d'une maison privée—peut-être s'agit-il d'une sorte de trésor récupéré dans les ruines après une destruction de la cité—fera l'objet d'une étude précise qui prendra en compte la place que tient cette série dans une production qui dépasse les limites du pays d'Ugarit. Quant aux séries céramiques elles serviront peut-être à préciser les observations stratigraphiques faites au cours de la fouille et qu'il convient de corroborer au moyen d'autres sources.

Dans cette publication l'architecture sera traitée selon la part qui lui revient naturellement et l'architecture funéraire, tout particulièrement, formera une section notable puisque les enseignements tirés de la fouille renouvellent complètement le problème. Mais je prévois à terme une étude plus conséquente sur l'architecture d'Ugarit, ses caractéristiques propres, les influences qu'elle a subies et sa place dans le contexte de la Méditerranée orientale. Ce travail viendra en complément des recherches plus techniques engagées par l'équipe de Mme Yon.

* * *

Mme Yon assume en effet la direction de Ras-Shamra depuis le début de 1978. Elle y a mené une première campagne au mois de mai de cette même année avec l'ouverture d'un sondage en A-1/D-1. Au mois d'octobre elle est revenue sur le site en compagnie de l'architecte de la mission et d'un topographe. A la suite de ces travaux préliminaires, Mme Yon a établi un programme de recherche dont elle a bien voulu me communiquer les lignes générales pour que je puisse en faire état devant votre assemblée. Sous réserve que des découvertes infléchissent dans un sens ou dans un autre les directions de recherche définies, ou même en créent de nouvelles, ce programme doit être considéré comme un engagement des activités de la mission pour plusieurs années.

L'objectif essentiel est de chercher à connaître aussi précisément que possible ce qu'était une grande ville de la côte syrienne à l'époque du Bronze Récent et ce dans une vision très large à savoir "comment s'organise l'espace de l'activité humaine, comment se matérialisent les rapports sociaux, quel genre de vie est possible en fonction des conditions naturelles et comment s'est faite l'adaptation à ces conditions."

Pour remplir cet objectif, Mme Yon définit plusieurs directions de recherche; elles concernent l'urbanisme, les techniques d'architecture, l'outillage non métallique et la céramique locale.

1° / *L'urbanisme*

L'étude du tell dans sa configuration actuelle avec ses lacunes provoquées par l'érosion qui s'est naturellement exercée depuis la fin de l'occupation du site ou qui a été provoquée par diverses actions de l'homme (labours, constructions de fermes, plantations d'arbres, réutilisation des blocs de pierre ayant appartenu à des murs de monuments du Bronze Récent, trous de pilleurs de tombes, tranchées ou trous divers de soldats . . .), l'étude du tell donc, doit conduire à l'étude du tissu urbain, de son adaptation au terrain, aux limites précises des zones d'habitat, au tracé du rempart qui délimitait la cité chaque fois que cela est possible. A partir de là il sera plus aisé de définir l'organisation de l'espace, de préciser le rapport entre les masses construites et les espaces vides: d'une part on trouvera la superficie occupée par les grands monuments tels que les palais, les temples, les grandes résidences et l'habitat urbain—ville de la pente sud du tell par exemple—de l'autre les rues et les places. L'étude des voies de communication découle de cette direction de recherche; c'est elle qui permettra de dire jusqu'à quel point il y a une originalité de l'urbanisme d'Ugarit. Les conditions de l'existence quotidienne pour la population de la cité seront connues à partir de ces différentes données ainsi que de l'analyse de certains problèmes spécifiques comme celui de l'approvisionnement en eau pour chaque foyer.

2° / *Les techniques d'architecture*

La qualité de l'architecture de pierre de Ras-Shamra invite à une étude détaillée des techniques de travail. On cherchera à définir le mode de la taille des pierres par les traces laissées par les outils de taille et par l'étude des modules; les différents types d'appareillage, les modes d'assemblage, les marques éventuelles de montage seront répertoriés avec soin; l'usage du bois dans la construction, tant pour les chaînages que pour les poutraisons entre les étages ou celles des terrasses sera défini chaque fois que la documentation le permettra; le rôle de la brique crue, en particulier dans les superstructures, sera analysé avec le plus grand soin. On espère que de ces analyses pourront naître les fondements d'une théorie de l'architecture ugaritique.

3° / *L'outillage non métallique*

Les différents sondages ont fourni une quantité importante d'objets en os ou en pierre, en particulier des silex taillés; ce type d'outillage tenait donc dans la vie quotidienne une grande place en dépit de l'apparition du métal dans la vie courante un millénaire et demi plus tôt et de son usage de plus en plus répandu, ce dont témoigne le site même de Ras-Shamra puisqu'on y retrouve une très belle collection d'outils en bronze généralement dans un état de conservation extraordinaire. Avec la collaboration des préhistoriens, plus habitués à analyser le matériel lithique et osseux, on tentera de constituer une première documentation pour les niveaux du Bronze Récent; celle-ci devrait permettre de s'engager dans une meilleure interprétation des techniques agricoles, artisanales, voire "industrielles" d'une cité du XIIIe siècle; une vision plus précise du mobilier domestique, et donc du mode de vie quotidien, sera une autre conséquence de cette analyse.

4° / *La céramique locale*

Tout en utilisant les séries bien datées qui accompagnent les objets de fabrication locale, par exemple les céramiques mycéniennes ou chypriotes, ou les objets inscrits, afin de s'appuyer sur des chronologies assurées, on s'intéressera plus particulièrement à la céramique propre à la cité d'Ugarit en usant de toutes les possibilités qu'offre la technique moderne, physique et chimique, des laboratoires de céramologie, en particulier ceux du Centre National de la Recherche Scientifique, pour déterminer des séries, si possible les provenances et éventuellement les ateliers.

Pour réaliser ce programme Mme Yon prévoit:

a) Une mission topographique dans la suite de celle engagée en 1978. Il s'agit de réaliser un relevé général du tell afin:

- de préciser ses limites actuelles,
- d'établir les courbes de niveaux et de préciser le relief tel qu'il se présente aujourd'hui,
- d'analyser celui-ci en tenant compte des changements dûs aux fouilles antérieures et aux accumulations de déblais,
- de mettre en place avec exactitude dans le nouveau relevé les monuments et les secteurs d'habitat dégagés antérieurement.

b) Des missions de fouille; le choix du sondage ouvert en mai 1978 devrait être le départ d'une fouille de plus grande envergure au moins dans un premier temps. Son emplacement est en effet situé entre le quartier des Palais et des grandes résidences à l'ouest de la ville et celui de la Ville Sud, riche, structurée, avec une place, des rues, un matériel de qualité et des bibliothèques. Un tel secteur paraît devoir favoriser des recherches portant aussi bien sur l'urbanisme que sur le mobilier quotidien et le sondage 1978 a clairement montré qu'il y avait là des constructions organisées, avec un matériel varié et susceptible de répondre aux différentes questions du programme qui vient d'être défini.

* * *

Ainsi les deux programmes se rejoignent: le second poursuit, amplifie et complète le premier resté inachevé. Ils montrent la continuité des nouvelles actions parfaitement en accord avec les problèmes majeurs de la recherche actuelle sur la fin de l'âge du Bronze au Proche-Orient.

Part Two

LANGUAGE & LITERATURE

LITERARY CRITICISM, FOLKLORE SCHOLARSHIP, AND UGARITIC LITERATURE

JACK M. SASSON

The University of North Carolina at Chapel Hill

I. The search for a category in which to place a literary document and for a mode of interpreting ancient literary documents is not a frivolous enterprise. Far from being merely an academic response to classify whatever reaches our hand, the desire to locate a text within a literary category—some might say within a 'genre'—often permits us to highlight commonly shared themes and allows us to speculate on the extent of literary patterning.[1] More importantly, perhaps, a successful search for a literary genre permits us to delineate an agenda of inquiry that could be posed to individual documents once their literary context is established.

But our first task is certainly to become more precise in what this paper will entertain and hence to be more modest about the goals it seeks to achieve. 'Folklore scholarship' is an ambitious heading for what is, at best, a catch-all discipline which has yet to develop theories and perspectives acceptable to the majority of those engaged in its behalf. Moreover, rather than tightening its focus, folklore has witnessed an expansion of interest within the last decade to incorporate approaches and viewpoints derived from anthropology, psychology, sociology, and linguistics.[2] But as a working definition, we might describe folklore as a discipline which explores and charts the presence of conventions and behavioral manners shared by groups of peoples and often transmitted, orally or in writing, through time and across space. Because in the study of the Ancient Near East evidence comes from moribund civilizations, we can safely avoid those folkloristic avenues that permit an evaluation of the folk-life of contemporaneous societies, and concentrate on those which analyze the literary remains of past cultures. But here we must add that whereas folklore has borrowed much from the approaches of

[1]Frye (1957) 247-48.
[2]See Burns (1977) 109-11.

literary criticism, it differs from the latter in its broader scope of inquiry; whereas the former is interested in the origins, development, and spread of literary traditions, the latter tries to investigate the interrelationship that exists among the tale, the teller, and their audience.[3]

Similarly, 'Ugaritic literature' is too amorphous an entry in our title. Folklore research has almost nothing to say about the study of political, legal, administrative, and 'scientific' archives. Folklore might contribute marginally to the analysis of cultic, magical, and 'wisdom' documents. But as we shall try to show, it can be insightful in its elucidation of those half-a-dozen or so texts which we consider as belletristic. While we will refer to *Keret, Aqhat,* and *Baal,* the main thrust of this paper will be programmatic rather than pragmatic, suggestive rather than illustrative. But two caveats should be inserted at this point:

1. The interpretative tools available to the folklorist can be applied only when Semitic philology has provided tolerably dependable renderings of the Ugaritic narratives. Even as we admit to major failings in comprehending particular passages within the texts at our disposal, it can nevertheless be stated that general scholarly agreement prevails over the contours, outlines, and understanding of large portions of their contents.
2. The narratives at our disposal are, regrettably, 'one-dimensional.' By this I mean that, unlike the situation that obtains in the discovery of other Near Eastern narratives, e.g. Gilgamesh and Etana, no more than one exemplar each of *Keret, Aqhat* and *Baal* has so far been recovered. We are, therefore, constrained to consider these Ugaritic narratives only within the archaeological context in which they were found, and to limit our discussion only to the written form in which they have reached us. While this may seem obvious as an initial principle, it will have wide ramifications as we draw other conclusions.

In the past century a number of avenues, delineated by folklorists, have been applied to the interpretation of Biblical as well as ancient Near Eastern societies.[4] It is generally agreed that the methods advocated by the so-called 'functionalists,' scholars dedicated to uncovering the manner in which myths codify actual beliefs and promote order among the cultists as well as interested in describing the manner in which legends and epics propagate an existing social order, are sustained by an excessive amount of circular reasoning. For it cannot be reasonably maintained that mythological and literary imageries have a basis in

[3]Max Lüthi (1976) 19.

[4]A useful survey of approaches taken by folklorists, albeit not centered around Biblical and Near Eastern scholarship, is in Richard Dorson (1963) 93-110. An invaluable collection of essays dealing with a wide range of folkloristic topics, with useful bibliographical updating, is in Alan Dundes (1965).

empirical reality as long as that reality is itself often reconstructed on the authority of the literary texts. Another way of airing this criticism is to say that the texts questioned by the functionalists always confirm the explanations they offer, for the simple reason that there is usually nothing in those explanations which was not derived, to begin with, from the texts themselves.[5]

Another approach, advocated most commonly by those on the perimeters of active research in the Ancient Near East, is derived from the symbiosis which occurred between followers of the so-called Cambridge school and advocates of Jungian psychology. While extremely seductive, the elaborate symbolic language, which is meant to psychologically chart primordial 'archetypes' deeply etched in the common consciousness, can be accepted only by those predisposed to a particular interpretation of the complexities of the human psyche.[6] Lastly I mention an approach that, derived from Scandinavian folklorists, has become best known to Biblical scholarship in the highly refined form elaborated by Hermann Gunkel. Atomistic, this approach tried to isolate brief, tolerably self-contained episodes. These are then compared and placed in parallel with similar ones extracted from other (mostly near Eastern) documents. Criticism of this method is at least twofold. It tends to neglect the contexts from which the various motifs are culled and ignore the motivation which impels the (re)telling of the narrative in which they are set. A more severe criticism, however, can be levelled. It is altogether unclear to me how relevant is a method which compares motifs, albeit similar in shape and content, to the understanding of a literature. The discovery of a set of motifs from two differing tales should barely cause the raising of an eyebrow. Even the identification of a series of such motifs in the same two tales would be merely an interesting discovery. In my opinion, only when sequences of motifs, each of which is important to the development of the plot, are recovered from within two narratives can we begin to profitably assess a literature and usefully apply the tools available to the folklorists. But one who agrees with this observation and sympathizes with the criterion it establishes would no longer be considered as an 'atomist'; rather, he is better located among those espousing 'structuralist' modes of interpretations.

Structuralists, of course, do not form a homogeneous group, and it would be foolhardy to describe the various enterprises that are launched under its banner. Suffice it to say that at least two interpretive channels

[5]See Kluckholn (1942) 45-79. Criticisms of this approach are collected by Kirk (1970) 8-31.

[6]See, for example, the survey presented by Fischer (1963) 235-92, and the appended critics of a number of commentators. The approach has been criticized by many folklorists; see Dorson (1963) 105-9.

can be distinguished. The first attempts to gain an insight into the 'deeper' meaning of a text by reallocating contrasting components of a narrative into paradigms of opposites. The other channel confines itself to establishing the literary genre of a given narrative by noting the manner by which plot-motifs are chained sequentially, some might say syntagmatically—to form a whole. It can easily be perceived that while, in the first approach, a presupposed interpretation quickens a redefinition of the structure of a given text, the second avenue is merely descriptive, allowing interpretation to begin only when the literary genre of a narrative is seen to follow a pre-described sequence.[7]

The second approach, sometimes allocated to the 'formalists,' has been championed by slavic scholars. Although much refined and elaborated in recent times, the work of V. Propp is seminal to that enterprise. In his *Morphology of the Folktale*,[8] Propp moves away from the conventional approach of focusing on characters who fit a type common to a number of narratives (e.g. the wicked stepmother, the evil uncle, etc.), to one in which they are chosen solely on their immediate role in propelling the plot of a particular folktale. These tale-roles, in turn, are seen to influence units, labelled functions, which string themselves to form the whole narrative. Propp thinks that not only are these functions invariable in their location within a tale, but that they are limited in number. With this in mind, Propp defines a folk or fairy tale as any narrative which proceeds from an initial situation either through a hostile act against a hero (or his sponsor) or because of a manifest lack in the fortune of the hero (or his sponsor)—childlessness, famine—which progress through a sequence of proscribed functions, and which ends either in a marriage of the hero (or his sponsor) or in a successful resolution of those lacks. A tale can arise from the skillful arrangement of a series of originally independent folktakes, as long as the initial conditions that propelled the first in the series of tales are not satisfied or fulfilled until the last tale within that series. An excellent example of such an occurrence can be noted in the Biblical *Ruth* where Naomi's lacks (no heir, hunger) sets Ruth towards her ultimately successful searches, for food (end of chapter 2), for a husband (end of chapter 3) and, through him, for a redeemer (end of chapter 4).[9]

I believe it can be shown that portions of *Aqhat*, *Keret*, and some segments in *Baal* fit nicely within the sequential scheme developed by Propp. But my objectives here are not merely to establish more precisely than has heretofore been done, the genre to which Ugaritic narratives

[7]Useful introductions to the subject are found in Scholes (1974) and, more relevant to Biblical studies, in McKnight (1978).

[8]Note also the important correctives to the English edition, "The Problem of 'Tale Role' and 'Character' in Propp's Work," in Jason (1979) 311-20.

[9]See Sasson (1979) 203-14, 226.

belong, but to present guidelines for interpretations of these texts once their literary category is recognized. The latter goal is particularly relevant since many scholars, unfamiliar with Propp's presentation, and not infrequently, with folklore methodology, have nevertheless recognized that folkloristic elements lay embedded within our texts. I shall therefore reserve a detailed Proppian analysis of Ugaritic narrative, which would absorb much space, for another occasion and use the remaining pages to offer the following synthesis.

II. Approaches that seek to locate a category for the Ugaritic narratives help us to differentiate between two levels of inquiries, and hence to clarify the demands that we make upon our texts. We might first differentiate between investigations which allow scholarship to critically assess the information available from the perspective of (social) historians, and inquiries that permit speculations on the meaning and purpose of these documents from the perspective of those who wrote and circulated them. When dealing with literary texts, these two levels of inquiries can rarely be satisfied by the same sets of questions.

I begin by discussing the limitations and difficulties confronting the (social) historian as he tackles *Keret, Aqhat* and *Baal,* and proceed by outlining the contexts which can be assessed on the basis of folkloristic guidelines.

A. If a narrative is found to fulfill 'formalistic' requirements, and hence, to belong to a folk (or fairy tale) category, then an important limitation would be imposed on the interpreter. Folktales do not ordinarily preserve an accurate memory of a single historical event or that of a particular stage in the development of cultures. All activities contained within are normally levelled and smoothed out to give the appearance of exemplary or paradigmatic behavior.[10] With this point in mind, five assessments can be presented.

1. Proceeding from the contents of the Ugaritic texts, and judging by the mortality of the protagonists, scholars have labelled *Baal* as a 'myth', and *Keret* as an 'epic'. But if a narrative is analyzed on the basis of its structure and form, and categorized on the role the protagonists play in shaping each of its sequences, and if this approach is seen as equally applicable to *Baal* as to *Keret,* then the distinctions that we make between myth, on the one hand, and epic, legend, saga, on the other, would be retained with minimal benefits, as minimal as those obtained by the distinction folklorists make between folktales, which are said to involve humans, and fairy tales, which are said to introduce non-human characters. Blurring this artificial demarcation might, at the very least, resolve the minor difficulty experienced by those who seek a proper

[10]Eliade (1963) 196-97.

designation for *Aqhat* whose contents allowed it to span, in the old terminology, the realms of myth and epic.[11]

2. An often repeated assumption is that *Baal* was 'composed' earlier than either *Aqhat* or *Keret* and that all three are earlier than the archaeological context would suggest. Since linguistic evidence, always difficult to assess even for a vocalized text, are convincingly mustered only rarely, it falls upon an inspection of the contents to buttress this theory.[12] The observation made above, that narratives of this type do not recall a precise moment of the past, would make it unlikely that, on the basis of information currently available, Ugaritic tales can either be 'dated' [except for establishing the *terminus ad quem*] or located within a linear development in literary creativity.

3. Because of the paucity of data from Ugarit, scholars have combined evidence from belletristic literature with those derived from administrative archives to reconstruct diverse aspects of Canaanite culture.[13] It is perhaps noteworthy that this effort is frequently made by those who would compare Canaanite to Hebrew institutions. The opinion expressed above should warn against an approach which would only result in a composite of partial compatibility with actual occurrences.[14] For example, to resort to *Keret* and *Aqhat* for evidence of Canaanite kingship would, in my opinion, only yield testimony on the most platitudenous of sentiments; for the information on this topic contained within these narratives has been largely harmonized and homogenized to please esthetic, and not historical sensibilities. Furthermore, if it is perceived that not only portions of *Keret* and *Aqhat*, but even of *Baal* fall into a literary pattern which pleases because it nurtures no expectations that are, ultimately, left unfulfilled, then it becomes less likely that any of the texts were destined to function as vehicles for the propagation

[11]Cf. Kirk's sub-chapter, "the Relation of Myths to Folktales," pp. 31-41 of his *Myth*. Kirk disagrees with Stith Thompson and other folklorists who do not make a clear distinction between myths and fairy tales, though he agrees with the opinion that there is much "mobility from one genre to another" (p. 40). Gibson shares Kirk's perspectives (1975) 63.

[12]The criteria for 'dating' Ugaritic belletristic efforts are of differing merits, and are often promoted with more faith than reason. See the collection of opinions concerning the dating of *Baal* in de Moor (1971) 48-58. Albright (1968), has this to say: "... Baal, Aqhat, and Keret, were put into approximately their extant form between the seventeenth and the fifteenth centuries in the order given ..." (p. 4). See also p. 4, n. 9: "The myths [Baal and Aqhat] are naturally (*sic*) older [than Keret]."

[13]It is especially hazardous to confer an 'early' dating for these texts simply because their contents differ linguistically from those found in the administrative and epistolary archives. [So, Albright (1968) 101-2; Cross (1973) 113, n. 42]. Indeed, one would not expect literatures, so differing in genres and purposes, to be at all stylistically similar.

[14]An example of such a method is available in A. Van Selms (1954).

of cultic festivities, to explain seasonal fluctuations, or to celebrate the apotheosis of eponymous ancestors.[15]

4. Scholars have recently tested the 'historical' memory of Ugaritic poets and, on the basis of personal and place name, have suggested that Ugarit's dynastic ancestry either had Mitannian roots or could be reconstructed and retrojected to Upper Syria of the Middle Bronze Age.[16] But such conjectures should recall that folk tales as well as fairy tales *do* create protagonists who never existed and *do* assign them tasks that have no historical bases. More commonly however, we either find protagonists with modest actual achievements matched with extraordinarily heroic deeds or the reverse condition: actual deeds assigned to imaginary heroes. Whatever the eventual mix, the tales are then, understandably, loaded with 'historicizing' touches, such as interesting foreign locales, worthy opponents, often drawn from neighboring cultures, and complicated tribal affiliations. Because of their 'one-dimensionality' as well as because of the paucity of confirmations from administrative texts, it becomes hazardous to extract historical information from Ugaritic tales.

5. An important point to consider is that folktales, because they follow a predictable pattern of development, need not be created solely in rural or peasant milieus. Thus, narratives such as *Keret* and *Aqhat*, as well as *Baal*, need not have been elaborated outside of palace temple confines. Since, as it has been dramatically shown by Ruth Finnegan, recourse to formulaicity—stylistic or thematic—repetitions of whole segments of narrative, paronomasia, and, I might add, textual errors, can rarely identify a written from an orally transmitted narrative,[17] we

[15]de Moor (1971) 9-28 offers a good history of *Baal* interpretations. His own conclusions include the observation that *Baal* "embodies an early attempt of man to give a comprehensive explanation of the mechanism of the climate in [the Ugaritian's] surroundings" (p. 249).

De Langhe (1958) 122-48. See De Vaux's sober, bibliographically rich, pages on this topic (1971) 135-48. De Vaux, however, speculates when he differentiates between the credulity of peasants and that of the Upper Classes (p. 147).

[16]Astour (1973) 23-39; de Moor (1976) 324-35; Kitchen (1977) 141-42. Note that W. F. Albright, mostly on the basis of revocalizing Krt as Kirta, attributes Keret to Hurro-Mitannian inspiration (1968) 103 and n. 19; Cf. also Pope (1977b) 179.

[17]I would object to the all-too-easily achieved lumping together of the terms 'folklore' and 'oral literature/tradition,' on which see Finnegan (1977) 35-40. To begin with, the first is usually applied to a discipline which is most useful when it suggests *interpretative* avenue, whereas the latter is a term that properly belongs to literary categorization.

A most impressive aspect of Finnegan's book, mentioned in this footnote, is the manner in which she charts the difficulties in assuming the existence of an oral style (chapter 4), and in making distinctions between modes of transmitting 'oral' and written narratives (chapter 5). Her cautionary conclusions (see also her concluding remarks on pp. 272-75) based on a study of societies that have given us evidence from written as well as from spoken sources, should be even more relevant and sobering when applied to cultures known to us solely from written sources.

should not dismiss the possibility that our material from Ugarit was formulated by a scribal intelligentsia, and that it circulated only among the elite circles. Moreover, the fact that our texts are 'one-dimensional,' renders it impossible to make pronouncements on orally transmitted materials and their use in finalizing the versions available to us.

B. While folk or fairy tales are limited to a specific number and order of functions and seem severely impoverished in the tale-roles which shape these functions, it does not follow that their creators were esthetically hamstrung. To begin with, Propp allows for a number of alternatives for each one of his functions. Moreover, despite the pre-determined structure of the folktale, opportunities for inventive and individual touches abound: in describing the characters, their surroundings, and their motivations. A folktale can also be filled with secondary characterizations which do not advance the plot but creatively round the proportions of a given narrative; past actions could be remembered in a manner than might differ slightly from their first appearance. The opportunities for creativity even within a sharply conventionalized literary form, can be (as we know it from the study of Arabic poetry and to a lesser extent from that of acrostically shaped poems) what permits a great storyteller to rise above his colleagues.

If so far I have sought to underscore the manner in which categorizing belletristic literature limits the range of historical pronouncements that could properly be made, I would like to outline the avenues of inquiries that folklore research can open. In particular, I would like to emphasize the interpretive contributions to establishing the contexts, social, cultural, and political, in which this literature is set.[18]

Social Context

Under this heading, folklorists try to assess the relationship that exists between the teller and the audience. The brunt of our information must come from the narratives themselves; but, because we are dealing with a society that is no longer extant, because we are dealing with texts that are 'one dimensional,' and because the Ugaritic scribe did not leave us with his own categorizing terminology, our difficulties are increased. Below, I entertain some considerations which, although they may not yet be satisfied by the present state of Ugaritic research, may be applicable to other corpus of Ancient Near Eastern literature.

The nature of the *audience* might be gauged by the following:

[18]In outlining the contexts for folkloristic interpretations, I am indebted to Bascom's fine essay, republished in Dundes (1968) 279-98.

TEXTUAL EVIDENCE

α. *The archaeological setting in which the texts were found.* While it may matter that documents are found in a place archive, temple library, or private quarters, a number of other considerations must also be entered: are the texts found with others similar or dissimilar in genre? Can one perceive any systematic arrangements for the tablets found in one setting? Were the segments of a simple narrative dispersed in different parts of a temple, palace or private quarters? Can one, on the basis of archaeological discoveries decide, with some certainty, on the *function* of the room in which the texts were found?[19]

[19]The following chart may help in locating the find spots whence literary tablets were recovered. It will be noted that despite my chart, precise determinations of these find spots will not be possible. This chart is to accompany the map published in *Ugaritica III*, p. 265, fig. 216 [=Courtois, *Supplement, Dictionnaire de la Bible*, 1175-76; cf. also his comments on the recovery of the texts, 1156-60]. The drawing reproduces the so-called "Library of the High Priest," located between the temples of Baal and Dagan/El. The cardinal points in my chart are given with respect to this building's central courtyard, since no numbering system had been devised for the many rooms found within it. I could not locate the find spots for the tablets uncovered in 1933. The information on color of tablets, handwriting, etc., comes from Herdner's discussions in CTA. I use "*ᵓlmlk*" as a convenient term for a handwriting that is substantially similar.

Text No. [CTA/UT]	Year found	Place found	Color	Handwriting
Baal & Anat				
1/ᶜnt [IX,X]	1931	S.E.	Beige	*ᵓlmlk?*
2/68-129-137	1931	S.E.	Beige	*ᵓlmlk*
3/ᶜnt	1931	S.E.	Ocre	*ᵓlmlk*
4/51	1930/1931	N.E./S.E.	Ocre	*ᵓlmlk*
5/67	1930/1931	N.E./S.E.	Gray	*ᵓlmlk*
6/49+62	1930/1933	N.E./ ?	Gray	*ᵓlmlk*
7/130+131	?	?	Ocre	large, "grossière"
8/51 frag	1931	S.E.	Gray	large
9/133	1933	?	Brown	"grossière," large
10/76	1931	S.E.	Gray	*ᵓlmlk?* [nice]
11/132	1931	S.E.	Gray	*ᵓlmlk?* [as 10]
12/75	1930	N.E.	Beige	very small
13/6 [Hymn]	1929	N.W.	Gray	"grossière"
Keret				
14/Krt	1930	N.E.	Beige	*ᵓlmlk*
15/128	1930/1931?	N.E./S.E.	Beige	*ᵓlmlk*
16/125-127	1931	N.E.	Ocre	*ᵓlmlk*
Aqhat				
17/2Aqht	1931	S.E.	Beige	*ᵓlmlk*
18/3Aqht	1931	S.E.	Beige	*ᵓlmlk*
19/1Aqht	1931	S.E.	Shaded Ocre	*ᵓlmlk*

These questions will permit speculations on the ease and alacrity with which tablets could be retrieved and brought before an audience, scribal or aural, and can thus allow speculation on the periodicity of such a gathering process. If tablets from the same narrative, especially ones that have so far been found in only one exemplar, have been kept hither and yon, one may assume that storage was expected to last for long periods; or at least that they were not destined for a cultic activity that took place regularly, at brief intervals.

β. *The colophon.* The subscription that is attached to texts is of special importance. We have a rather full colophon at the end of CTA 6 [a text belonging to the *Baal* cycle] which tells us that this text was dated to the time of Niqmad, king of Ugarit, who may have sponsored its inscription. This may mean that the text was available to the elite at Ugarit. Moreover, as reconstructed by *some* scholars, this colophon occurs at an important juncture of the cycle. If this particular reconstruction is adopted, it would indicate that *Baal* aimed to please a *reading* audience, and that it was destined for the desks of scribes, since it is unlikely that the colophon was recited, declaimed, intoned, or sung.

γ. *Rubrics within the texts.* The instructions given to the scribe or the reader are noteworthy. If they urge that one should return to a certain line of the text, and if that line belongs to a different tablet, then a scribal audience might have been involved. If that line to which the attention is drawn occurs at a dramatic juncture, this might indicate that the audience's suspense is being carefully nurtured and this might point to a listening rather than a reading aucience. Unfortunately, the rubrics found in Ugaritic texts are rarely easy to interpret and have, so far, not born instruction to return to narrative that is currently available to us.

δ. *Headings and heavily lined separations.* These may be of importance; especially if the last ones occur in the midst of an unbroken narrative. For they might allow us to note the moments that were considered by the composer or scribe to contain logical breaks in the narrative. Again, if we perceive these breaks to have dramatic functions, e.g. to stop at an exciting moment of the narrative, then these may have been introduced to make declaiming or singing more effective.

Rephaim				
20/4Aqht=121	1930	N.E.	Beige	ᵓ*lmlk*
21/122	1930	N.E.	Gray	ᵓ*lmlk*
22/123+124	1930	N.E.	Brown	ᵓ*lmlk*
Šaḥar & Šalem				
23/52	1930	N.E.	Whitish	peculiarities
Nikkal				
24/77	1933	?	Ocre	heavy hand

NARRATIVE CONSIDERATIONS. See below.

The nature of the *teller* can be evaluated by the following data:

TEXTUAL EVIDENCE.

α. *The colophon.* A prosopographical study of the personal names found in the colophon might be beneficial. In that of CTA 6, the names of *ᵓelmlk and ᵓatn prln* [or however one decides to break up this name] might be subjected to such an analysis.[20] Likewise, a study of the town of *šbn* (cf. UT #19.2379), its citizenry, and its connection to Ugarit and its palace might yield some information of import.

Unfortunately the connection between *ᵓelmlk* and the High Priest *ᵓatn prln,* so crucial to any decision on the transmission and composition of *Baal,* depends on a proper understanding of the terms *spr, lmd* and *ṯᶜy.* If one were to adopt the translation 'apprentice' (as I believe it to be the case) for *lmd* rather than the often preferred 'dictated', then the issue of oral transmission of *Baal* becomes more difficult to uphold without further evidence, and we might have to retain the possibility that *ᵓelmlk,* a student of a High Priest, actually composed (diverse segments of) *Baal.*[21] As to *ṯᶜy,* Deitrich and Loretz once proposed a rendering 'collated' which would, of course, imply that a master copy existed with *ᵓelmlk* merely copied.[22] However, most scholars either render the term 'sponsor, donor', as applied to Niqmad, or consider it, rightly in my opinion, as an as yet uniquely attested ethnicon, applied to *ᵓatn prln* (paralleling *šbny*).[23]

β. *Handwriting.* It would appear that *Keret,* and *Aqhat* were written or copied by the same scribal hand. *Baal,* however, shows that same hand to be involved only in CTA 1-6. Scholars have had little difficulties in acknowledging that CTA 2-6 belonged to the same cycle. Whether or not CTA 7-9, in a different handwriting, and 10-11, in yet a third manuscript, belonged to that cycle is a matter of discussion.[24] This issue is important, for if CTA 7-11 are seen as part of that same cycle, then it

[20]Cf. Gröndahl (1967) 236, 367, 369-70.

[21]A full discussion on the term *lmd* is to be found in Hillers and McCall, Jr. (1976) 19-23. Their strictures are very sound and should be consulted. I might only add here that the colophon of the Erra Epic [see lastly Cagni (1977) 60] would confirm the fact that the scribe, Kabti-ilani-Marduk, *composed* the poem, albeit under divine inspiration. That Kabti-ilani-Marduk might have used material that had circulated earlier is possible, but this in no way should prejudice the conclusion that he was indeed the author of *Erra.*

[22]1972: 32.

[23]See Hunger's discussion (1968) 22. But cf. C. H. Gordon, UT 19.2713, who nevertheless renders "donor (=sponsor)" in his recent (1977) 117. Similar understanding is found in Driver (1956) 151. For discussion of the titles *rb khnm* and *rb nqdm,* see Yamashita (1975) 63-64.

[24]Discussion on the perimeters of *Baal* is found in de Moor (1971) 36-43 and in Van Zijl (1972) 6-12.

would undermine the likelihood that ᵓ*elmlk* was its author; rather, he would have been charged, as did others, with making a new copy of an existing text. This issue is complicated, however, by at least three other features.

1. The handwritings of CTA 7-11 are sensibly less esthetically pleasing than those of ᵓ*elmlk*. While one ought not to confuse literary with scribal artistry, it may nevertheless be that CTA 7-11 were the products of students under ᵓ*elmlk's* directions.
2. Whether or not CTA 2 ['Baal vs. Yamm'] is to be separated from other texts of the cycle because it allocates words and columns differently than CTA 1, 3-6, is yet another issue that has to be taken into consideration.[25] The handwriting is certainly that of ᵓ*elmlk*, but so is that of CTA 1 which many scholars regard to be a separate rendition of many of the themes displayed in the cycle.
3. That a few fragments, some of which were found in 'private' quarters[26] and differing in handwriting from the texts mentioned above, may belong to *Baal* is a possibility that has been entertained by some scholars.[27]

One more datum needs to be taken into consideration under this heading. A list, compiled by Horwitz, gives the occurrences of words that are spread over two lines in the cuneiform alphabetic texts. It is striking that CTA 2-6, clearly the works of ᵓ*elmlk*, should contain all the occurrences of that phenomenon available to *Baal*. The same idiosyncrasy is also noticeable in CTA 14-16 [*Keret*] and in 17, 19 [but *not* 18—all belonging to *Aqhat*], texts believed also to display ᵓ*elmlk*'s handwriting.[28] Since this propensity to split words between two lines seems to be so singularly 'Elemilkian', one might offer the following conjectures: 1. It is likely that a scribe *copying* a text from an 'original' that lies before him would try to avoid such an idiosyncrasy; rather, his eye would permit him to estimate the amount of additional room needed to complete a word, and hence to avoid splitting his vocabulary. 2. It is not likely that dictations, which depend on mouthing *whole* words, if not a full phrase at one time, could account for this idiosyncrasy. For these two reasons, one *might* conclude that ᵓ*elmlk* was responsible for putting together, i.e. composing, most of the version of *Baal* that is now

[25]See A. Van Selms (1970) 251-52.

[26]Discussion in Van Zijl (1972) 11-12.

[27]PRU II, p. xlii; PRU V, pp. 1-2.

[28]W. J. Horwitz (1977) 126 n. 17. Note that CTA 1 and 7-11, commonly regarded as belonging to *Baal*, as well as CTA 20-22 [*Repha'im* cycle], do not display such idiosyncrasies. Except for CTA 1, these are clearly not penned by ᵓ*elmlk*. CTA 24 [Nikkal], also note in ᵓ*elmlk's* handwriting, however, does evidence this peculiarity.

at our disposal.[29] This of course need not imply that he *created* the contents that were used in that composition.

γ. *Errors*. S. Segert studied scribal errors in literary and non-literary texts from Ugarit.[30] His conclusion is that, generally speaking, there seems to be little distinction between the mistakes that are presumed to come from dictation and those that originate from copying.[31] Cross believes that many errors, including mistransposition of paired formulae, could be ascribed to singing or dictating.[32] It should be stated that some of the 'errors' compiled by Segert have received plausible explanations and that others may merely attest to semantic or grammatical variants. More importantly, however, it is almost impossible to determine the reason, cause, or source of an error. To criticize one example cited by Horwitz,[33] only western ears would regard the phonemes *ʾaleph* and *ʿayin* as indistinguishable when pronounced by a dictating scribe. Additionally, we should also remember that authors of texts commit errors, even as they compose.[34]

NARRATIVE CONSIDERATIONS. Stylistic evidence permits evaluation on the nature of the audience as well as that of the teller.

α. *Paronomasia*. We should differentiate between 'oral' and 'visual' word-play. While the presence of examples from the first category, which include 'equivocal' [word play that depend on homonymy], 'parosonantic' [play on roots which share two or three radicals], 'etymological', 'assonantic', 'onomatopeic', and 'antanaclastic' [same word, different meaning in differing contexts] paronamasia can be an indication that oral presentations are at stake, attestations of examples from the second category ('visual') often betray a scribal audience. For it is not likely that this last type of paronomasia, which includes 'gematria', 'notrikon', [acronymic use of single consonants], 'epanastrophe' [last consonant of a word repeated, often in reverse order, in the following word], and 'anastrophe' [upsetting the usual word order to emphasize a play on words], would be readily caught by a listening audience.[35] It must be admitted, however, that Ugaritic scholarship has not reached the stage in which paronomastic evidence is clearly recognized.

[29] Horwitz (1977) 127, uses the same evidence to conclude the opposite.

[30] Segert (1958) 193-212; (1959) 23-32. A Pioneering study on this topic is F. Rosenthal (1939) 215-25.

[31] See also Segert (1971) 415.

[32] 1973: 117, n. 18.

[33] 1977: 124 n. 10 (on *pḫr mʾd / mʿd*).

[34] On this, see Segert (1971) 415, n. 7.

[35] On the terminology, see IDB *Supplement*, pp. 968-70.

β. *Rhetorical devices.* As used by Biblical scholars, this heading conveys two markedly different approaches. The first deals mostly with stylistic devices (inclusio, ambiguity, chiasmus, stereo-typed phrases, (fore)shadowing, *leitwortstil,* repetition, rhetorical questions, etc.) a number of which are exposited by James Muilenburg and his students.[36] The goals, but not necessarily the forms, of their enterprise are shared in Europe by Alonso-Schökel and Wolfgang Richter.[37] The second approach tries to reactivate Aristotelian concepts in order to evaluate the manner in which an audience is persuaded by a writer/speaker.[38]

The scholarly literature on these topics, when it comes to evaluating Ugaritic documents, is conspicuously small. Yet, successful discussions on these points might well reveal the type of audience that welcomed *Baal, Keret* and *Aqhat.* While it cannot be ruled out that declaimed or orally presented literature can be well stocked with rhetorical examples, the fact that these rhetorical devices are essentially the product of skillful and learned expositors *might* be an indication that a scribal audience, rather than a listening one, was involved.[39] To concentrate on one example, the difference that occurs in the repetitions found in the so-called ABA pattern, that is those that occur when large segments of a narrative are taken up once more (by messengers, by the undertaking of a mission as per instruction, command, etc. . . .), are well worth noting since they might include variations, often imperceptible to a listening audience, which would delight a copyist or a reader.[40] Were we to possess a complete text for the Ugaritic belletristic creations, on the other hand, we might decide whether a repeated section (A) is made to cut into the flow of narration (B) in such a manner as to heighten expectation of an audience by delaying the resolution of a particular sequence.

γ. *Performance.* We have alluded already to the rubrics as possible sources for information on this topic. From Ugarit, only CTA 23 [*Šaḥar and Šalem*] provides us with obvious indications that a dramatic performance was at stake.[41] But this text, it is interesting to note, falls outside the category of folk/fairy tales. It is possible that the ratio of dialogue to descriptive narrative within a given text might be used to

[36]Cf., conveniently (1969) 1-18 and the essays assembled by Muilenberg's students, in Jackson (1974).

[37]Alonso-Schökel (1965); Richter (1971).

[38]Gitay (1978). For a bibliography on the issues, see p. 71-72 and nn. 186-87.

[39]Welch (1974) 421-34, and especially 424-25. On the ABA pattern, Welch states, "[it] provides us with strong evidence for a well disciplined yet broad perspective enjoyed by ancient authors as they commanded the execution of their literary works. The counter-balancing shifts in style and subject matter were performed intentionally and served a valuable purpose in unifying and framing the message of the passage as a whole" (p. 427).

[40]Note also Welch's (1974) 427, good injunctions against claiming textual corruption on the basis of differences in the repeated portions of a narrative.

[41]The point has been made by almost every commentator who dealt with this text.

recover the performability of a narrative. Although a dialogue can be imbedded within ancient narrative only *seriatim*, it could nevertheless be investigated for contents which gain dramatically by the accompaniment of gestures. Many of the exchanges between Aqhat and Anat, preserved in *Aqhat*, as well as those between Yaṭpan and Anat—even the soliloquies of the bereaved Danel—could be accentuated by bodily movements and by voice modulations.

Cultural Context

Under this heading, folklorists evaluate evidence which witnesses the relationship between narratives and the cultures that produce them. One of these concerns is the documentation of the manner in which a literary text mirrors a particular culture, preserving information on values, attitudes, behavior, sanctions, which might be shared by a people. However, any conclusion that is entertained must take into consideration the startling and disturbing realization that characters in folktales are often made to act in a manner that defies conventions, that is often despised, even prohibited in daily practice. This is so because folk narrative often becomes a vehicle in which society alludes to taboos, sexual and otherwise, which are normally suppressed in more 'elevated' writings.[42]

With this in mind, the problems that confront the analyst are at least twofold: *a*. how does one recognize the distinguish between sanctioned and prohibited mores? and, *b*. how does one explain the inclusion, within a narrative, of prohibited activities? Although they are concerned with separate issues, these two questions can be broached simultaneously. Below, I shall but touch on these:

a. In approaching the first of these queries, it might be best to pursue two separate avenues. Returning to the concept of 'function' as delineated by Propp, one can begin by isolating those episodes in the narrative which seem to contain individual 'scenes'; that is, sequences which describe an activity that begins, develops, and ends even as it initiates another sequence. However hyperbolically stated, many of these episodes will be seen to reflect activities that are either commonplace or unlikely to challenge our conceptions of normative human enterprises; hence, these will be judged to require no further elucidation. If however, the sequence that is isolated is deemed to contain quaint, esoteric, preposterous, obscene, or unusual practices we might subject it to further analysis by testing its contents against the evidence of non-literary documentation. If the last procedure offers no confirmation or support from that documentation, then the activity, found within a

[42]Bascom in Dundes (1965) 285-98.

sequence, might be ranged among those that a society discouraged in actual life.

Evaluation of the religious contents of Ugaritic texts would profit by this approach. Above, we criticized the tendency to promote a cultic or a seasonal application for the whole cycles of *Baal* and *Aqhat* because, in our opinion, these particular narratives were meant to satisfy literary, rather than religious, sensibilities. But one can, nevertheless, isolate a particular sequence from within these narratives, one which retains the terminology for a specific cultic act or rituals (e.g. terms for sacrifice, vows, prayers, incubation, etc.) and evaluate it in the light of attestations available in the non-literary tablets.[43]

b. Locating the activities which might be at odds with the established norms of a given society can, admittedly, be a highly speculative enterprise. This is especially so since many of these activities are, in the Ugaritic texts, attributed either to superhuman or to divine protagonists. Despite the difficulties that are encountered, the undertaking might yet be worthwhile, above all because it might permit a balanced appreciation of Canaanite culture, an appreciation that has been marred, in modern scholarship, by unflattering comparison with Hebraic civilization. It may matter enormously, for example, whether or not we take the sexual relationship between Anat and Baal at face value. For if we do so, we not only risk accusing the Canaanites of tolerating incestual cohabitation—a union which, incidentally, has never been documented outside of literary texts—but of glorying in an excess of libido that has, repeatedly, been invidiously compared with the behavior of the Hebrews. Similarly, an appreciation of the fact that folkloristic texts do retain, and do refrain from condemning, activities that were prohibited in a living society, might prevent facile generalizations on Canaanite practices such as bestiality, human sacrifice, covetousness, cruelty, and immorality: before such occurrences can be attributed to them, it might be best to parallel the documentation in non-literary contexts.

'Educational' and Political Contexts

This very broad category provides us with an umbrella under which we can consider the various benefits that accrue to a society when it is shown that a particular literary text is put in circulation. Certainly any piece of literature fulfills an educational need. On the one hand, it forces the composer/creator to probe his heritage and to test his learning even as he presents his audience with satisfying works. On the other hand, it permits the audience to glory in the activities of ancient heroes, to share

[43]That the enterprise can be beset with difficulties can be gathered by the discussion that Baruch Levine offers on the term *šlmm* (1974) 13-20.

vicariously in the drama of changing fortunes, to gather lessons from worthy behavior, and to accept the consequences of ill-starred ventures. If there is any evidence that the material is also destined to justify religious institutions and to explain cultic activities, it is within this category that it is best understood; for this perspective narrows down the usefulness of functionalist interpretations, criticized above, to the point where they would no longer be regarded as establishing, scientifically and objectively, chapters in the history of West Semitic religions, but rather, where they would be considered as revealing to us the perception that a particular folk, living at a specific time, had of the meaning of its faith and the origin of its rituals.

One other need if fulfilled by folk narratives. It permits the listener, as well as the teller, to indulge in propagandistic activities, with consequences that are of benefits not only to the permanence of an established dynasty, but also to the health of the city-state. I shall lightly touch upon this by considering *Keret*.

While, above, we disputed the likelihood that *Keret* could inform the modern historian on the activity of Middle Bronze Age West Semites, this heading allows us to speculate on the meaning that it had for those that were acquainted with its contents. For, however, historical, historicizing, or fictitious we judge its various episodes to be, we might yet consider them to afford the Ugaritian a paradigm on the persistence (and probable triumph) or a dynasty despite the succession of devastating blows. It should be noted that such lessons could be learned even if the heroes are not regarded as immediate ancestors of the folk that is benefitting from their experience. (An example that comes to mind to sustain this observation is Gilgamesh, a native of Uruk, whose exploits were celebrated in many cities and among differing cultures.)[44] This perspective might make it reasonably clear why *Keret* fails to link its hero to Ugarit, a city which, nevertheless, enjoyed and partook of his fame.

But it will not suffice to stop here! To adequately probe the political advantages gained by circulating *Keret*, I suggest that we might have to supplement the interpretive guidelines that are derived from studying the manner in which a dynasty actualizes itself through the activities of a paradigmatic hero. *Keret* seems also to belong to a genre of literature which one might call 'political biographies'. Whether quickened by actual events (e.g. 'the Apology of Hattushilish', the story of Idrimi, possibly, the story of Sinuhe) or inspired by verisimilitude (e.g. the Biblical Joseph), these accounts play a role, in the propaganda of

[44]Or, to take a Biblical example, note how the story of Job, a man from Uz, was used by the Hebrews to teach important lessons.

individual cultures, which can be profitably investigated. But in order to do so, it would be very useful to first establish a syntax and a morphology of such biographies. But that, obviously, is a charge that must be taken on another occasion.

UGARIT AND THE BIBLE: PROGRESS AND REGRESS IN 50 YEARS OF LITERARY STUDY

P. C. CRAIGIE

Department of Religious Studies
University of Calgary

I. *Introduction*

It is some fifty years since the first tablets were found at Ras Shamra, bearing the alphabetic script and language now identified as Ugaritic. Although fifty years is a short span of time in the context of archaeological systems of measurement, it may seem to be a sufficiently long period of time in which to have formed a firm and objective judgment of the relevance of the Ugaritic texts for the study of the Bible, and of the Bible for the study of the Ugaritic texts. And yet in fact, after half a century, it is by no means certain that we are in a position to come to a firm evaluation of the interrelationship of Ugaritic and Hebrew literary texts. There are at least two reasons for such uncertainty. First, the 50-year period is artificial, in that discoveries have continued to be made down into the present decade;[1] each new collection of texts discovered has necessitated new study and a re-evaluation of old positions. Second, during the last twenty-five years several new "schools" or "traditions" of scholarship have emerged, which have proposed particular interpretations or avenues of approach to the Hebrew and Ugaritic texts; these "schools" are still in the process of growth and have not yet (in my judgment) undergone the radical criticism and evaluation which may be necessary before an assessment of their real contribution can be made.

While there can be no doubt that fifty years have marked the growth of the comparative discipline of Hebrew-Ugaritic literary studies, there is some doubt whether that growth has been entirely healthy. During the last two decades, a number of voices have been raised in protestation

[1]For example, during the 1978 season, the joint Syrian-French mission at Ras Ibn Hani, just south of Ras Shamra, recovered approximately 60 texts, though almost all are fragmentary.

against the phenomenon of "pan-Ugaritism,"[2] and it is this protest which in turn raises the issue of health in the growth of comparative studies. Has the recent boom in comparative Hebrew-Ugaritic studies really resulted in progress? Or is there indeed an epidemic of "pan-Ugaritism," namely regress disguised as progress? These are the questions which are the central concern of this paper. But the focus is specifically upon comparative *literary* studies, not upon all areas of comparative Hebrew-Ugaritic research. Our task then is to seek a diagnosis of the state of the art and, more tentatively, to suggest a prognosis. I begin the first part of that task with a brief survey of comparative Hebrew-Ugaritic studies; the survey is inevitably selective, given the mass of publication in the field, but from that mass of material I have sought to discern certain trends and developments.

II. *Survey of Comparative Hebrew-Ugaritic Studies*

The first two decades following the discovery of the Ugaritic texts were marked by both progress and error. The novelty of the materials discovered inevitably led to hasty conclusions in some cases and erroneous judgments in other cases. Yet, taken in broad perspective, the first two decades of comparative studies were not characterized by excess. J. W. Jack read a paper before the S.O.T.S. in Edinburgh in 1934, which appeared the following year in amplified form as a monograph;[3] although he forwarded a number of observations and proposed parallels which have since been rejected, Jack was careful in his judgments, aware of alternative explanations and of problems in the data, and could certainly not be criticized for latent or incipient "pan-Ugaritism." Rene Dussaud, whose comparative study was first published in 1937,[4] went somewhat further than Jack and in retrospect may be judged as a little rash with respect to historical judgments based on the Hebrew and Ugaritic texts, yet even Dussaud's mild excesses may easily be forgiven. He was writing soon after the initial discoveries, and it must be remembered that were it not for Dussaud's involvement and support, the excavations at Minet el-Beida and Ras Shamra might never have been started. It was the same widely ranging mind that in 1928 anticipated possible benefits from the excavation with such extraordinary success, that also at a later date indulged in occasional, but understandable, excesses in the comparative study of Hebrew and Ugaritic texts.

Other early comparative studies were also moderate, given the excitement of new discoveries. Robert De Langhe's massive two-volume

[2] See, for example, Driver (1965a) 117; De Moor and van der Lugt (1974) 3-26; and Craigie (1977a) 33-49.

[3] Jack (1935).

[4] Dussaud (1937, 1941).

study[5] contains many observations on Hebrew-Ugaritic matters that are now out-of-date; nevertheless, his work is still of value, principally because of the enormous primary research De Langhe undertook pertaining to the Ugaritic texts themselves, quite apart from their relevance for the Bible. Other early works and studies, such as those of Patton on the Psalms[6] and W. Baumgartner's on the state of scholarship,[7] are now dated, but nevertheless they mark the path of the real progress which was genuinely being achieved during the first two decades following the discovery of the Ugaritic texts. Popular and balanced surveys may be found in the monographs of Kapelrud, Jacob, and Pfeiffer;[8] a more detailed account, containing much creative and original work, was written by John Gray.[9]

But the caution of most comparativists of the early decades was gradually reduced in the work of later scholars. An old and familiar process could be seen taking place: carefully phrased hypotheses became "established facts," simply by virtue of seniority, and conjectural readings in the footnotes of the thirties became the accepted texts in the speculations of the sixties and seventies. This trend can be illustrated clearly in the following example:

> *Cooking a kid in its mother's milk* (Deut. 14:21). This obscure piece of legislation in the Mosaic law appeared to have been provided with clarification in the Ugaritic texts. In Charles Virolleaud's *editio princeps* of *CTA* 23 (*UT* 52).14, he restored a difficult text as follows:
>
> *ṭḇ{ḫ . g}d . bḥlb*
>
> Virolleaud noted carefully that his restoration was simply conjectural and translated: "Fais (cuire un che)vreau dans le lait."[10] H. L. Ginsberg later drew attention to the apparent biblical parallel[11] and almost all scholars since that time have followed and accepted the proposed parallel uncritically.[12] Only in recent studies has it become clear that: (a) the restoration is probably incorrect, and (b) even if correct, the translation of *ṭbḫ* and probably also of *gd* (as proposed by Virolleaud), is almost certainly wrong.[13]

[5]de Langhe (1945).

[6]Patton (1944).

[7]Baumgartner (1940); (1941); (1947). For all his caution, Baumgartner reiterated Dussaud's earlier statement to the effect that the discovery of Ras Shamra was the most important ever made for Biblical Studies [(1941) 181].

[8]Kapelrud (1965); Jacob (1960); Pfeiffer (1962).

[9]Gray (1957), second edition, 1965.

[10]Virolleaud (1933).

[11]Ginsberg (1935), esp. 72.

[12]Schoors (1972) 29-32.

[13]See Craigie, (1979a).

In the decade of the '60s, however, certain major new developments began to take place which are thoroughly relevant to the present discussion. It may be convenient to summarize these new developments by referring to the three geographical areas in which they have flourished: (i) Rome; (ii) Claremont (California); (iii) Münster (in Westphalia). Such a selection of only three places will doubtless irritate some (one could add Paris, Cambridge [Mass.] and the Scottish Universities); nevertheless, the limitations on length must justify the focus on these three places. Let me summarize briefly these traditions or projects, while delaying critical comments to a later stage.

Rome: the School of Mitchell Dahood

The school is defined partly in terms of the numerous works of Mitchell Dahood himself,[14] and partly in terms of the research of his present and former students.[15] While this tradition in scholarship has made considerable contributions to Ugaritic Studies *per se*, its principal emphasis has been on the study of Hebrew texts in the context of Northwest Semitic language and literature, principally (though not exclusively) Ugaritic. In general terms, the approach has involved a new understanding of Hebrew grammar, philology, etymology, etc., based upon the new knowledge of Northwest Semitic languages, to which the Ugaritic texts have made such an enormous contribution. Thus, far more is involved in this comparative approach to the Hebrew texts than simply drawing upon Ugaritic resources for parallel material or general illumination of the Biblical world. In effect, Hebrew language must be relearned in the light of the new data, and very often that means that the structure and meaning of the language, as conveyed by the Massoretes, must be unlearned. Thus, in the study of a psalm, the Ugaritic texts may affect the understanding of the Hebrew poet's imagery, the poetic structure, the grammatical structure, the etymology of key words, and consequently the form and meaning of the entire passage. In short, the approach of the Rome School is a radical approach; for its proponents and adherents, it involves fundamentally new understanding of the Biblical texts in matters as diverse as comparative etymology and historical theology. Of all the comparativist approaches currently in vogue, this is the most far-reaching in its implications, and indeed the tradition which evokes from some the most critical opposition.

[14]Dahood has written a large number of articles on the subject. A convenient index to his earlier works is provided by Martinez (1967). On grammatical matters, see Dahood (1965). His most sustained contribution to the field is to be found in his three-volume commentary, *The Psalms,* in the Anchor Bible.

[15]See, for example, Cathcart (1973), and Kuhnigk (1974).

Claremont: the Ras Shamra Parallels Project

This project, officially entitled the "Ugaritic and Hebrew Parallels Project," was initiated in 1965 under the direction of Loren Fisher; it was one of several programmes sponsored under the auspices of the Institute for Antiquity and Christianity. Fisher had perceived the need for a single work which would provide scholars with immediate and critical access to the vast amount of data pertaining to comparative Ugaritic-Hebrew studies; thus, he proposed that the project "list and discuss the parallels between the Ugaritic and Akkadian literature from Ras Shamra and the Hebrew Bible."[16] Specifically, the project is directed primarily to literary and cultural parallels, classified into eleven categories (e.g., motifs, phrases, formulae, literary structures). The first two volumes of this project have already been published[17] and the third is approaching publication and should appear before the end of 1980.

The publication of the first two volumes of *Ras Shamra Parallels* has made it clear that the project has undertaken far more than simply listing the parallels already proposed. Both the first volumes contain new and creative work, parallels proposed for the first time in publication. And it is the new contributions which have appeared in these volumes which have evoked the most powerful criticism, specifically the charge of "Pan-Ugaritism."[18] The plurality of contributors to the "Parallels Project" is such that it cannot be described as representing any single "school" of scholarship,[19] beyond that of very serious emphasis upon the value of Ugaritic for studying the Hebrew texts. But the Project has demonstrated on the one hand the enormous potential value of the Ugaritic texts for the study of the Hebrew Bible, and on the other hand the vast amount of very critical work which needs to be done before any Hebrew-Ugaritic parallel can be accepted as valid.

Münster: Ugarit Forschungen

A team (*Forschergruppe*) was set up in Münster, West Germany, to conduct basic research in Ugaritic. It is led by Professors Manfred Dietrich and Oswald Loretz, who at the same time edit the series *Alter Orient und Altes Testament*, the companion series *Alter Orient und Altes Testament—Sonderreihe*, and the annual *Ugarit-Forshungen* (volume 1, 1969). Also on the team is Herr Joaqin Sanmartín, as *wissenschaftlicher Mitarbeiter*. The project is financed by the Deutsche For-

[16]RSP I xiii.

[17]RSP I and II.

[18]See de Moor and van der Lugt (1974) which is a review article of RSP I.

[19]Thus, each of the first two volumes contains lengthy contributions from M. Dahood, and in that sense may be said to represent the "Rome School," but the volumes as a whole certainly do not represent the approach of the "Rome School."

schungsgemeinschaft, Bonn. The principal long-term aim of this project is the preparation of an *Ugaritisches Handwörterbuch*, which has involved a complete listing of all published material pertaining to Ugaritic (*Ugaritische Bibliographie 1928-1966* and *1967-1971*) and an edition of all texts in alphabetic cuneiform: *Die keilalphabetischen Texte aus Ugarit* (AOAT 24/1, 1976).[20]

From a certain perspective, the work of this research team is strictly primary research into Ugaritic, but for two reasons, it is relevant to the comparative study of Hebrew and Ugaritic materials. First, the comparative study, insofar as it involves Ugaritic texts, must depend on good primary resources (reliable text editions, dictionaries, etc.) before valid comparisons can be undertaken. In this context, the Münster team is contributing on a large scale to the necessary tools for undertaking comparative studies (though this is not their primary purpose). Second, in both the annual (*UF*) and study series (*AOAT*), numerous comparative studies are being published; Oswald Loretz's "Psalmenstudien" in the volumes of *UF* provide a prime example. Thus, in two significant ways, the *Forschergruppe* in Münster is making a contribution to comparative Hebrew-Ugaritic studies.

This survey of traditions and projects pertaining to comparative studies sets a perspective on the contemporary situation. Though there are many, both persons and groups, falling outside this threefold classification, the majority of the critical issues are raised, in one form or another, in relationship to them. In order to form a critical assessment of the strengths and weaknesses of the various approaches to comparative studies, it is necessary now to turn to some of the problem areas and methodological questions which pertain to such comparative studies. Although the following points are of a fundamental nature, they tend to be either implicit or ignored in the majority of comparative studies.

III. *Problem Areas in Comparative Studies*

Linguistic Relationships:[21] In the comparative study of any two bodies of literature, it is useful *a priori* to have some data pertaining to the linguistic interrelationship of the languages concerned, namely Hebrew and Ugaritic. It is not merely a matter of pinning accurate labels on the two languages (e.g., that they are northern and southern dialects respectively of the Canaanite section of Northwest Semitic languages). One could be wrong with the label and still have the appropriate and relevant data: viz. the degree of overlap in lexical stock, the similarities and differences in grammatical structure, the extent to which similarities

[20]The details were provided in a report by W. G. E. Watson in his (1977b).

[21]This topic is examined only in summary form here, and is treated in greater detail in Craigie (1971), esp. 5-7.

are to be expected *a priori*, etc. A single example will illustrate the nature of the problem and the importance of attempting to determine the linguistic relationship between the two languages:

Hebrew-Ugaritic Parallel Word Pairs. There are a large number of Hebrew-Ugaritic parallel word pairs, common to the poetry of both languages and involving the use of cognate terms; the study of this phenomenon is a major part of the approach of the "Rome School" and has also received prominence in the Ras Shamra parallels project. According to Mitchell Dahood, the occurrence of such common word pairs points to the existence of a common Canaanite "thesaurus"; both Hebrew and Ugaritic poets drew from its resources.[22]

It must be granted that there are indeed a large number of common parallel word pairs: an example would be "heaven//earth" (Ug. *šmm*// *ʾarṣ*; Heb. ארץ//שׁמים).[23] But how does one determine the significance of comparative data such as this? With respect to the Hebrew parallel word pairs, there are at least three possibilities: (a) the Hebrew word pairs arose independently of the Ugaritic word pairs; (b) if Hebrew and Ugaritic were sufficiently closely related, linguistically, to be mutually intelligible, it is conceivable that the Hebrew poets may have read/heard Ugaritic poetry and *borrowed* such parallel word pairs for their own use (ignoring, for the moment, chronological problems); (c) a close linguistic relationship between Hebrew and Ugaritic might imply a common cultural background to each, and thus it might be proposed that there was indeed a "Canaanite thesaurus," the resources of which were utilized by both Hebrew and Ugaritic poets. But how does one determine which—if any—of these three possibilities is correct? First, a broader perspective is needed; it is provided by the observation that similar word pairs also occur in Akkadian poetry, Egyptian poetry, Arabic poetry,[24] and in the poetry of certain other languages such as Finnish and Chinese.[25] Thus to return to the example of "heaven//earth," note the following:

Akkadian:	*šamû* // *erṣetu*	(Atrahasis I. 13f)
Arabic:	*samāʾ* // *ʾarḍ*	(Qur'an 53:32)
Egyptian:	*pt* // *tꜣ*	(Ani II. 10-11)

From this type of data, it might be assumed that in the poetry of any language in which parallelism is employed, parallel word pairs will appear, and that a degree of commonality in human experience, and therefore in human poetry, will contribute to *common* parallel word pairs in the poetry of various languages. If this argument is correct, then one is left with the strong possibility that common parallel word pairs arise

[22]See Dahood (1972) 74.
[23]Dahood (1972) 356.
[24]See Craigie (1977b) and (1979b).
[25]Cf. Kalevala (1907); and Newman and Popper (1918). On parallelism and word pairs in Vedic poetry, see Gonda (1959), esp. 29-36.

independently in various languages and the prior question pertains to the origin of parallelism as such; once parallelism is employed, common parallel word pairs are to be expected. Against this view, it might be argued that the large number of *cognate* parallel word pairs common to Hebrew and Ugaritic poetry make a special case for interrelationship, e.g. a common background or "Canaanite thesaurus," to use the language of Dahood. But now the question of linguistic relationships comes into play again; however one defines the linguistic relationship of Hebrew and Ugaritic, it is at least clear at the outset that they share a high proportion of lexical stock; therefore, *a priori*, it is to be expected that they will share a large number of *cognate* parallel word pairs. Thus, while the possibility of a common "Canaanite thesaurus" remains, the probability of the independent origination of Ugaritic and Hebrew parallel word pairs is quite strong.

Chronological Relationships. The comparative study of literary texts (unless it be purely phenomenological or aesthetic) should take into account the relative chronology of the texts under comparison; only then can the comparative data be appropriately interpreted, e.g. in terms of polygenesis or monogenesis of literary forms, in terms of the significance or non-significance to be attached to similarities, and in terms of literary priorities. Furthermore, the chronological gap between texts under comparison provides a necessary perspective for the evaluation of comparative data, particularly when direct or indirect literary interrelationships are being proposed. It is fairly safe to say that the Ugaritic texts always have chronological priority over the Hebrew texts in comparative studies, though the chronological gap in such studies varies from ca 100 years to 1,000 years, depending upon the identity of the texts under comparison.

Geographical Relationships. A part of the issue here is simply the proximity (or non-proximity) of the geographical areas in which the relative texts were written and/or survived. But a more significant question pertains to the cultures which they represent and the possibility of interrelationship between those cultures. Thus, combining chronological and geographical data, the Kingdom of Ugarit was situated far to the north of the territory held by the Hebrews, never bordered on it, and ceased to exist before the Hebrew Kingdoms entered the arena of history. All this is obvious, but the corollary questions pertain to *representativeness*; may the Ugaritic literature be held to be representative of Canaanite literature, both *geographically* (viz. representative of Canaanite literature and oral poetry current in the southern "Canaanite" city states) and *chronologically* (viz. representative of the later Canaanite literature and oral poetry of the distant region)? These are questions not easy to answer with precision for a number of reasons. (a) Ugarit, during its Golden Age, was a cosmopolitan centre, multi-lingual, representing on the one hand developed forms of the arts and on the other hand the natural processes of cultural and literary syncretism. (b) Although there is evidence of the use of Ugaritic script in the south (of Ugarit),[26] and of historical interrelationships (e.g., the recent Akkadian tablet found at Tell Aphek[27]), there is at best indirect or sparse evidence of the nature of Canaanite literature and oral poetry in the south in pre-Hebrew times and during the Hebrew Kingdoms. Thus, although there is not an absence of evidence, the nature and paucity of the evidence is such that it is still only possible to speak cautiously of the representative nature of the Ugaritic texts *vis-à-vis* Canaanite literature and oral poetry as a whole. Consequently, there must be caution in any comparative studies which propose direct, or even indirect, literary relationships.

Literary Matters. It must further be added that there are severe difficulties in the conduct of comparative studies with respect to *genres* or literary forms. In broad terms, the Ugaritic literary texts may be classified as myths and legends in poetic form, to which may be added the semi-poetic form in parts of certain religious (ritual) texts and epistles. In contrast, the bulk of Hebrew literature which falls under comparison is prophetic or psalmodic poetry and narrative prose. Ugarit has provided no prophetic poetry. It has left us no unambiguous examples of psalmody, with the exception of those passages which might be identified as originally hymnic, but have survived only through integration within different and larger literary forms (myth or legend),[28] and it has no extensive examples of literary narrative prose. This observation is important, for it means that virtually all Hebrew-Ugaritic comparative studies involve the comparison of *different* literary forms.[29] The observation constitutes a warning concerning the necessity of caution, not a ban on comparative studies, but it is a warning which is only neglected with peril.

The Nature of the Ugaritic Texts. Fifty years of research have had immensely valuable results in one particular area with respect to comparative studies; the Ugaritic texts are better known and better understood now than they were before, as a result of massive, minute and

[26]Beyond the city of Ugarit, there is evidence of the use of the script (or forms of it) from a variety of locations: Tell Sukas, Sarepta, Mt. Carmel, Beth Shemesh, Tell Taanach, Kamid el-Loz, Tell Nebi Mend, Tabor, and Ras Ibn Hani.

[27]*The Jerusalem Post International Edition*, August 22, 1978.

[28]I exclude the so-called Canaanite "psalm-fragments" [cf. Jirku (1933)], partly because in terms of literary form, it is hypothetical whether or not they ever were actually a part of psalms, and if they were, they have undergone literary adaptation of such a kind that the form *per se* can no longer be identified with certainty.

[29]In my judgment, the comparison undertaken by L. R. Fisher and F. B. Knutson falls into this category. See Fisher and Knutson (1969) 157-67, and cf. Craigie (1971) 11-15.

fundamental research. (This is one of the areas in which the Münster project has already made a great contribution, as will be evident to all those who have utilized *KTU* and the volumes of the *Bibliographie*.) But for all the progress, a reminder is necessary. Many of the Ugaritic texts are broken, illegible or incomplete; the reading of some texts was difficult at discovery, and checking the readings becomes more difficult with the passage of time as a result of the gradual process of deterioration. To this may be added the relative paucity of texts, the uncertainty as to the vocalization of the texts as a whole (the variant forms of the *aleph* providing at best limited evidence with respect to total vocalization and chronological or regional dialects), and other difficulties. The difficulties are not such as to undermine the possibility of comparative studies, but they do require caution, and too few comparativists remember the cautionary perspectives provided by Donner a little more than a decade ago.[30]

The Nature of the Hebrew Texts. The difficulties engendered by the Hebrew texts in the context of comparative studies are of a different nature, resulting from the different method of transmission and survival. The "palimpsestic" nature of the Hebrew texts creates particular difficulties for certain types of comparison. The original consonantal text may be assumed to have survived (subject to the usual copyist errors, manuscript problems, etc.), but the older texts have been overlaid by a system of *matres lectionis* and all the texts have been modified by the vocalization systems of the Massoretes. The vocalization of a consonantal text creates particular problems for a comparative study, particularly in the context of poetry. Does the vocalization reflect accurately the meaning of the original texts? More importantly, with respect to such matters as meter, does the Massoretic vocalization reflect pronunciation in the time of the Massoretes only, or does it reflect a genuinely ancient system of pronunciation and therefore provide some insight into the sound of the ancient Hebrew poetic texts? There are means of providing provisional answers to these questions with respect to certain portions of the Hebrew texts, but there is insufficient data to provide complete answers. It is precisely this area of uncertainty which contributes to the debate over the relative merits of the "Rome school" in comparative studies and to the comparative study of Hebrew-Ugaritic metrics.[31]

In the light of the aforementioned areas of difficulty and problems of method, some assessment must now be made of the extent to which real gains have been achieved in the comparative study of Hebrew and

[30]Donner (1967). Donner also raises the issue clearly of the representative nature of the Ugaritic texts in the context of the Late Bronze Age.

[31]See, for example, Stuart (1976).

Ugaritic literature, and those areas in which the process of regress may be evident.

IV. *Areas of Progress and Regress*

To begin with a broad statement of assessment, the overall picture is one of progress, in two directions. In matters such as comparative Hebrew-Ugaritic philology and comparative literature, fifty years of study reflect enormous advances. Inevitably, however, the progress has been somewhat circular. In the first place, it was Hebrew language and literature which contributed to a knowledge of Ugaritic language and literature; then, as the latter was better understood, the reverse process began and Ugaritic data began to provide help with difficult aspects of Hebrew language and literature. If the focus is narrowed, however, it may be possible to determine somewhat more accurately the areas of the study of biblical literature in which there has been either progress or regress. The following areas are selective and by no means comprehensive.

The Language and Forms of Poetry. Almost all the Ugaritic material which deserves the term *literature* is poetic in form. The study of Ugaritic poetry has thus created a better understanding of the nature of Syro-Palestinian poetry, poetic structure, poetic devices and the like. This broad general knowledge provided by Ugaritic poetry has been of more assistance in the general study of Hebrew poetry than has, for example, the study of Akkadian or Egyptian poetry, for with respect to both language and poetic forms, Ugaritic poetry has generally the closest affinity to Hebrew poetry. These advances are aptly illustrated in the growth in knowledge of the nature and forms of parallelism which has resulted from a study of the Ugaritic texts.[32]

Poetic Motif and Imagery. Again, there have been areas of real advance. The tracing of the motifs of the Baal myth, in its various parts, has contributed greater sensitivity to the religious and literary art of the Hebrew poets. Examples may be seen in the analysis of motif in the Song of the Sea (Ex. 15:1-8),[33] the Helel myth (Isa. 14:12-14),[34] or in Psalm 104,[35] to use only a few illustrations. An example of the comparative study of imagery may be seen in a study of the imagery of Anat, through which Deborah is presented, in the poetry of Judges 5.[36]

[32]The following selected studies illustrate, by way of example, different aspects of the current study of Ugaritic and Hebrew poetry; Ceresko (1978) [*cf. CBQ*, 38/3 (1976) 303-11]; Watson (1976a); and Margalit (1975).

[33]For example, Cross (1973) 112-44.

[34]Craigie (1973) 223-25.

[35]Dahood (1970), and Craigie (1974).

[36]See Craigie (1978).

Essentially, in these instances, the Ugaritic texts are providing insight into the religious and cultural thought-world of the Hebrew poets and are thus providing background data necessary for an understanding of the subtler aspects of the Hebrew poet's art. Here, there as not only been progress, but there remains scope for considerably more research and further progress.

Parallel Word Pairs in Poetry. This is a field of study which, in my judgment, is currently in a "pan-Ugaritic" phase (see further section III above). The earliest contributions in the field were marked by considerable caution (see especially the work of U. Cassuto[37]), whereas the most prolific current exponent of the art, Mitchell Dahood,[38] has gone too far in his application of data and the consequent re-interpretation of the Hebrew texts.[39] For all my criticism of Dahood in this matter, however, the fact remains that even if one were to reject 75% of all Dahood's contributions on this topic, we should still be left with a major contribution to comparative scholarship.

Poetic Meter. The comparative study of Hebrew and Ugaritic meter appears to be currently in a phase of profitable growth, as reflected for example in the works of D. K. Stuart, F. M. Cross and D. N. Freedman.[40] From a critical perspective, however, there remain too many areas of uncertainty: the problems of vocalization, with respect to both the Hebrew and Ugaritic texts, the related problems of phonology,[41] the problems associated with dating the texts under comparison, and the consequent uncertainty as to any precise system of metrical measurement, are enormous. I would not describe this as an area of "pan-Ugaritism," but I am yet to be convinced that lasting progress is being made in the comparative study of Hebrew and Ugaritic metrics.

Poetry, Myth and Ritual. The myth and ritual tradition (in a technical sense) in the comparative study of Ugaritic-Hebrew literature is no longer so dominant as it was;[42] it continues to exist, however, in modified forms,[43] though it is presented with more subtle and sophisticated argumentation. On this topic, I would say that there is not currently a state of "pan-Ugaritism" in vogue, though there has been in the past. But it is hard to form an accurate judgment concerning what

[37]Reprinted in Cassuto (1971) 25-32; first published in 1942/43.

[38]Major contributions appear in RSP I and II; the third volume (to be published in 1980) will contain a further contribution from Dahood on this topic.

[39]See de Moor and van der Lugt (1974).

[40]See particularly D. N. Freedman's "Prolegomenon" and bibliography in the reprint of G. B. Gray's *The Forms of Hebrew Poetry* (=Gray 1972).

[41]Cf. Gibson (1978) 140.

[42]For an earlier review of the topic, see de Langhe (1958).

[43]For example, in de Moor (1971).

real progress has been made in this area of study. In my judgment, there is still too little known about religion in Ugarit, and specifically about the relationship between the religion of the temples and that reflected in the religious texts,[44] to permit too extensive conclusions of a comparative nature concerning Hebrew religion and the potential mythic/ritual background to the Hebrew texts. This is a subject which needs further extensive study, though of a kind marked by considerable caution and a willingness to admit the uncertainty of any conclusion.

V. *Conclusion*

What is the state of the question? How far have we come and how much further is there to go in the comparative study of the Ugaritic texts and the Bible? A great deal of progress has been made over the last 50 years. In the last 20 years alone, that progress has gained additional momentum, both through an increase in the number of scholars working in the field, through refinement in method, through the development of certain scholarly projects and schools of thought, and as a result of the recovery of further textual materials in Ugaritic from Ras Shamra and various other sites. Without doubt, there is some evidence of the existence of "pan-Ugaritism," and though it may be unhealthy as such, in the longer term it should contribute to progress in comparative studies. Thus, the reaction to those who might be diagnosed as characterized by the flushed and feverish state of "pan-Ugaritism," should not be to ignore them; critical reaction and evaluation are required. The manic aspects of "pan-Ugaritism," modified by the depressive reaction of criticism, can result ultimately in real progress.

But still there remains much to be done and a long way to go. The biblical texts still contain many difficulties and obscurities; they are still not as well understood as we should like them to be. The same is true of the Ugaritic texts. But real progress in comparative studies always presupposes the continuation of primary research in each of the respective disciplines. And with respect to the Ugaritic texts, their potential value for the study of the Hebrew texts is directly contingent upon the advance of our knowledge concerning the Ugaritic texts *per se*. So I do not call for a halt, or even a "go-slow," in comparative studies. I simply urge that they be conducted in conjunction with primary research of a non-comparative nature and issue a reminder of the necessity for all comparative results to be subject to constant and rigorous criticism.

[44]For example, the presence of numerous stone anchors in the Baal temple at Ugarit leads one to suppose a strong maritime element in Ugaritic religion, yet it is not clearly demonstrated in the mythological literature (with the exception of the references to *Ym* which are ambivalent in this context). See Frost (1969) 235-45.

UGARITIC AND HEBREW METRICS[1]

DENNIS PARDEE

The University of Chicago

The primary concern of this paper is one of definition. The term 'meter' has been used quite frequently in the modern study of Hebrew poetry, and more recently of Ugaritic poetry, to refer to the quantitative and/or rhythmic aspect of the poet's art, as opposed to 'parallelism,' used to refer to the primary stylistic feature of Hebrew and Ugaritic poetry. As a neophyte in metrical studies, I do not wish to propose a new theory of Hebrew (and Ugaritic) metrics, but simply to discuss the feature of past theories which consist of using the word 'meter.' The reasons for this study are two: 1) When reading various studies on Hebrew and Ugaritic metrics I am frequently struck by the degree of arbitrariness which goes into the erection of the system, one which often leads to unacceptably extensive transformations of the text (hence a certain scepticism towards any metrical system); 2) Even when the metrical systems are erected and applied to the text, they appear to me not to meet the accepted definition of the word 'meter' as used in describing the structure of poetry in other languages. Conclusions similar to these were reached for Ugaritic poetry already three decades ago by G. Douglas Young.[2] I take up the cudgels again, in the first place, because I arrived at the present conclusions independently, on the basis of my own study of Ugaritic and Hebrew poetry, and, second, because the two recent attempts to find metrical systems in Ugaritic poetry discussed below do not really respond to Young's arguments. One of my main purposes, then, is to establish that generally accepted criteria for determining meter do exist in the study of poetry, especially that of the Western languages all the way from Greek poetry to that of the present. It is my belief that Young's strictures were in agreement with

[1]This is a general and theoretical presentation of positions reached in the study of a particular Ugaritic text, *UT* 607 (*KTU* 1.100) in "*m^{e}roră̆t-p^{e}tanîm* 'Venom' in Job 20:14," forthcoming in *ZAW* 91 (1979), and "A Philological and Prosodic Analysis of the Ugaritic Serpent Incantation *UT* 607," forthcoming in *JANES*.

[2]Young (1950).

these generally accepted criteria, while the attempts discussed below to find a metrical structure in Ugaritic and Hebrew poetry are not.

The present discussion will be divided into two main sections: A presentation of how the term 'meter' is used in describing the structures of poetry in several languages with which most scholars of the ancient Near East are acquainted; 2) An examination of two recent theories of Ugaritic (and Hebrew) meter.

METER

There are two primary senses of the word 'meter' which are used in the analysis of poetry, the first derived directly from a specific use of the Greek term *metron* 'measure' and referring to a metrical group, specifically a dipody,[3] the second a broader usage describing the measure of a line of poetry and hence of the predominant metric system of an entire poem. These meanings are given very clearly but succinctly in the article "Mètre" in *La Grande Encyclopédie*:[4]

> Un mètre comprend nécessairement deux parties, l'une forte ou accentuée, l'autre faible, qui peut être même représentée par un silence. Ces deux éléments sont nécessaires pour que le rythme puisse être saisi. Un mètre peut être représenté soit par 1 pied, c.-à.-d. par un groupe de deux ou trois syllables, soit par un groupe de 2 pieds intimément unis à l'aide d'un frappé plus fort. Dans le premier cas, les mots *pied* et *mètres* sont synonymes. . . . Par extension, on appelle encore mètres la forme du rythme prédominant dans une oeuvre poétique; ainsi l'on dit le mètre dactylique, anapestique, lyrique, etc. Le mot mètre est alors à peu près synonyme de vers. Il est toujours facile de saisir dans lequel de ces sens le mot est employé."

Since in classical poetry the lines are usually relatively independent (without rhyme or parallelism to link two or more lines together), 'meter' is occasionally defined specifically as the rhythmical pattern of a single line of poetry.[5] This must be understood, however, as an abbreviated formulation of the second usage described above, because of the fact that most Greek and Latin poetic works are composed in a metrical pattern—which means that, *grosso modo*, identifying one line of a classical poem tells one the meter in which the poem is composed. On the other hand, this definition is a very useful one in its own right, for even within a given classical metrical structure the individual lines may have many different combinations of foot types, placements of caesura, etc.

[3]*The Oxford English Dictionary*, "Metre," para. 4.

[4]Vol. 23, 802.

[5]Halporn, Ostwald, and Rosenmeyer (1963) 125-26.

My contention in this paper is that neither of the two primary meanings of the term 'meter' is properly ascribed to Ugaritic and Hebrew poetry: that these poetic systems do not have anything corresponding to the classical foot, and that there is not discernable in them a "predominant form of rhythm." In a purely descriptive sense, however, the third usage of 'meter' just given would be useful (i.e., the quantitative or rhythmic analysis of a given line of poetry), but since that meaning is only properly used within the context of a regular metric system, it is improperly applied to Ugaritic and Hebrew poetry if they do not have such a system.

One feature of meter that must be stressed is its regularity, its preconceived, patterned, and predictable nature: though an entire poem may not be written according to a single metrical system, a large portion of the poetry produced in the Western world before the extensive use of free verse may be analysed according to one or more systems in a patterned and meaningful structure.[6] René Wellek and Austin Warren,[7] in a discussion of the differences between rhythm and meter, imply a definition of the latter by its "periodicity." C. M. Bowra[8] speaks of "the repetitive element which is the basis of metre." Roger D. Abrahams and George Foss[9] define meter and rhythm as follows:

> The organization of rhythmic impulses into preconceived patterns of predictable occurrence is meter. Rhythm, then, is the actual relationship of consecutive impulses and exists both in and outside of art; meter is the organization of rhythmic units and exists exclusively in art. There may be rhythm without meter but meter is merely an artistic concept of rhythmic patterns based on repetition and predictability.[10]

[6]*Encyclopaedia Britannica* (15th ed.), Macropaedia, vol. 8, p. 945 ("scansion"): "Because few poems are absolutely regular, metre is usually determined by the type of foot that appears most frequently. . . ." For a striking example of metrical ascriptions of poems, see Appendix A, "Metres and Their Poets," and Appendix B, "Poets and Their Metres," in Bennett (1963) 151-302.

[7]Wellek and Warren (1942) 151.

[8]Bowra (1962) 85.

[9]Abrahams and Foss (1968) 133.

[10]In a later section of this chapter, devoted to "metrical rigidity" (pp. 140-42), Abrahams and Foss present a spectrum of speech forms ranging from metrically free (utterance) to metrically rigid (dance song). They also allow for a "wide range of metrical variability in folksong from the strictest adherence to time values and stress patterns to an arrangement of stresses only slightly suggestive of a constant meter." Given their definition of 'meter' cited above, I believe that it is safe to say that a work lacking "preconceived patterns of predictable occurrence" would not contain true meter, though hints of metrical regularity known from other song types might lead one to see influence in non-metrical works from the metrical works. In the environment where the Ugaritic poetry was composed, one where true meter has not been demonstrated for any work, such a spectrum from rigid to flexible is ruled out. At best, if one wished to retain the term 'meter' for

George Young[11] speaks of the "recurrences necessary for verse." L. Quicherat[12] identifies 'verse' as "un assemblage de mots arrangés suivant certaines règles fixes et déterminées." W. Theodor Elwert[13] speaks of "séries rythmiques qui, pour être considérées comme des vers, doivent être reconnaissables comme séries identiques." Later he stresses this point further and makes clear the relationship between 'verse' and 'meter':

> Si le vers est une entité linguistique telle que sa structure peut être imitée, c'est-à-dire répétée, et que les répétitions peuvent être perçues par l'auditeur comme identiques, cette structure doit être stable; et les principes d'après lesquels cette structure est créée doivent, par conséquent, être intelligibles, ou, suivant l'expression usuelle, mesurables. Il faut qu'il soit possible de déterminer la dimension (lat. *metrum*, du grec *metron* "mesure") de chaque type de vers; le terme latin *metrum* est passé au français comme *mètre*, employé dans le même sens de "dimension d'un type de vers" (et puis dans le sens de "type de vers"). Si dans notre texte nous n'employons que rarement le terme *mètre* au lieu de *type de vers* c'est pour éviter que le terme *mètre* ne ranime des souvenirs de versification latine.[14]

H. G. Atkins[15] describes meter as follows: ". . . the relation between the separate rhythmic units is so definite that they can be 'measured,' and that we can predict from those under review the nature of those to follow." In distinguishing meter from prose he says: "Prose, i.e., artistic prose, has rhythm, but no metre; that is to say, the movement is not of a measurable, metrical form. We cannot determine or predict the system of recurrence."[16]

I wish to argue that it is this regular, predictable, or at least observable recurrence which is lacking in Ugaritic and Hebrew poetry and that it is this lack which renders usage of the term 'meter' inappropriate.

Though the linguistic features which are measured in a metrical system may be described in different fashions by different authors, three primary systems have been recognized: alternation of short and long syllables in various kinds of 'feet,' syllable count irrespective of length or stress, and accented syllable count. The first is perhaps most clearly

---

Ugaritic poetry, as it is known today, one would have to propose a flexible meter—which appears to me to be an invalid procedure without a rigid point of comparison.

[11]Young (1928) 4.

[12]Quicherat (1850) 1.

[13]Elwert (1965) 8 (translated from the German, *Französische Metrik* [Ismaning-Munich, 1961]).

[14]Elwert (1965) 12, para. 12.

[15]Atkins (1923) 15-16.

[16]Atkins (1923) 16.

exemplified in Greek poetry, the second in French,[17] the third in Germanic (usually linked with alliteration, rhyme, or both).[18] A fourth system combines the last two types, with the stressed syllable as the primary feature but accompanied by a given number of unstressed syllables (exemplified by much English poetry and German poetry of certain periods).[19]

A further contention of this paper will be that none of the types listed above, nor any combination of types, can properly describe Ugaritic and Hebrew poetry as we have it preserved today.[20]

TWO RECENT THEORIES OF UGARITIC METER

Syllable Count

Douglas K. Stuart has recently proposed that Ugaritic and early Hebrew poetry can be scanned according to syllable count (irrespective of syllable length or stress) and the very title of the book, *Studies in Early Hebrew Meter*,[21] leaves no doubt that he considers the Ugaritic and early Hebrew systems to be metrical. I contend that the degree of

[17] Cf., e.g., Deloffre (1973) esp. 15-17. The ten-syllable line is also the preferred form of the Yugoslavian oral poetry which has received so much attention with the work of Parry and Lord. See Lord (1965) 17, 21, 37-38.

[18] Cf., e.g., Lehmann (1956) 36-41, 51; Atkins (1923) 65-143. Cf. note 15, above.

[19] For a summary discussion, see *Encyclopaedia Britannica*, Micropaedia, vol. 6, 842 ("meter"). For German poetry, see Atkins (1923) 143-222; and Bennett (1963). Cf. note 6, above.

[20] To my knowledge, no one has proposed a system of feet, in the classical sense, for Ugaritic poetry. Syllable count will be discussed below. A system of accented syllables accompanied by a set number of unaccented syllables appears to me to be out of the question for Ugaritic, or Hebrew poetry. On the other hand, Ugaritic poetry, the lines of which are on the whole more regular in length than those of Hebrew poetry, could have a meter based on accented syllables only, if we assume that long words could have more than one accent and that short words could combine to furnish one accent (see below, the discussion of word accent, for related concepts). Since this is undeterminable owing to our ignorance of Ugaritic vocalization, without mentioning poetic intonation, such a system cannot be proven. The same may be said of the more regular of Hebrew poetry. A large amount of Hebrew poetry, however, has lines which vary a great deal in length, and none of the accepted metrical systems may be easily applied to such poetry, i.e., no metrical system which I have seen can scan a significant portion of Hebrew poetry, without emendation, and come up with anything approaching a predictable pattern, or any kind of regularly repeated pattern. J. Kurylowicz' isolation of a Masoretic system of poetic notation according to major and minor accents is intriguing, but it does not result in a patterned metrical system for any number of Hebrew poems (i.e., one may come up with 3 + 3, 3 + 2, 3 + 4, etc., but Kurylowicz has not claimed that any number of complete poems has a regularly repeating combination of cola) [Kurylowicz (1972) esp. chapter 10, "Three Semitic Metrics"].

[21] Stuart (1976). He is, of course, heavily indebted to the work of his mentor at Harvard, Frank Moore Cross, Jr., and to David Noel Freedman. See, for example, Freedman (1972) and Freedman (1977).

regularity attained by Stuart is artificial and that even if one grants him the regularity he alleges, it is not sufficiently patterned to merit the term 'meter' as commonly used.

The most important of Stuart's text critical principles for scansion of Ugaritic poetry is the following: ". . . case endings may have been omitted at the whim of the composer in the context of construct chains and proper nouns."[22] Closely allied, in practice if not in theory, is the interchange of *yaqtul* and *yaqtulu* verbal forms (with no apparent syntactic basis, but purely *metri causa*). The other criteria are invoked less frequently and vary in plausibility in each case (though they are adduced almost exclusively, like the first two principles, *metri causa*): the elision of particles (e.g., *w* in 14[*Krt*].1.24), the restoration of particles (e.g., *b* in 14[*Krt*].1.34), the omission of words (e.g., *ʾmr* 'lamb' in 14[*Krt*].2.67), transposition of particles (e.g., *k/km* in 14[*Krt*].2.103-.3.105), etc.

As a comparison, I give here a few lines from the *Krt* text as vocalized and scanned by Stuart, followed by my version of the same text.

26. *yaʿrubu baḥadrihu yabkiyu*	10	He enters his chamber, he weeps
baṯani rigamīma wayidmaʿ	10	In the . . . . . . and sheds tears.
28. *tinnatikna ʾudmaʿātuhu*	9	His tears pour out
kamā ṯiqalīma ʾarṣaha	9	Like shekels to the ground,
kamaḫmašāti miṭṭatahu	9	Like pieces of five on his bed.
31. *bamā bakyihu wayīšanu*	9	In his weeping, he falls asleep,
badamʿihu nahamimatu	9	In his tears, slumber.
33. *šinatu talʾuʾannu wayiškab*	10	Sleep overtakes him when he lies down,
<*b*>*anahamimati wayaqmuṣu*	10	Slumber when he curls up.
35. *wabaḥulmihu ʾilu yaridu*	10	And in his dream El descends,
badahratihu ʾabū ʾadami	10	In his vision, the father of man,
wayiqrab bašaʾāli kirta	10(!)	And he approaches, asking Kirta,
38. *minnu kirta kiyabkiyu*	8	"What ails Kirta that he weeps,
yidmaʿu nuʿmān ǵulm ʾili	8	Weeps the beloved lad of El?

[22]Stuart (1976) 25. This principle is introduced by the phrase, "Thus in many cases represented in the following chapters it becomes clear that case endings may have been. . . ." This is, of course, valid only within Stuart's system (and is thus somewhat of a *petitio principii*): Ugaritic can only be shown to have lines of equal length within cola if the case endings are omitted (and many other changes made) at the whim of Stuart; when he omits them *ex hypothesi*, the hypothesis proves itself. Unfortunately, there is very little internal corroborating evidence (e.g., I cannot remember a single case of an orthography with *aleph* at the end of a word supporting Stuart's position on case endings, though, in spite of some difficult forms, there are many final *aleph* forms which indicate that the case vowels were used consistently and correctly in the construct state).

41. *mulka ṯōri ᵓabīhu yaᵓarrišu*	11	Is it the kingship of Bull, his father, he desires,
himma darkata kaᵓabī ᵓadami	11	Or dominion like the father of man?"[23]

My version:[24]

26) *yaᶜrubu biḥadrihu yabkiyu*	3/10/23[25]	a b c
27) *biṯanî rigamīma wayidmaᶜu*	3/11/25	d^2 c'
28) *tannatikāna ᵓudmaᶜātuhu*	2/10/24	a b
29) *kama ṭiqalīma ᵓarṣah*	3/8/19	c d e
30) *kama ḫamišāti matṭṭatah*	3/9/21	c d' e'
31) *bima bakāyihu wayašānu*	3(2)/10/22	a^2 (= x + y) b
32) *bidamāᶜihu nahmamatu*	2/9/20	a' (= x^{-1} + y') b'
33) *šinatu talᵓuᵓannu* (34) *wayiškabu*	3/11/25	a b c
nahmamatu (35) *wayaqmiṣu*	2/8/18	a' c'
wabiḥulāmihu (36) *ᵓilu yarada*	3/11/23	a b c
bidahratihu (37) *ᵓabu ᵓadami*	3/10/21	a' b'^2
wayiqrabu (38) *bišaᵓāli kirta*	3/10/23	c' d e
ma ᵓatta (39) *kirta ki yabkiyu*	(4)3/9/21	a^2 b c
40) *yidmaᶜu naᶜmānu ǵalmu* (41) *ᵓili*	4/10/24	c' b'^3
mulka ṯôri ᵓabihu (42) *yaᵓarrišu*	4/11/25	a b^2 c
himma darkata (43) *kaᵓabi* *adami*	4/11/24	d a' b'^2

Stuart achieves regularity of the first unit (lines 26-27, a bi-colon) by vocalizing the first two verbs as *yaqtulu*, the third as *yaqtul*;

[23]Stuart (1976) 54-55.

[24]To save space, I omit my translation, which does not differ from Stuart's in any major points.

[25]The three figures represent word count, syllable count, and "vocable count" (a short vowel and a consonant are counted as one unit, and a long vowel as two; this method of counting was proposed by D. N. Freedman in his (1974), esp. p. 169. He has since abandoned this method of counting [see his (1977) 12], but I find it a useful means, alongside word and syllable counts, of indicating the approximation of length of line in Ugaritic poetry).

the second unit (lines 28-30, a tri-colon) by vocalizations which are as plausible as mine (except, perhaps, for the alternation of *-ha* and *-hu*);

the third unit (lines 31-32, a bi-colon) by vocalizing the infinitive in line 31 (*bm bkyh*) as an 'infinitive construct' though in line 38 he vocalizes *bš*ᵓ*al* as an 'infinitive absolute' (in the same syntactic construction);

the fourth unit (lines 33-35, a bi-colon) by vocalizing the *w*-verbal clauses differently (*yaqtul* versus *yaqtulu*) and by restoring a *b* before *nhmmt* (in defiance of the parallelism and of the syntax of the bi-colon, in my opinion);

the fifth unit (lines 35-38, a tri-colon, though not necessarily so, as Stuart notes) by vocalizing *ḥlm* as a 'segholate' (with Aramaic [*ḥelmâ*] *and Arabic* [*ḥulm*] against Hebrew [*ḥălōm*]). Notice further that Stuart either misvocalizes or miscounts the third line of the tri-colon (*wayiqrabu* gives ten syllables; Stuart vocalizes *wayiqrab* but still gives the syllable count as ten);

the sixth unit (lines 38-41, a bi-colon) by omitting the case endings from *n*ᶜ*mn* and *ǵlm* (the first omission is probably not valid even according to Stuart's criteria, for *n*ᶜ*mn* is probably in apposition rather than in construct, though it could be a genitive of name or title like Hebrew *nĕhar pĕrāt*); the emendation of *m*ᵓ*at* to *mn* is probably inspired by motives other than meter;

the seventh unit (lines 41-43, a bi-colon) by vocalization with which I agree.

The extent of our agreement in the interpretation (and even of the basic vocalization) of the text is an encouraging sign. I believe, however, that the regularity of syllabic count is attained in too many cases by an arbitrary and unverifiable variation in vocalization. The extent of arbitrary vocalization (in the example cited four out of seven units are rendered uniform by internally inconsistent means[26]) appears to me to invalidate the method.[27]

Furthermore, even if we were to accord to Stuart that his criteria of vocalization and scansion are correct, his results still do not indicate that 'meter' is a correct term for the description of Ugaritic poetry for the reason that no pattern is discernable among Stuart's cola. His syllabic values in the portion of the *Krt* text given above are: 10 + 10 / 9 + 9 + 9 / 9 + 9 / 10 + 10 / 10 + 10 + 10 / 8 + 8 / 11 + 11. This overall pattern is not

[26]Yet another is uncertain because of a mistake (the fifth unit, lines 35-38—see note above).

[27]This point is made, though less forcefully, by Stuart's reviewers, e.g., Good (1978), and Culley (1978).

repeated in the *Krt* text nor does any other pattern overlap the section quoted. Indeed Stuart makes no claim for repetition among cola. This lack of repetitive pattern, according to the generally accepted criteria discussed above, disqualifies the *Krt* text from being described as having 'meter.'[28] All that one can say, on the basis of Stuart's figures, is that most cola have the same number of syllables in each line (all cola are internally uniform in this section, but others are irregular even in Stuart's sytem) and that the number of syllables may vary from eight to eleven (as low as seven syllables and as high as twelve elsewhere in the *Krt* text, as low as five and as high as twelve in texts from the Baal cycle) with no discernable pattern of repetition.[29] With a consistent vocalization, of course, the statement based on Stuart's figures becomes invalid and we are left with a poetic structure which must be accounted for in terms of intra-colon syllabic irregularity and non-repetition.

Though Stuart's criteria for the reconstruction of Hebrew poetry (pp. 26-28) certainly have much to commend them, there is a certain degree of arbitrariness in their application here as there was in Ugaritic. Since my own concerns at this point lie with Ugaritic rather than with Hebrew poetry, I will only point out that Stuart's reconstructions often vary significantly from the Masoretic form of the poems—i.e., however correct Stuart may be in his reconstructions, we end up separated from the most important ancient tradition for the vocalization of Hebrew and with very little explicit ancient corroborating evidence for many of the

[28]I do not mean to imply that variation is not possible in a metrical system, only that the variation has to occur within a pattern, otherwise there is no meter. For a discussion at the level of the non-specialist such as myself, I refer the reader to Danchin (n.d.) 26-27, an analysis of the irregularities in Wordsworth's iambic poem "The Solitary Reaper."

[29]Good (1978), in reviewing Stuart's (1976), apparently does not demur at Stuart's use of the term 'meter' but nevertheless finds the method lacking: "This work is certainly the best exemplar I have seen of the syllable-counting metric. Only one serious problem remains, a problem serious enough to prevent my buying the method: with syllable counting, meter has ceased to be a mode of analyzing poetic rhythm. It solves the difficulty posed in scanning internal feet (i.e., inner-line rhythmic patterns) by paying no attention to accents (p. 11). The line or couplet is the thing, and when you have two lines of 9 syllables each (9:9), that is metric regularity—all the metric regularity you are going to get out of this analysis." The problem pointed out by Good is that Stuart's method only finds regularity within a given colon, not from colon to colon. From my introductory discussion, it should be clear that a scanning system which only finds regularity within individual cola, without a repeating pattern of cola, would not be paralleled in the metrical systems of any of the languages discussed. This is a moot point, however, for even regularity within individual cola cannot be proven (as shown above). All that can be said is that there appears to be more approximation of length of line within a colon than among lines from different cola (i.e., 3/10/25 + 3/9/24 next to 3/7/19 + 3/6/18 is more likely than 3/10/25 + 3/6/18 next to 3/9/24 + 3/7/19, though all varieties of distribution do occur).

changes.[30] I cite as an example the Simeon and Levi section of Jacob's blessing in Gen. 49:[31]

Stuart	*MT*	
7	7	
7	9	(*mkrtyhm* revocalized)
9	8	(switches *bsdm* and *bqhlm*)
9	10	
8	8	
8	9	(omits *w*-)
6	6	
6	8	(omits *w*- and final syllable of *qšth*)
7	7	(with Stuart, not counting the *ḥatef-pataḥ* in *y*^{c}*qb*)
7	8	(omits *w*-)

Whatever the value of Stuart's reconstructions may be (and in this case some have little motivation other than meter), one must in any case make the same point here as was made with regard to the Ugaritic analysis: even if Stuart's counts are accepted, the result does not qualify as 'meter.' The same degree of irregularity of syllable count between cola and the same lack of patterning of poetic units is observable here as in the Ugaritic section, with the same conclusion necessary for the validity of the term 'meter.' It should probably be added at this point that if Stuart's system cannot be proven for Ugaritic poetry, which on the whole is more regular in length of poetic line than is Hebrew poetry, and if Hebrew poetry is considered to follow in the line of Canaanite poetic structure,[32] Hebrew poetry should not be expected to be constructed according to syllable count. I believe, on the basis of my study of Ugaritic poetry, that neither body of poetry was formed with an explicit or implicit goal of producing cola with the same number of syllables, and certainly that neither culture can be shown to have produced poetry with a repetitive pattern of syllable count which would merit the term 'meter.'

[30]I realize the slenderness of this point when compared with the previous sections, since our Ugaritic vocalization is a virtually complete reconstruction, but the point deserves to be made nonetheless.

[31]Stuart (1976) 139.

[32]Stuart (1976) 28: "It is our general theory that the poetry of the early Israelites was in the Canaanite tradition . . . they *both* partook of Northwest Semitic musical and poetic traditions."

Word Meter

B. Margalit[33] has proposed a system of Ugaritic metrics[34] based on "word-metre."[35] In spite of this term, however, it appears to me that the real metrical element which emerges from Margalit's discussion is the "verse-unit," for only those words function as verse-units which meet certain criteria: they must be between two and five syllables and must occur in certain syntactic environments. Thus words of the 'normal' length of two to five syllables may appear in various combinations and with monosyllabic words in three-word sequences which have only two verse-units, while various two-word combinations may have only one verse-unit.[36] It appears to me that a system which necessitates so many expansions, contractions, and bridgings of words (= *metra*) is not based on the word as the basic unit of poetic structure, but on the fact that many words in Ugaritic happen to fall within certain lengths. Thus words which do not fall within these lengths do not qualify as verse-units. One must conclude that what the poet was seeking was not to use a certain number of words, but a combination of words which would give the line its proper length (and, in my opinion, it is very likely that

[33]Margalit (1975).

[34]Margalit states at the beginning of his study that ". . . we present the rudiments of a system of structural-prosodic analysis, more commonly (though less precisely) labelled 'metrics.' " This might imply that he is shying away from a metrical analysis of Ugaritic poetry, but his regular use of the term 'meter' in his own discussion and in his defense of Ley's metrical system (to describe which, 'meter' is used in the narrow sense of a single element of a poetic line [cf. definitions, above] and in the broad sense of a metrical system) indicates that he is not abjuring its use. Substituting 'prosody' is no real improvement, however (and here I regret the title of my article to appear in *JANES*, cf. n. 1, above), for *The Oxford English Dictionary* defines 'prosody' as: "The science of versification; that part of the study of language which deals with the forms of metrical composition. . . ."

[35]*Cf.* Margalit's introductory remarks, pp. 289-91.

[36]It should be noted, for whatever value it may have, that nothing approximating Margalit's "word-metre" may be deduced from the use of word dividers in the Ugaritic texts themselves (i.e., the word dividers are not distributed according to Margalit's "verse-units"). Note that William J. Horowitz does not take considerations such as Margalit's into account in his theory that the word dividers mark the metrical line; indeed, the two systems are mutually exclusive, as a glance at Horowitz' long example shows [Horowitz (1972) 96-99, discussion 88-104]. As for Horowitz' claim that the irregular uses of small vertical wedges mark meter, it is based on statistical analysis, an argument which I am unable fully to appreciate. His suggestion that the small vertical wedge was a stress marker (p. 90) seems unlikely because of the number of particles and pronominal suffixes which are marked off by it, and because of the number of independent words which are not marked off by it (e.g., for the former, *wl* . *ᶜpr*, and, for the latter, *kṯr ṣmdm*: 2.4[68].5 and 11). Moreover—once again the argument of regularity and predictability—even if Horowitz' theory about the distribution of the small vertical wedge is correct, this still does not constitute meter, for there is no regular pattern in Horowitz' results (3 + 3, 3 + 2 + 1-2, 2^{+} + 3 . . .).

the proper length was perceived intuitively and approximately, not scholastically, predictively, and precisely).

Furthermore, the same conclusion must be drawn with respect to Margalit's use of the term 'meter' as with Stuart: even if the word-meter system is accorded validity,[37] the resulting "verses" and "strophes"[38] do not reveal the regularity and predictability of metrical verse. 18(3 Aqht).4.19-37, for example, is scanned (p. 303) as

3 + 3 / 3 + 2 / 3 + 2 / 3 + 2 / 3 + 2 + 2 / 4
3 + 3 + 2 / 3 + 2
3 + 3 / 3 + 2 / 3 + 2 / 3 + 2 / 3 + 2 + 2

This is one of the most regular units that Margalit isolates and, in spite of the irregularities which do occur (the 4 at the end of the first division of the "strophe," the irregular middle line), if all Ugaritic poetry were this regular, one might be convinced of Margalit's proposal. But 17(2 Aqht).6.20-39, which Margalit describes as containing "particularly fine specimens" of the 3 + 3 verse (p. 306) is scanned as

3 + 3 / 3 + 3 + 3 / 3 + 3 + 3 / 3
4 + 3 + 2 / 3 + 3 / 2 + 2 + 2 / 3 + 2 / 3
2 / 2 + 3 + 2 / 2 + 2 + 2 / 3 + 3 / 3 + 3 / 3

It does not take a classically trained metrician to determine that there is no repetition of pattern here, no predictability of occurrence of the verse-units. Rather, what we have is an almost random sequence of threes and twos in single units, bi-cola, and tri-cola, with one four thrown in for good measure. Though Margalit speaks of "a basic (3 + 3) strophic-theme" (p. 308), I see nothing in the distribution of these numbers but a higher concentration of threes than of twos and fours (four only occurs once in the unit cited, but is more frequent elsewhere). If virtually all Ugaritic lines consist of verse-units of two, three, and four, the greatest number of lines, other things being equal, will have three units, and fewer will have two and four.

I must conclude, then, that the concept of word-meter does not fit the Ugaritic texts because 1) there is too high an incidence of verse-units being divided in one word or spread over two or more words to permit the conclusion that the Ugaritic poet was thinking in terms of word count; and 2) the regularity attained by Margalit's system is not sufficient to permit the use of the term 'meter' in describing that system.

[37] If it is reformulated as some form of accentual system it at least appears plausible.

[38] For a discussion of the inappropriateness of the term 'strophe' for Ugaritic poetry, see my article which is to appear in *JANES* (cited n. 1, above).

CONCLUSIONS

Of the four metric systems which are generally accepted among scholars as predominant in the poetry of the Western world, it appears to me that three are ruled out for Ugaritic poetry: the purely quantitative systems based on syllable distribution in feet or on simple syllable count, and the quantitative plus stress system which includes a set number of unstressed syllables. The remaining metrical system, that based on stressed syllable count with no fixed number of unstressed syllables, is possible for Ugaritic poetry but unprovable because of our lack of knowledge of the spoken form of the language, and hence of the vocalization of the poetic texts and of any special features of poetic diction.

It appears just as likely, however, that the poems were originally recited in song form.[39] The song form, and thus the poetic form, could have been ametrical[40] or metrical.[41] If the song form was metrical, the poetic form could have been ametrical, but the individual lines would have been of approximately the same length to permit the slurs and groupings of syllables necessary to fit the words to the music. Here I rejoin Stuart, who remarks that: "Chanting allows for the pairing of almost any number of syllables and words to a given melody note and thus conveniently handles any poetry or prose regardless of formal meter."[42] And in the conclusion of his introduction he reiterates this theme:

> It is interesting to note that Lord and Parry's recordings of Serbo-Croation [sic] folk-poets' songs reveal that the number of distinct notes in each melody is usually greater than the number of syllables in the words sung. This means, of course, that some syllables are held while the voice intones a multiplicity of sounds, as in the music of all ages.[43]

[39]". . . sung delivery is the most common characteristic of oral poetry" [Finnegan (1977) 13]. For the characteristics of oral poetry, see Lord, (1965) and Finnegan (1977). Ugaritic poetry was probably originally oral judging from poetic characteristics alone. From an historical perspective, it should be noted that none of the texts predates the Late Bronze Age, whereas most scholars agree that the poems themselves date from a much earlier period [e.g., W. F. Albright (1961), 31].

[40]"By conditioning, we think of music as inherently metrical, but there exists in other cultures today, and there existed in Western culture until the twelfth century, music without meter. That is, music whose rhythmic components defied organization into the larger framework we call meter" [Abrahams and Foss, (1968) 134 n.]. (Cf. n. 9, above).

[41]This would correspond to Atkins' second stage in the development of verse, when the "irrational proportions [of words] would be reduced to the rational proportions of music," but before poetry was severed from music, and the "linguistic material alone had . . . to be the bearer of the rhythm" [Atkins (1923) 13-14]. Cf. n. 15, above.

[42]Stuart (1976) 18.

[43]Stuart (1976) 38.

I would only add that 1) these remarks imply that a poetic system of syllabic uniformity is really not necessary and it is, therefore, somewhat fruitless to seek one out at the expense of inconsistent vocalization; and 2) Stuart's system, which results in equality of lines within cola but relatively great disparity among cola, is no more easily associated with a musical performance than is a poetic system which only calls for approximately comparable length of lines.[44]

At the present state of our knowledge of Ugaritic poetry, then, I believe that it is wisest to be very hesitant about the use of the term 'meter.' We can say that poetry was formed primarily in units of x + 1 (+ n . . .) lines which were structured by parallelism. The length of the lines was to be only approximately comparable, with a closer approach to uniformity visible within cola than among cola. Attempts to locate meter should probably focus on stress patterns, though these appear fruitless to me with our present knowledge, or lack of knowledge of general pronunciation and of poetic diction. If we attempt to link the poetry with song we can hypothesize either that the music was ametrical or that it was metrical and the words only approximately so (i.e., close enough in syllable count to fit the musical meter by slurring and grouping of syllables). Any method of descriptive 'scansion' (i.e., quantitative analysis) is useful in showing up the tendency toward approximate comparability of length of line within cola as well as the quantitative relationships among cola. This quantitative analysis may be applied to words, syllables, or the individual phonetic units (Freedman's "vocable count") but such an analysis is purely descriptive and may only be called 'metrical' in the broadest sense of the term. This statement implies that parallelism was the primary structural principle of Ugaritic poetry and that length of line was only prescriptive in the general principle of approximation.[45]

[44]I.e., the sequence of the section from the *Krt* text analyzed above is no more analyzable as a musical meter than as a poetic meter. If Stuart's system results in neither a poetic nor a musical meter, then one might as well abandon the inconsistent vocalization, and work with lines of only approximately comparable length, since the latter could as easily fit a musical performance as Stuart's lines.

[45]In defense of the position that Ugaritic and Hebrew poetry need not be metrical, I cite Finnegan (1977) 90:

> The most marked feature of poetry is surely repetition. Forms and genres are recognised because they are repeated. The collocations of line or stanza or refrain are based on their repeated recurrence; metre, rhythm, or sylistic features like alliteration or parallelism are also based on repeated patterns of sound, syntax, or meaning. . . .
>
> The prosodic system is perhaps the feature which most immediately gives form to a poem. We tend to think of this mainly in terms of *metre*, because of the influence of Greek and Roman models. Certainly metre does constitute one aspect. But as

Roughly the same situation holds for Hebrew poetry as for Ugaritic poetry, though there are differences because of the Masoretic vocalization of Hebrew, the transmission of the text with ensuing textual problems, the variety of poetic genres (practically excluding epic poetry, the main Ugaritic genre), the oral forebears of the present texts, and the chronological span of the oral texts and of the original writing down of texts with and without oral original forms. In general, however, one can refer to parallelism as the main structural element in Hebrew poetry and approximately comparable length of line as the main quantitative element. R. E. Bee has recently[46] proposed a statistical basis for the assertion that Hebrew poetry should be scanned according to stress patterns. He studiously avoids the term 'meter' and only holds that there is statistically more regularity of stress than of syllable count. With regard to the fact that the stress counts do not fall into repetitive patterns he asserts that "Approximate constancy may have a statistical basis" (p. 63). If Bee's conclusions are correct (and they may certainly be applied to much Hebrew poetry, though not all), then my assertion that approximate comparability of length of line is the only quantitative element in Ugaritic and Hebrew poetry would have to be applied to stress counts rather than to word counts, syllable counts, or vocable counts.[47] This points up again the difficulty of comparing the two

---

> soon as one analyses the ways in which verse can be structured, one has to extend prosody to cover alliteration, assonance, rhyme, tonal repetition or even parallelism. It becomes clear that what in some languages or poetic cultures is achieved by a metre based on quantity is in other achieved by, say, alliteration; one can compare quantity in the Homeric hexameter with the elaboration of alliteration in Old English poetry (*Beowulf* for instance), assonance in the Old French epic, or the parallelism and word pairs of the Hebrew poetry in the Bible. For a full understanding of the prosodic characteristics of any poetic tradition one has to look beyond the mere counting of beats, syllables or quantities—the traditional model of a 'metre'—and look to a range of other factors which may perform a comparable function.

Notice especially that Finnegan moves from "stylistic features" in the first paragraph cited, to "structured" and "prosody" in the second. Though I am now somewhat hesitant about the appropriateness of the term 'prosody' to describe non-metrical poetic principles (cf. n. 34, above), there is no doubt that poetry can be 'structured' without 'meter.' On parallelism as a structural feature in languages other than the Semitic languages, see Finnegan (1977) 98-106, 127-33.

[46]Bee (1978a); and Bee (1978b).

[47]As a point of comparison with Bee's results for Hebrew poetry, I asked my colleague George R. Bateman, Senior Staff Analyst in the University of Chicago Computation Center, and Lecturer in Statistics in the Graduate School of Business, to conduct a statistical analysis of word count/syllable count/vocable count in Ugaritic. For the present he has analyzed only the sixteen lines of the *Krt* text discussed above in this paper. The method he used was The Coefficient of Variation analysis, a descriptive method:

bodies of poetry, for the lack of a traditional vocalization of Ugaritic poetry has deprived us of a tradition regarding stress patterns (though we could just as easily, I suppose, reconstruct stress patterns as syllable or vocable patterns—for this purpose much of Margalit's work would be useful).

Finally, a word about parallelism. If the basic thesis of this paper is correct, that quantitative requirements on Ugaritic and Hebrew poets were only approximate, parallelism emerges as at least equally as important as quantitative and rhythmic concerns. Yet here much remains to be done. Bishop Lowth, of course, dealt long ago with the three main semantic categories of parallelism. Since the discovery of Ugaritic much has been done in isolating parallel pairs.[48] William R. Watters[49] has shown, however, that much remains to be done in the analysis of the origins and uses of parallelism. Though I believe that his virtually total rejection of a traditional basis for the use of parallelism must itself be rejected out of hand,[50] he has shown that there are too many 'non-

---

$$\text{C.V.} = \frac{\text{Sample standard deviation}}{\text{Sample Mean}} \times 100\%$$

The results attained are: the coefficients of variation are 21.08%, 10.37%, and 9.77% for word count, syllable count, and vocable count, respectively. The much higher relative variation for word count as compared with the other two seems to indicate at least that word count was not the primary structural feature of Ugaritic poetry. Syllable count and vocable count, on the other hand, show less relative variation. This is, at least, partially because vocable count is based directly on syllabic structure. Because of a lack of reference point with which to compare the coefficients of variation, however, we are not at the present time prepared to assess the significance of the roughly 10 o/o coefficient of variation for syllable count and vocable count. We are preparing for future publication a statistical analysis which compares the various quantitative analyses of Ugaritic poetry, as well as the degree of uniformity within and among cola.

[48]See Dahood (1972) 71-382, and (1975) 1-39, with bibliography. For strictures on Dahood's method, see reviews by de Moor and van der Lugt (1974); Loewenstamm (1975); and Pardee (1977).

[49]Watters (1976).

[50]See Edwin M. Good's review, Good (1978). It is best to hew a middle road between Watters' total rejection of a traditional basis for the use of parallel pairs, and his opponents whom he depicts (caricatures, I fear, in some cases) as limiting the use of parallel pairs to a stock repertoire. I quote again from Finnegan [(1977) 72] (*cf.* n. 39, above): "The basic insights [of the oral-formulaic school] remain stimulating and fruitful, and the demonstration that the oral bard composes with and within traditional patterns of various kinds will stand as a landmark in the study of oral literature. Provided that the more ambitious claims of some exponent are treated with caution, the Lord-Parry school provides a body of work which cannot be ignored by any student of comparative oral literature." The debate concerning individuality versus tradition is an old one in literary criticism, and cannot be pursued here at any length [cf. Hall (1963), esp. 167-70 on T. S. Eliot]. Nonetheless, I believe it safe to say that the Ugaritic poets worked both within and beyond the traditions of their predecessors with varying degrees of individuality. On the appearance of original

traditional' parallel structures to allow for an entirely traditional basis of usage. To put it another way, we need a thorough discussion of Ugaritic and Hebrew parallelism which gives an extended treatment of semantic parallelism (e.g., 'heaven // earth,' 'widow // orphan') versus positional parallelism (e.g., verbs which hold comparable slots in parallel lines without being semantically parallel). In assigning letters to parallel lines, one is constantly torn between assigning a prime value or a new letter to words that are positionally or grammatically parallel. For example, in the text cited above (14[*Krt*].1.26-43), in lines 35-38 there is the parallelism of *yrd* and *wyqrb*. I assigned these words the values of c and c′. Dahood, however, lists no other examples of this parallel pair in Ugaritic and only prose collocations in Hebrew.[51] Thus this pair must be described in the *Krt* text, at least on the basis of present evidence, as an *ad hoc* parallelism, one necessary for the telling of the story, but not one established in poetic usage. A different problem arises in 3(ᶜ*nt*).1.4-6. It reads

qm yṯᶜr wyšlḥmnh	He arises, prepares, and serves;
ybrd ṯd lpnwh	He cuts the breast before him.

Is the parallelism here *a a′ a″ // a‴ b c* or is it *a b c // d e f*? To my knowledge, no one has ever proposed an extensive set of criteria for determining when parallelism is present or not which would solve problems of the type just adduced and which would provide a reasoned categorization of types of parallelism.

---

formulae even within a tradition which does not prize originality, it is worthwhile to cite Lord himself [Lord (1965) 44-45 (cf. n. 17, above)]:

> In order to avoid any misunderstanding, we must hasten to assert that in speaking of 'creating' phrases in performance we do not intend to convey the idea that the singer *seeks originality* or fineness of expression. He seeks expression of the idea under stress of performance. Expression is his business, not originality, which, indeed, is a concept quite foreign to him and one that he would avoid, if he understood it. To say that the *opportunity* for originality and for finding the 'poetically' fine phrase exists does *not* mean that the *desire* for originality also exists. There are periods and styles in which originality is *not* at a premium. If the singer knows a ready-made phrase and thinks of it, he uses it without hesitation, but he has, as we have seen, a method of making phrases when he either does not know one or cannot remember one. This is the situation more frequently than we tend to believe (note especially the last sentence!).

Further, with the respect to formula manipulation, Lord remarks (p. 131): "It would be fantastic to expect that a gifted poet who has thought in poetic form all his life should not have sufficient mastery of that form to be able not only to fit his thought into it but also to break it at will."

[51]Dahood (1972) 214, para. 257.

A further area of parallelism which has received more study but which deserves even more is the distribution of parallelism in the lines into various forms of chiasmus (*a b c // c′ b′ a′*, *a b c // c′ a′ b′*, *a b c // b′ c′ a′*, etc.) and into various repetitive forms (a^2 [= $x + y$] *b* // a'^2 [= $x + z$] *b′*, etc.).[52] When one considers the possible variations over cola of different numbers of lines (x + 1 [+ n . . .]) and the possible variations of numbers of words per line, one realizes that the possible variations of parallelism go into the scores if not the hundreds. Though I doubt that a predictive pattern would emerge from analysis, it is quite possible that a statistically significant pattern would emerge. In any case, the scholarly urge to analyze and systematize should certainly be exercised on this aspect of Northwest Semitic poetry more than in the past.

[52]I am thinking of something along the lines of Gray (1972) 35-83, but much more complete.

THE GEOGRAPHICAL SETTING OF THE *AQHT* STORY AND ITS RAMIFICATIONS

BARUCH MARGALIT

University of Haifa
Haifa, Israel

I. Introduction

1.1 The attempt to locate the Ugaritic poems of *Krt* and *Aqht* in time and in space has accompanied Ugaritic studies from the beginning. The initial euphoria generated by the epochal discoveries at Ras Shamra a half century ago was in some measure at least due to the conviction staunchly defended by two of the foremost Ugaritic scholars of the day, Virolleaud and Dussaud, that the *mise-en-scène* for one of the principal works (the *Krt* poem) was biblical Canaan. Keret himself was assumed to be "king of Sidon" and the military campaign which he led against the king of Udm was fixed in the Negeb region, Udm itself assumed to be identical with biblical Edom. This interpretation of the Ugaritic materials was then used to support a theory of the Negebite origins of the Phoenician people as well as the Israelites.[1]

1.2 Dissent from what came to be known as the "Negebite hypothesis" took two forms: the strong and uncompromising denial by Albright (and eventually the scholarly community at large);[2] and the counter-thesis expounded by de Vaux (and supported by others, notably de Langhe)[3] according to which the locale of the Keret epic was to be sought not in the Negeb of Palestine but rather in the Galilee region of the same country, close by the Sea of Kinnereth and the Mount of Beatitudes.[4]

1.3 Shortly after de Vaux's paper on the geographical setting of the Keret poem, G. A. Barton published a similar essay on the *Aqht* tale.[5]

[1] *Cf.* Dussaud (1933), and Virolleaud (1936) 18-19.

[2] Albright (1936) 26-32; (1938) 18-24, esp. 22ff.; and (1940) 253-56.

[3] de Langhe (1945) 132-47, and (1958) 146-47.

[4] de Vaux (1937a), and (1937b) esp. 540-41.

[5] Barton (1940) [=JBL 60 (1941) 213-25].

The principal thesis, no doubt influenced by de Vaux's but based on putative evidence culled from within the *Aqht* poem itself, was that the area between the Sea of Kinnereth and the Hermon was the *mise-en-scène* for the activities described in the tale of Danel and family. Barton was the first to suggest the word at the end of CTA 19 (= 1 Aq):147 be read as *bknrt*, referring to the Sea of Galilee (OT *yam kinneret/kinn^e^rôt*). He was also among the first to suggest a concrete localization of *Ablm*, the home of *Yṭpn* and the site of Aqht's murder, identifying it with Abel-Beth-Maacah (mod. Abil el-Qamḥ), near Dan (Tell el-Qadi).

1.4 Looking back at these developments from the vantage point of several decades, it is clear that time has not been kind to the aforementioned geographical and historical hypotheses and their allegedly far-reaching implications for Old Testament study. The Asherites, Zebulonites, Terachites and Negebites have all vanished from the scene, a historical memory at best. Only the Galilean hypothesis survived into the post-war era to claim a few adherents. But by 1957/58, de Vaux had renounced his earlier conclusions relating to the Keret epic. Completely ignoring Barton's similar views on *Aqht*, de Vaux observed, somewhat wistfully, that the Kinnereth hypothesis was simply "too good to be true."[6] The *coup-de-grace* to this hypothesis was delivered by M. Astour.[7] Not only did Astour present plausible—if inconclusive—evidence for a North-Mesopotamian background to the Keret story, he failed to so much as list a *knrt* entry in his notable chapter on Ugaritic toponymy in RSP.[8] The uninitiated reader of RSP is thus likely to be unaware that E. Ullendorff[9] argued for interpreting the phrase *bmdgt . bknrt* (CTA 19:147) to mean "in the fishing-grounds of (the Sea of) Kinnereth," an interpretation which the editors of HAL cite as possible evidence for a Ugaritic cognate of the biblical toponym.[10] But Ullendorff did not derive any far-reaching conclusions from this for the setting of the *Aqht* story as a whole.

2.1 The evidence for a Kinnereth background to the *Aqht* tale was re-examined by the present writer in a study published in UF 8.[11] Taking as our point of departure the reading *bknrt*—a reading justified *prima facie* by Virolleaud's hand-copy of the text (*cf.* CTA, fig. 61)[12] and subsequently corroborated (for the most part) by the recent KTU edition—and persuaded of the fundamental truth of Ullendorff's exposition,

[6]de Vaux (1957) 313.

[7]Astour (1974) 29-30.

[8]Astour (1975) § VIII. It is clear from p. 255 that Astour knew of Barton's paper. I am not certain that he knew of Ullendorff (1962), to which I found no reference in the chapter.

[9]Ullendorff (1962) 342-43.

[10]Baumgartner *et al.* (1967) 463, *s.v. kinnereth.*

[11]Margalit (1976) 172-77. *Cf.* also 177-88.

[12]Cf. de Langhe (1945) 169: "un rapide examen de la copie confirme cette lecture (=*knrt*)." *Cf.* also Driver (1956) 62.

we argued that the Sea of Kinnereth, and the area at its southwestern shore, were both directly and indirectly referred to throughout CTA 18-19, most explicitly in the twenty-odd text-lines immediately following the explicit reference in line 147; indeed, that these lines could not be correctly understood without such a presupposition, the lack of which had fatally flawed all interpretations and translations hitherto.

2.2 Reading the text exactly as preserved we offered the following rendition of lines 148-51 and 152-54:

> "He raised his voice and cried:
>
> The wings of eagles Baal will break,
> Baal will break their pinions;
>
> If they fly over the grave of my son,
> If they disturb him from his sleep (midst) the pool-of-water."[13]

From this text-segment alone it was a legitimate inference that Danel had disposed of Aqht's (mangled) remains by casting them into the water, the same body of water presumably as was alluded to in line 147: *yqbr . nn . bmdgt . bknrt.* Any doubt that might still have lingered was necessarily dispelled by the immediate continuation. Turning his attention from the eagles (*nšrm*) to the sea proper, the bereaved Danel utters a most telling curse (lines 152-3):

> "Thy down-grade[14] be dammed,[15] woe-to-thee water-pool;
> For by-thee was slain Lad *Aqht*"

followed immediately (lines 153-4) by a parting benediction for his late and lamented son:

> "Dwell (*Aqht*) in El's House till the end-of-time,[16]
> Now, and through eternity;[17]
> Now, and forever."

2.2.1 The curse of the Kinnereth takes its inspiration from the unique topography at the southwestern corner where the sea's outlet

[13]For *qr* = "pool," *cf.* CTA 16:I:26-27—. . . *bn* [27]*qr* ᶜ*nk*, "from the pool of your eyes."

[14]*mlk* = *mêluka*, Ar. *mayl*, "inclination, declivity, slope." The choice of term plays skillfully on the name "Jordan" (Heb. *Yarden*) assumed to derive from √*yrd*, "go down(wards)." The hitherto prevalent interpretation of this term as "king" must accordingly be abandoned, and with it, the only source for Danel's kingship.

[15]*yṣm*; *cf.* Ar. *ṣamma*, "stop, plug," MHeb *ṣamṣēm*, "constrict."

[16]*amd*; Ar. ᵓ*amad*, "end (of time;" *cf.* already al-Yasin (1955) 40.

[17]ᶜ*nt . brḥ . p*ᶜ*lmh*; lit. "now, yesterday [*cf.* Ar. *al-bariḥa*(*ta*), "yesterday"], and unto eternity (ᶜ*lm* + terminative -*h*)."

marks the beginning of the lower Jordan. The original outlet was indeed blocked as the sea forced an outlet to the south of the tell. In MB-LB Palestine this situation must have been in its incipient stages, the final blockage transpiring about 1000 A.D.[18]

2.2.2 The blessing of Aqht is also a decisive confirmation of the lad's burial at sea. It is well-known that the superannuated head of the Ugaritic pantheon, El, dwells underwater, *mbk nhrm / apq thmtm* "(at) the beds of the twin-rivers / the channels of the twin-deeps." Danel, having cast *Aqht's* remains into the sea, anticipates that they will make their way to the domicile of the venerable deity renowned for the qualities of compassion and benevolence.

2.3 It was further argued that the site designated *ablm qrt zbl yrḫ* "*Abl(m)*, city of his majesty Yariḫ" was a thinly veiled allusion to the very tell on which Danel must have stood when he cursed the sea and took leave of his son, a tell which though in ruins throughout the biblical period was still known in Hellenistic and Talmudic times by its Canaanite name, Beth Yeraḥ. Finally, it was suggested that the assassin named *Yṭpn* hired by Anat to slay *Aqht*, and described as dwelling in the vicinity of *Ablm*, was a Sutean nomad (*mhr št*) whose very name, *Yṭpn*, was based on a middle-weak root meaning "wander about."[19]

2.4 The importance of these conclusions, if correct, for our understanding and appreciation of the *Aqht* tale hardly needs elaboration. But their ultimate significance—assuming veracity—transcends the bounds of any individual Ugaritic poem. The seemingly incontrovertible evidence for a Kinnereth localization of a Ugaritic epic poem whose principal *dramatis persona* is labeled throughout "man of Rapha/ Rapiᵓu" or "Raphaite gent" must be seen in a wider context. Prior to the '*Aqht*-Studien' in UF 8, we published a brief study of a short poetic text (RS 24.252) which Virolleaud had edited in *Ugaritica* V.[20] In this text we proposed to identify the Bashan localities of (OT) Ashtaroth (Tell Aštara) and Edrei (Deraᶜa). The text, which describes a divine banquet in honour of a personage (or deity) named *rpu* and designated *mlk ᶜlm*, shows definite affinities with the so-called Rephaim texts (CTA 22-24) which scholars have long connected with the *Aqht* tale by virtue of the explicit reference to Danel contained in them (CTA 20:B:7-8). From here it is a relatively small step to the tenacious, yet generally suspect, OT traditions of a Rephaim people who established a kingdom

[18]Ben-Aryeh (1965) 45-52 (Hebrew).

[19]Ar. *ṭāfa* [$\sqrt{}$*ṭ(w)f*], "walk about, roam." The root $\sqrt{}$*ṭfn* (Ar. "kill") is precluded by the hypochoristic *yṭp* (CTA 18:IV:7). Contrast, *e.g.*, Gese (1970) 89, n. 137. For the literary phenomenon, *cf.* the PNs *Maḥlôn, Kilyôn,* and *ᶜOrpā* in the *Book of Ruth*.

[20]Margulis (1970).

in the Bashan region—the "Land of the Rephaim"—during the Middle-Late Bronze Age (Gen 14, etc.), a kingdom centering on the "royal cities" (Jos 13:31) of Ashtaroth and Edrei (Deut 1:4, etc.).[21]

3.1 Our aim in this paper is twofold: first, to present additional evidence from the *Aqht* poem in support of the Kinnereth hypothesis and to suggest in the course of exposition a possible location for the residence of the hero Danel and his family; secondly, to draw out some of the implications of this as well as other related data (*e.g.*, the recently published RS 34.126) for some long-standing problems of Ugaritology, including the hitherto unsolved riddle of the close, at times uncanny, connections of Ugaritic poetry with that of the Hebrew Bible.

II. New evidence for the Kinnereth setting of the Aqht *story*

1.1 The evidence furnished by the burial scene in CTA 19:III:145ff, and the data relating to the identification of *ablm* and the characterization of the Sutean *Yṭpn*, are the principal supports for the Kinnereth hypothesis in the tale of *Aqht*. The attempt to ferret out additional proof may be compared with the work of the geologist who, after discovering the initial mineral lode relatively near the surface, continues to seek secondary deposits in the adjacent area. These secondary deposits, once discovered, usually require more intensive efforts of extraction.

1.2 One such secondary deposit is to be found in the account of Danel's visit to the second of three sites cursed for their proximity to the scene of the crime. The place is enigmatically designated *mrrt tǵll bnr*. Its proximity to the south-western shore of the Kinnereth is assured by the following considerations:

1.2.1 the accusation-formula *d^{c}lk . mḫṣ . aqht . ǵzr* "For by (= beside) thee was slain Lad Aqht" is applied to it as to the Kinnereth (= *qr . mym*) proper and the adjacent *ablm . qrt . . . . yrḫ* (= Khirbet Kerak);

1.2.2 it is the second of the three places visited by Danel. Since the first and third are identified as situated close to each other, it is probable that the same is true for the middle-named place;

1.2.3 the absence of the typical "long-distance-travel" formula (*hn . ym . wṯn*) from the description of Danel's peregrination (*^{c}db . . . mṭ ydh*) also (*^{c}db . . . mṭ ydh*) implies that all three places are within relatively short walking distance of each other, and that less than a day's walk separates the two furthest points.[22]

[21]For further discussion of this material, *cf.* § IV, below.

[22]We note parenthetically that the long distance formula is similarly absent from the description of Danel's return home (line 170). *Cf.* § III, 1.2, below.

1.3 The first clue to the identity of *mrrt tǵll bnr* is deducible from the contents of the curse leveled at it by Danel (lines 159-60): *šršk . barṣ . al . ypᶜ / riš . ǵly . bd . nsᶜk.* "May your root not grow in the ground / (May) you bow (your) crown in the hands of your chopper." The references to 'root,' 'crown,' and 'chopper' (or 'uprooter') make it clear that the site in question is distinguished by a tree or tree-like plant growing in the immediate vicinity. This characterization cannot but bring to mind the several OT place-names containing names of trees, the majority of which have as their initial element the word *ᵓēlôn* or its derivatives. Such place-names, be it remarked, occur with particular frequency in the pre-monarchic strata of biblical tradition: the Patriarchal narratives and the period of conquest and settlement.

1.4 The suspicion that the Ugaritic toponym in question may contain the word *ᵓēlôn* (or its derivative) as its first element is the direct result of considering the signification of the word *mrrt*. The latter gives the impression that it is formed of a root √*mrr* whose basic meaning is "strong" (cf. Arabic), secondarily (and thus in Ugaritic) "bless" (literally, perhaps, "confer strength").[23] The use of such a term as an allusion to a tree occasions no surprise: trees are self-evident symbols of strength and majesty, as the poetic diction of the Hebrew Bible indicates on numerous occasions. The surprise lies in the realization that, viewed through the prism of folk-etymology if not comparative Semitics, a semantically identical root may be presumed to underlie the Hebrew word *ᵓēlôn* "oak," viz., √*ᵓ(w/y)l* "be strong."[24] It is just this association which prompts the prophet-poet Amos to choose the oak as a similitude of strength (Am 2:9): "I destroyed the Amorite . . . / Whose height was like the cedars / whose strength like that of oaks (*ᵓallōnîm*)." And then, echoing the Ugaritic passage at hand, the prophet adds: "I destroyed his fruit above, and his roots beneath."

1.5 The word *tǵll*—from √*ǵll* "immerse, wade, etc."—occurs but once elsewhere in Ugaritic poetry: *kbrkm . tǵll . bdm . ḏmr* (CTA 3:II:13-14), spoken of Anat wading knee-deep in the gore of soldiers fallen in battle. The collocation of this root with the preceding *mrrt*, assumed to designate a tree, is admittedly odd, at least at first sight and without the recognition that, here as elsewhere, the Ugaritic bard is indulging his penchant for complicated word-plays and conundrums. But before seeking an answer to this riddle we must consider the third and final word, *bnr*.

[23]It is possible that *nmrt* of RS 24.252, if derived from √*mrr*, may preserve the original denotation, "strength." Note the subtle irony evoked in the *Aqht* text by the connotation "blessed one" (*mrrt*) in a curse context.

[24]This is also a common modern derivation. *Cf.* HAL, 52. The Hebrew *ᵓēlôn* is cognate with Aramaic *ᵓilān*, "tree." *Cf.* also Hebrew *ᵓēlaʰ*, conceivably from an identical root. For Hebrew *ᵓyl*, "strength," *cf.* Ps 88:5, and the idiom *(l)ᵓēl yad* "power-of-the-hand; ability."

1.6 The word *nr* "light" or "flame" occurs regularly in Ugaritic in connection with celestial luminaries, especially (and almost exclusively) with the sun-goddess *Špš*, who is formulaically designated *nrt ilm* "Luminary (or: Torch) of the gods"; and on one occasion (RS 34.126) *nyr ṭbt* "beneficent luminary." Accordingly, the phrase *tǵll bnr* lends itself to literal translation as "wades-in-(sun)light," and the cognomen in full as "Mighty(-one)-wading-in-(sun)light."[25]

1.7 Enlightened by the knowledge that the site nicknamed *mrrt tǵll bnr* must lie within short walking distance of Khirbet Kerak and the sea, we shall now venture a solution to the riddle.

1.8 Emptying into the Jordan river at a point approximately midway between Khirbet Kerak and Tell el-Ubeidiyeh (or Abeidiyeh) 3 kms. to the south, is Wadi Fejjas (modern Naḥal Yavniel) which at this point coincides with the ancient trade and travel route known in later times as the Darb el-Ḥawarneh (cf. fig. 1).[26] Overlooking the Wadi Fejjas from the south, about 3 kms. west of the Jordan, from a height of about 150 m., is the Bronze Age site of Khirbet Šemsin (I), whose toponymic equivalent in Canaanite-Hebrew is of course **Bit*(*u*)-*Šamši*/Beth-Shemesh. Whether in fact the site of OT Beth Shemesh (in Naphtali/ Issachar)—Josh 19:22, 38: Judg 1:33—identical with *b-u-ti-š-m-šu* of the Egyptian Execration texts,[27] is this Khirbet Šemsin, or (as generally assumed) Tell el-Ubeidiyeh itself,[28] is of little consequence here. At Khirbet Šemsin we are standing either at, or within 3 kms. of ancient Beth-Shemesh-in-Naphtali. Now, at the foot of the present-day ruins of Khirbet Šemsin (I) is a grove of ancient *sidduria* trees (among the oldest in the country) known in Arabic as Sejerat-el-Kelb "Grove-of-the-(spring-of-the)-Dog," modern Huršat Ya^cala. Some 500 m. to the west, along the aforementioned travel route of el-Ḥawarneh, is another Khirbet Šemsin (II)—the only one so designated on the British Mandatory Map—in the midst of which there looms today a solitary, and most majestic . . . oak tree.

[25]*Cf.*, also, *nyr rbt* (note feminine modifier!) in CTA 16:I:37-8, in reference to the sun goddess [*cf.* Margalit (1976) 154-56]. For a different interpretation of the place-name, cf. W. G. E. Watson, *Or* 45 (1976) 441.

[26]*Cf.* Saarisalo (1927) 23ff., 115ff., de Vaux (1937) 370-71; and Oded (1971) 191-97 (Hebrew). This was the principle land-route between the Bashan/Hauran, and the Plain of Acco.

[27]Helck (1971) 60, and literature cited therein.

[28]*Cf.* Saarisalo (1927) 118-20 [following Alt (1914) 34, and (1926) 51] who adopting this view, suggests that with the destruction of Ubeidiyeh the name wandered from there to the adjacent Khirbet Šemsin site(s). Note Saarisalo's observation that el-Ubeidiyeh is probably the successor to Khirbet Kerak/Beth Yeraḥ rather than its contemporary. This tallies with our conclusion [(1976) 187] that Beth Yeraḥ was in ruins at the time of the *Aqht* legend. In our estimation, the Ugaritic epic reflects an intermediary period when *both Beth Yeraḥ* (Kerak) and Ubeidiyeh (Beth Shemesh) were abandoned, and the area between them a nomadic camping site.

1.9 It is now possible, I believe, to reconstruct Danel's itinerary as related in CTA 19:III:155ff:

1.9.1 The casting of *Aqht's* ingested remains into the sea, and the pronouncement of the initial curse, took place near the estuary of the Jordan at the northern edge of Tell Beth-Yeraḥ/Khirbet Kerak. After bidding his son a tearful farewell (153-54), Danel takes walking-stick in hand (*ᶜdb . . . mṭ . ydh*)[29] and proceeds due south a distance of 3-4 kms. to Ubeidiyeh. Turning west onto the Darb el-Ḥawarneh, Danel proceeds another 3 kms., whereupon he beholds (at a distance of about 500 m. to his left) the grove of Ein-Kelb, while straight ahead, at an equal distance, may well have loomed an MB ancestor of the lonely oak standing today. Both sites afford a view (partly obstructed) of the valley between Khirbet Kerak and Ubeidiyeh, and the southern rim of the sea. Since both were thus eye-witnesses (hence in some sense accomplices)[30] to the murder of *Aqht* at *Ablm*, he pronounces a curse here as well, grounding it in the fact that *dᶜlk . mḫṣ . aqht . ǵzr* "by-thee was murdered Lad *Aqht*."

1.9.2 Having concluded, Danel turns back in the direction of Ubeidiyeh and *Ablm*. The latter, through which the Jordan percolates ever so gently as it follows its tortuous course,[31] is in effect the principal victim of the curse pronounced by Danel over the Kinnereth. For if the Jordan outlet is blocked, the lush pastures between Khirbet Kerak and Ubeidiyeh are doomed to extinction. Not satisfied however with this doom-by-proxy, Danel pronounces his third and final curse. The curse of "blindness" (*ᶜwrt*), quite senseless when taken literally, is in fact a literary pun on the homonymity/synonymity of Semitic *ᶜ(y)n* "eye; well-spring, water-hole," perhaps playing also on the signification "one-eyed" of the root *ᶜ-w-r* (cf. Arabic). The real meaning of the curse is "drought," *i.e.*, it serves to reinforce the consequences of the initial curse.[32]

1.9.3 Having unburdened himself emotionally, a grieving Danel sets out for home (lines 169-71), fording the Jordan at modern Um-Jouni

[29]Ullendorff (1962) 343f. seems to have been the first to suggest this simple and perfectly convincing explanation, now confirmed by RS 24.247 (cf. *Ugaritica* VII, 54). Contrast Caquot *et al.* (1974) 453, and de Moor and van der Lugt (1974) 8. *Cf.* now also *Eretz Israel* 14 (1978) 20.

[30]Note the language of the oath taken by the elders of the town in whose vicinity a murder-victim has been found (Deut 21:7): "Our hands have not spilled this blood, *nor have our eyes seen.*"

[31]The etymology of *abel/ablm* is probably √*ybl*, "soak, drench" = Hebrew √*ybl*, "stream," Arabic √*wbl*, "pour, soak, drench." The Ugaritic root is verbally attested (*hapax legomenon*) in CTA 4:I:38, *yblhm ḫrṣ*, "he [=Kothar] drenches them [=*nᶜl* + *qblbl*] with gold." *Cf.* our forthcoming AOAT monograph, *A Matter of 'Life' and 'Death'* (AOAT 206) 19-20. As a noun, cf. KTU 1.19:IV:60-61: *p*[*mla* .] *km . ybl. lbh* "His (=*Yṭpn*) heart [swelled] like a stream" (*cf.* Margalit, AOAT 206, 85n.; *idem.*, JNSL VIII [1980] [forthcoming]).

[32]*Cf.* Margalit (1976) 180-81.

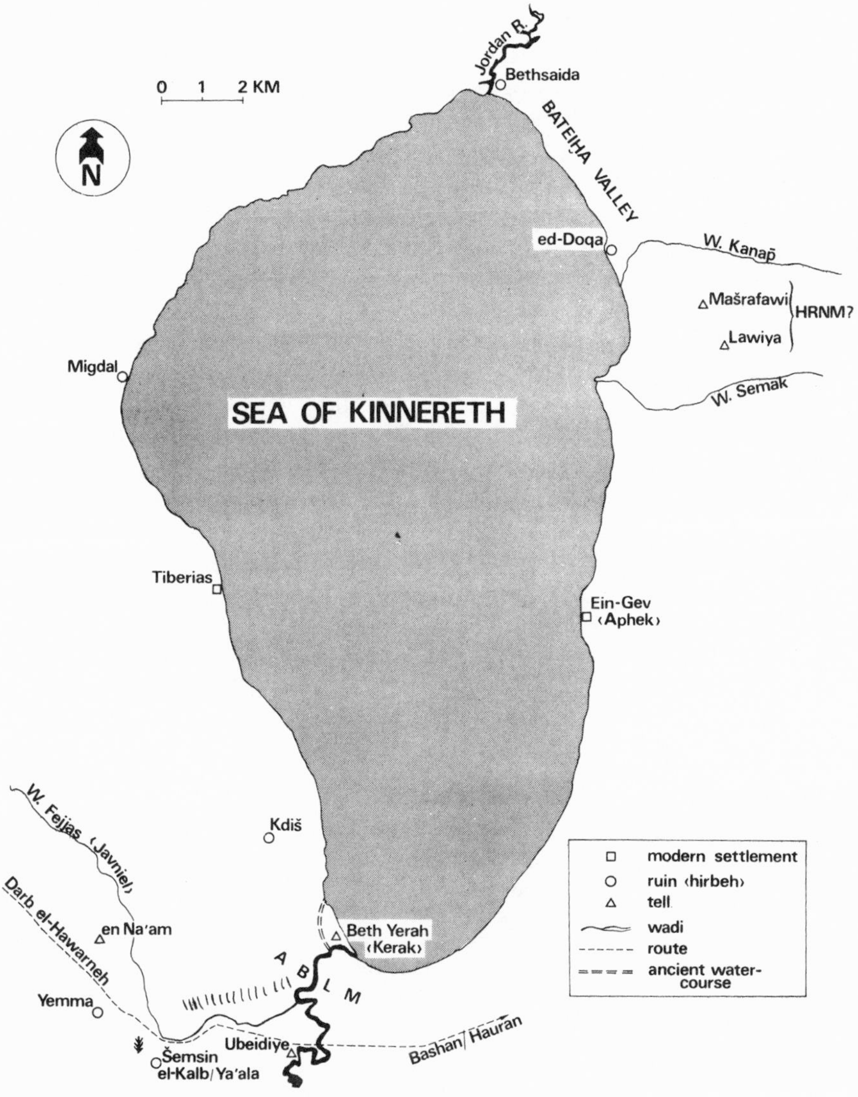
Jordan R.
Bethsaida
0 1 2 KM
N
BATEIHA VALLEY
ed-Doqa
W. Kanap̄
Mašrafawi
Lawiya
HRNM?
Migdal
SEA OF KINNERETH
W. Semak
Tiberias
Ein-Gev
‹Aphek›
Kdiš
W. Fejjas ‹Javniel›
Darb el-Hawarneh
en Na'am
Beth Yerah
‹Kerak›
A B L M
Yemma
Ubeidiye
Šemsin
el-Kalb/Ya'ala
Bashan/Hauran
modern settlement
ruin ‹hirbeh›
tell
wadi
route
ancient water-course

Figure 1

beside Ubeidiyeh on his way to the eastern shore of the Kinnereth, as will be presently seen.

1.10 But the identification of *mrrt tǵll bnr* with Khirbet Šemsin does not stop with the Ugaritic story. The matter goes further. It will be recalled that the element *mrrt*, considered etymologically, suggested itself as the semantic counterpart of Hebrew *ʾēlôn* [Ugaritic **ʾil(ā)n*]. It so happens that several scholars, most notably the late Yoḥanan Aharoni, have argued for identifying OT *Ēlôn Beṣaᶜanna(n)im* —the camp-site of the Kenite tribe headed by Ḥeber—between Mt. Tabor and the Jordan. Aharoni's first choice in fact is none other than the Sejerat-el-Kelb.[33] The merits of Aharoni's proposal, to our mind considerable, cannot be discussed here; nor is the identification crucial for establishing the vicinity of the *sidduria*-grove as the site of *mrrt-tǵll-bnr*. However, the three-fold equation, if acceptable, does serve to clarify perhaps two additional features of the Ugaritic account otherwise unexplained: (a) the exceptional length of the cognomen chosen by the poet to designate the site in question; (b) a possible reason for the poet's choice of √*nsᶜ*—rather than *√*krt*,[34] √*ksm*,[35] √*ḥtk*,[36] or *√*nsẖ*[37]—to denote the act of felling a tree.[38]

1.10.1 If the identification of *Ēlôn Beṣaᶜanna(n)im* with *mrrt tǵll bnr* is correct, then the length of the cognomen can be viewed as a deliberate attempt by the poet to capture something of the length and flavor of the original and authentic name. Note the assonantal-alliterative similarity between the two: . . . *t-ǵ-LĒL-B-N-r-* . . . *ʾĒL-N-B-ṣ-ᶜ-n-(n-)m*.

1.10.2 As for the preference of √*nsᶜ* over other vocables meaning "cut" or "chop," one might assume (granted the identification), that the

[33]Aharoni (1957) 79 (Hebrew); (1967) 204, 238; and *Encyclopedia Judaica* vol. 10, 665. *Cf.* also Y. Press, *Enc. Miq.*, vol. 1, 327-28, and Saarisalo (1927) 122-24; F. M. Abel, *Géographie de la Palestine* (1938) 2:439.

[34]The usual term (along with √*ḥtb*) for tree-chopping in OT Hebrew. *Cf.* Deut 19:5, Isa 14:8, *etc. Cf.* however, Job 19:10, *wysᶜ . kᶜṣ . tqwty*, "He removed my hope like a tree." Note that √*ḥtb* in Ugaritic appears to denote a woman's job (foraging for kindling?). *Cf.* CTA 14:III:12 and note 7 [KTU 1.14:III:8 reads *ḥtbt* (*Rasur:h*)], and Clines (1976) 26.

[35]*Cf.* Akkadian *kasāmu* (AHw 453, CAD K 240-41). *Cf.* also Ugaritic *ksm mhyt* (CTA 5:VI:5 = 16:III:4), "edge-(lit., 'cut')-of-the-waters," denoting the edge of the earth's surface (Hebrew *qeṣôt haʾar(e)ṣ*,<√*qṣṣ*, "cut").

[36]Hebrew √*ḥtk*, "cut," and most likely the base-meaning of *ḥtk*, "sire, child," (referring to the severance of the umbilical cord?).

[37]Recently suggested as an emendation in RS 24.244 for *ysynh* (read *ysẖ!nh*), also in connection with felling a tree. See Young (1977) 294.

[38]In CTA 6:VI:27 (& par.), √*nsᶜ* denotes the forcible removal, or wrenching out, of a post (*alt*), comparable to Ju 16:3, and *Azit.* III, 15, 17 (referring to gate-portals). If the view that √*nsᶜ*, "travel," originates with the notion of √*nsᶜ*, "pull-up (stakes)," is correct (*cf.* BDB, *s.v.*), then √*nsᶜ* is to be understood as nomad-terminology.

verb choice represents a subtle allusion to the name-element *B*^{e}*ṣa*^{c}*anna-(n)im*, believed (with considerable justice) to derive from a root √*ṣ*^{c}*n* meaning "wander-as-a-nomad" (cf. Arabic √*ẓ*^{c}*n*). This meaning is also widely attested for Hebrew √*ns*^{c}. In fact, there is evidence in the Hebrew Bible for the poetic as well as verbal synonymity of √*ṣ*^{c}*n* and √*ns*^{c}. In Isa 33:20, a verse replete with nomadic terminology, we read as follows: "Thine eyes will behold Jerusalem / a peaceful meadow (*nawe*^{h}) / an immobile (√*ṣ*^{c}*n*) tent / whose stakes will not be removed (√*ns*^{c}).

1.10.3 Accordingly, it seems not unlikely that the choice of √*ns*^{c} in the present Ugaritic context, like that of *mrrt-tǵll-bnr*, is motivated by the poetically welcome associations with the Hebrew place-name *Ēlôn-B*^{e}*ṣa*^{c}*anna(n)im*, *viz.*, the semantic overlapping of √*ns*^{c} and √*ṣ*^{c}*n* and the nomadic connotations common to both terms.[39]

2.1 It is against this backdrop that we now turn to consider the question of Danel's place of residence.

2.1.1 There is a certain *a priori* likelihood that Danel and family are residents of the Central Jordan Valley; otherwise we should have to assume that the murder of *Aqht* and the sequel activity by Danel (as well as Pughat) have all transpired at a considerable distance from home.

2.1.2 However, as matters stand, we are not dependent solely on deductive reasoning. A careful reading of the dozen-or-so lines at the end of the poem (as extant) points unmistakably in this direction.

2.1.3 But before proceeding to interpret this text we must comment briefly on the seemingly related, but ultimately irrelevant, problem of *hrnm*.

2.2 We are all familiar with Albright's view that the epithet *mt hrnmy* refers to Danel's home of origin, as with the thesis that the word *hrnmy* is a gentilic of *HRNM*, to be identified with Egyptian *Hrnm* / *Arnm* (modern Hermel), situated near Kadesh-on-the-Orontes.[40] This view has achieved wide currency and acceptance, even though a careful study of the quite brief exposition by Albright shows that the thesis is based essentially on a set of more or less probable suppositions rather than on incontrovertible facts: *e.g.*, the equation of Ugaritic *hrnm* with

[39] The nomad connection of √*ns*^{c} is most desirable to the poet if he is, in fact, thinking of *Ēlôn B*^{e}*ṣa*^{c}*anna(n)im*. One of the most attractive modern interpretations of *B*^{e}*ṣa*^{c}*anna(n)im* is the assumption of an original **bêt ṣ*^{c}*n(n)m*, "home of nomads," with assimilation of the *t* to the following *ṣ*, the *a priori* plausibility of which finds support in the reading *bethsennamin* of some LXX traditions (*cf.* B. Mazar, *Enc. Miq.*, vol I 328). As an interesting aside, *cf.* modern Hebrew *ṣo*^{c}*anî*, "gypsy," a Hebrew retroversion of European *ts/zegeuner*, itself (by all appearances) from Semitic *ẓ/ṣ*^{c}*n*. In RS 21.355 (Claremont), √*ns*^{c} occurs in the sense of "pay (money)," a usage worth comparing with that of the semantically related √^{c}*br* in the Hebrew idiom (*kesep*) ^{c}*ôbēr* (*lassoḥer*) = "negotiable currency."

[40] Albright (1953) 26-27.

Egyptian *hrnm/arnm* is only one of several linguistic possibilities.[41] Yet even if the equation is conceded, we cannot be certain that the Ugaritic place-name is identical with the Egyptian toponym, in view of the well-known propensity of identical *toponyma* to recur in widely scattered places.[42] Finally, it must be acknowledged that the very assumption of *hrnmy* as a gentilic toponym is just that: an assumption![43]

2.2.1 Yet even if all the foregoing points are decided in Albright's favor, it still does not follow as a matter of course that Danel is resident at *Hrnm* at the time of the *Aqht* tale. Albright, be it noted, was careful not to make such a claim when he entitled his paper "The *Traditional* Home of the Syrian Daniel" (emphasis added). He thus left open the question whether this site, *Hrnm,* was part of the story's geographical setting. It may be assumed that had Albright been able to confirm his identification of *Hrnm* with evidence from within the story itself, he would have dispensed with the qualification "traditional."[44]

2.3 The present investigation proceeds from one of two assumptions with respect to the *hrnm(y)* problem:

2.3.1 If it is granted that *hrnmy* is the gentilic form of a place-name *HRNM,* then (a) either *hrnm* is identical with Egyptian *HRNM/ARNM* near the Orontes (in which case it is Danel's place-of-origin, but not his place-of-residence at the time of the story); or (b)—the more likely of the two—Ugaritic *hrnm* is distinct from Egyptian *HRNM/ARNM,* in which case it may well refer to Danel's actual residence at the time of the story (if not the town proper, then the region thereof). If the latter is assumed [alternative (b)], then *hrnm* is to be located (as we shall argue) in the vicinity of the Kinnereth, along (or overlooking) its eastern shore.

2.3.2 We would emphasize however that irrespective of the foregoing alternatives, the *datum* furnished by *hrnm(y)* is, in the present

[41] *Cf., e.g.,* Helck (1971) 132, who considers Egyptian *h/a-r-n-m* a corruption of *h-r-(m)-ʾ-(e)-l* (modern Hermil) found in the list of Thutmosis III.

[42] *Cf., e.g.,* in the very case at hand, OT *bêt harān* (Nu 32:36) located in Transjordania, at the northern rim of the Dead Sea.

[43] *Cf.* the dissent registered in Driver (1965) 106, who renders "ancient one" (Arabic *harmala*). Furthermore, with thanks to S. B. Parker (1970) 100f, it cannot be taken for granted that the predication, 'Harnamite,' (if correct!) refers to Danel. The collocation *hrnmy dkbkbm* in CTA 19:186-7//193 is indeed difficult to reconcile with the assumption that Danel is *hrnmy*. Nor should we overlook the possibility that the *y* of *hrnmy* is part of the name. *Cf.* Richardson (1978) 298-315.

[44] Contrast Caquot *et al.* (1974) 402. We remark in passing that any attempt at localizing a place-name presumed to occur in a mythological or legendary text stands little chance of proving conclusive unless it can marshall evidence from *within* the story narrative. Unless the identification is self-evident, toponymic equations based on linguistic criteria only are insufficient.

state of our knowledge, of no importance for proving the Kinnereth location of Danel's residence at the time of the story.

III. The Kinnereth residence of Danel

1.1 The 'new' evidence for the Kinnereth residence of Danel and his family is found at the conclusion of the poem (as extant), lines 202ff. In lines 203, 204, and 205 respectively there are three unequivocal occurrences of the word *ym* in the meaning "sea." I am not aware of any attempt in the scholarly literature to elucidate these references.[45] Since it is increasingly recognized that the phrase *ǵlp ym* in line 204 denotes the murex shell-fish,[46] and in light of the geographical location of Ugarit, it is possible that the identity of the three *ym* references with the Mediterranean has been simply taken for granted. If so, then the assumption is mistaken, at least for two of the three allusions. Only the *ym* of *ǵlp ym* denotes the Mediterranean; the other two *must* denote a sea-body other than the Mediterranean. In light of what has preceded, the only logical candidate for this sea-body is the Kinnereth. Before proceeding to discuss the material in detail, it will be useful to recapitulate briefly the sequence of events leading up to lines 202-5.

1.2 At the beginning of col. IV (lines 8-9) Danel is back home, having laid his son's remains to rest in the sea and lustily cursed the vicinity of Khirbet Kerak and el-Ubeidiyeh. The formula *ᶜdb . uḫry . mṭ . ydh* "Thereupon he takes his walking-stick" used to describe Danel's movements to and from the proximately located sites referred to in the curses, is also employed in connection with the hero's return home. Not only is there no reference to animal transportation, there is no hint of extended travel (cf. above, § II, 1.2). In fact, one can easily gain the impression that *all* the activity described in col. III and the beginning of IV, including the hero's return to his domicile, has transpired within a single 24-hr. period.

1.3 At home, Danel commences the ritual mourning for his dead son (lines 171ff). The well-known women mourners, the symmetrical counterparts of the *kṯrt* midwives[47] who visited with Danel at the time of

[45]*Cf., e.g.*, Gordon (1966) 138; Gaster (1961) 372ff; Caquot *et al.* (1974) 456; and de Moor (1968) 212-15.

[46]*Cf.* already Ginsberg in ANET^2 155; and Caquot *et al.* (1974) 456. Ugaritic *ǵlp* = Arabic $\sqrt{}$*ǵlf*(II) = Hebrew $\sqrt{}$*ᶜlp*, "envelop, wrap, cover," denoting, of course, the turbinate shell housing the murex.

[47]Akkadian *šassurātu*. However the role of the *kṯrt*, designated *bnt hll*, "daughters of the moon-crescent," is to be understood more broadly as "patronesses of womankind," the divine counterparts of "ladies-in-waiting" (*rēᶜôt*). *Cf.* our discussion (in need of some revision today) in Margalit (1972) 52-61, 113-17.

Aqht's birth in col. II, spend a week-of-years in the hero's house.[48] After their departure (lines 182ff), Danel arranges a feast (*dbḥ . ilm*)—probably a *mrzḥ*—marked by music and dancing (cp. RS 24.252).[49] This event would appear to signify the official end of the mourning period.

1.4 Enter Pughat (l. 190), the wise daughter of Danel endowed with powers of divination (*yd^{c}t . hlk . kbkbm*). Approaching her father, she asks his blessing for the venture she is about to undertake: the 'redemption of the blood' of her brother Aqht.[50] From the immediate sequel, the section of primary interest for us here (lines 202ff), it emerges that Danel and Pughat (there is strangely no mention of mother *dnty* . . .) have meanwhile learned all the sinister details of Aqht's murder: the identity of the hired-sword, *Yṭpn*; his place of encampment; and the complicity of Anat in the crime.[51]

2.1 We now turn to lines 202/3-214, from which we intend to elicit the data sufficient to substantiate the claim for Danel's Kinnereth residence.

2.1.1 The text is at some points severely damaged. In 202/3-205 alone some 12-13 of a total 51-52 signs are missing. But the real obstacle to interpretation, in our estimation at least, has been the absence of proper stichometry, in addition to a certain lack of insight resulting from a blurred view of the story overall.

2.1.2 *[td]*[203]*d . ttql . bym* 3
trtḥ[ṣ ydm][204]*wṯkm* 3
tid!m . bǵlp . ym 3
[ṣdp][205]*dalp . šd* 3
ẓuh . bym . t[mt^{c}(?)] 3

[48]We should observe that when epic poets distort time or distances, they do so in the direction of hyperbolic exaggeration, and not in reverse.

[49]In fact, lines 188-89 of Aqht, although severaly mutilated, have often been cited in connection with RS 24.252, obv. 4-5, *btp . wmṣltm . bmrqdm . dšn*, which correspond to CTA 19:188-9 (*apud* KTU!) [---]*mṣltm . mrqdm . d . šn/tl/*[--]. On the basis of this correspondence, it has been suggested that *dšn* of RS 24.252 (which unlike CTA 19:189 is written as one word) is to be understood as *d* + *šn*, "of ivory," modifying *mrqdm*, "castanets." However, the KTU reading (CTA: *dš*[-]*l*[-]) makes it clear that the letter *d* is followed by a single word *exceeding* two letters (*wt^{c}n* in line 190 begins a new sentence), a circumstance precluded by the parallel in RS 24.252.

[50]There is much to be learned from this bit of information. Danel, for all his importance in the community, has no retainers whom he can commission to avenge his son's death. He himself, despite the title *ǵzr*, is apparently too old to undertake the job. Compare the patriarch Abraham (outside Gen 14!) who hides behind his wife's skirt-tails when in danger (Gen 13, *etc.*).

[51]*Cf.* CTA 19:II:89ff. The text as preserved does not mention *Yṭpn* and *Ablm*. This information was probably conveyed in the second exchange (lines 96ff), and now lost.

"[She (= Pughat) sets for]th;[52] she plunges[53] into the sea,
She wash[es hands] and shoulder(s),[54]
She rouges with sea-mollusk(s),
[Whelk(s)][55] from a thousand *šd* away;
She [immerses (?)][56] (her) tunic (?) in the sea."

2.2 The first, and decisive, point to be underscored is the clear implication that Pughat's point of departure—her home—is close by the sea. Note how soon after leaving—in the space of a single text-line—Pughat reaches the sea. By contrast, her journey to *Yṭpn* of *Ablm* (some 25 kms. away on our assumptions) is spaced over more than four text-lines (end of 208-12).

[52] *[td]d*: the root is probably √*ndd*, Hebrew, "wander, depart, flee, *etc*." The word occurs very frequently in the "Rephaim-texts" (CTA 20-22), in the formula **aṯr tdd rpum/ilnym*, "the shades/divine ones depart to (his) house." Another likely occurrence is in PRU V:4(=KTU 1.91):14, *k . tdd . bᶜlt . bhtm*, "when Baalat-of-the-palace proceeds (to). . . ." In addition to providing suitable sense, the restoration proposed satisfies both the epigraphic and alliterative requirements of the text. Both CTA and KTU presume a lacuna of two signs at the end of line 202. Alliteratively, *cf*. (. . . *umTK*||) *Tdd w TTQl* . . . (note too that *d* and *t* are alliterative 'allophones').

[53] *ttql*: the root is probably √*ql*, "fall down" (*cf*. the formulaic *thbr wtql* of the epics), the formation tD (Hithpa'el). A more remote possibility is √*tql* (=JAram/MHeb), "stumble," otherwise unknown in Ugaritic. The reading *ttql* follows CTA (the middle signs designated as less than certain) and KTU (without reservation).

[54] The restoration [*ydm*] at the end of line 203 (KTU:41) is a virtual certainty once KTU's reading *w*ṯ*k*m* (CTA: [--](*a/.t*)*dm*) is accepted (as it must!) for the beginning of line 204 (KTU:42). *Cf*.

CTA:14:II:62-64 (& par.)	CTA 19	
trtḥṣ . wtadm	*trtḥṣ*	*tid!m . bǵlp ym*
rḥṣ . ydk . amt	[*ydm*]	
uṣbᶜtk . ᶜd ṯkm	*wṯkm*	

Here as well, the restoration proposed commends itself alliteratively. *Cf*. below.

[55] [*ṣdp*]: Arabic *ṣadaf*, "sea-shell," in synonymous parallelism with *ǵlp ym* (on the latter, *cf*. de Moor (1968) 212-15). Here too, the contextual suitability of the restoration is complemented by considerations of epigraphic and alliterative compatibility. CTA allows for a lacuna of two signs at the end of line 204, but KTU more generously allows for three. From an alliterative viewpoint, the entire passage beginning with *trtḥṣ*, and concluding . . . *dalp šd*, constitutes a series of interlocking alliterative patterns. *Cf*. . . . [*yDM*] *wṯkM / tiD!M* . . . *yM*; [*yDm*] . . . / *tid!M* . . . / [*ṣDp*] *Dalp šD*; . . . *bǵLP* . . . / [*ṣdP*] *daLP* . . . Note also the linkage with the following (and strophe-terminative) monostich: [*ṢDp*] . . . *šD / Ẓuh*. . . , the sequences -*ṣd*- and -*dẓ*- partially alliterative. [On the technical terminology employed here and elsewhere on the subject of alliteration, *cf*. our forthcoming "Alliteration in Ugaritic Poetry. . . ," (Part I) in the Schaeffer Festschrift (UF 11) (edd. Loretz and Dietrich); provisionally, Margalit (1975) 310-13; and (1976) 191-92.]

[56] t[mtᵓ(?)]: restoration conjectural. *Cf*. CTA 4:II:6, *mdh . bym . tmtᶜ*, referring to Asherah laundering her garment (*md*) in the sea. This passage also points to the word *ẓu* as *membrum synonym* for *md* (Hebrew *maddîm*).

2.3 A second, seemingly moot, point is the identity of the sea in line 203 with the Kinnereth. The reference to the murex in lines 204-5 would seem *prima facie* to favor a Mediterranean location for the initial *ym* reference as well; for the murex is unknown in the Kinnereth area.

2.3.1 A close look at the text ought to dispell such a thought. Our poet-author, well aware of the natural habitat of the murex along the Phoenician coast, hastens to add (line 205) that the aforesaid murex originates at a distance of *alp šd* from where Pughat is standing. The phrase *alp šd,* along with its frequent concomitant *rbt . kmn.*, is a formulaic designation in Ugaritic poetry for long-distance. It occurs invariably when one divine personage visits another residing in a remote place, *e.g.*, the visit of Baal's couriers to the infernal kingdom of Mot (CTA 4:VIII:10ff; cf. lines 24-26) and Anat's visits to El, residing in the infernal depths (CTA 18:I:19-22), or to Baal atop Mt. Casius (CTA 4:V:84-86), or to Aegean Kothar-Hasis (CTA 3:VI:17-18). By extension, and as epic hyperbole, it is also used to describe perception at a distance (CTA 3:IV:81-84; 17:V:9-11) or the area occupied by a divine palace (CTA 4:V:118-19).[57]

2.3.2 Thus, the qualification *dalp šd* effectively precludes identifying the *ym* of line 203 with the Mediterranean; and if this is granted, then the sea of Kinnereth is immediately established as the number-one candidate. The murex in question would in any case have to be understood as part of Pughat's cosmetic kit; we can hardly assume that she would be personally engaged on this occasion in extracting the dye. What the poet is telling us in effect is that the heroine applied warrior-rouge to her body (cf. CTA 14:II:62ff; Nah 2:4),[58] using costly murex imported from afar (about 120 kms.), *viz.*, the Phoenician coast to the Central Jordan Valley and the Golan Heights.[59]

[57]Ugaritic *šd* = Akkadian *šiddum* = Hurrian (?) *kumani. Cf.* AHw 1230; Dietrich and Loretz (1969) 61-62; and Liverani (1974) 11.

[58]The murex dye, normally used for fabrics rather than as a cosmetic, was well-known in Ugaritic times: cf. C. F. A. Schaeffer, *The Cuneiform Texts of Ras Shamra-Ugarit* (1939) 38; M. Heltzer, *Goods and Prices . . . in Ugarit* (1978) 25f.; E. Ebeling, RLA 3:26f. It is a logical inference from here that Anat herself was portrayed with ruddy complexion and body-colour, befitting her bellicose nature. However, the attempt to deduce this datum from Ugaritic texts other than the present (*e.g.* CTA 3:II:1ff.) is unconvincing [*pace* de Moor (1968) 212n.]. de Moor adduces the phrase *kpr . šbᶜ . bnt* which he renders "henna of seven women." Aside from being barely intelligible, this rendering reflects a faulty stichometric division of the text: . . . *kpr . šbᶜ . bnt . rḥ . gdm . wanhbm . klat . ṯġrt . bht . ᶜnt*, ". . . camphor seven(?). Daughters of scent, Coriander, and Ambergris (?) / Twin porteresses of the House of Anat." Even if *kpr* = the *lawsonia alba* from which the henna is extracted, it is here more likely referring to the perfume derived from this same plant, as its biblical counterpart (Cant 1:14, 4:13). *Cf.* now Pope (1977a) 352-53.

[59]Assuming the murex to have originated at Tyre/Sidon, it would presumably have reached Danel's city of residence via the Darb el-Ḥawarneh route (*cf.* § II, 1.7.1, above).

2.4 The next sequence of actions, described in lines 206-12, portrays Pughat as she attires:

[206]*tlbš . npṣ . ġzr*	3
tšt . ḫ[št.] b[207]*nšgh*	3
ḥrb . tšt . btʿrth	3
[208]*wʿl . tlbš . npṣ . aṯt*	4

"She dons the garb of a warrior,
She places a da[gger][60] in her girdle,
A poinard she places in her belt;
And on top she dons the garb of a woman."

2.4.1 The purpose of this hybrid dress is clarified by Chester Beatty Papyrus VII (§ 1,5ff) which describes the goddess Anat as one "who is like a man, dressed like a man and girded like a woman,"[61] as well as by glyptic representations of the goddess in Egyptian art.[62] Pughat is about to impersonate Anat, a conclusion corroborated by the verbal similarity of lines 204-5 with CTA 3:II:42-43 // 89-90: ([86]. . . *tḥspn . mh . wtrḥṣ* . . .) [89]*ttpp . anhbm . dalp . šd / ẓu[ḫ . bym . t* . . .] (cf. KTU!).

2.5 Pughat is now set to travel. The three text-lines which follow describe her journey to *Ablm* and her arrival at the Sutean encampment.[63] It is from these lines that we elicit a most vital piece of information regarding Pughat's place of residence.

This bit of (indirect) evidence for commercial relations between the central Jordan Valley and the Phoenician coast during MB-LB may be connected, perhaps, with the OT notice (Nu 13:29), according to which the 'Canaanite'—as distinct from the Amorite—resided by the Mediterranean, and along the Jordan River. Arrayed in this manner, the Canaanites could control the East-West trade routes from Ḥauran-Bashan (the source of the foodstuffs) to the coast (the source of murex and artifacts, local and imported).

[60]The restoration *ḫ[ṣt]*, an *hapax legomenon* in Ugaritic, is cognate with Arabic *ḫušt*, a spiked weapon" (Dozy, *Supplément*, I 373), derived from √*ḫš*, "pierce, stab" (Lane, vol 2, 740, and Hava, *Al-Faraid* . . . , 189). Note the alliterative consequences of the restoration: *TŠT ḫ[ŠT] bnŠgh*, and . . . *ḫ[ŠT] Bnšgh / ḥrB . TŠT . BTʿrth.*

[61]Helck (1971) 461.

[62]*Cf.* Barnett (1969) 405-22, and (1978) 28*-31*. In light of the dominant role of Anat in the *Aqht* story and her demonstrable activity in the area of the Kinnereth (CTA 18:I:29-31; IV:5ff.; 19:I:2-8 [*apud* UF 11 (1979) 554-56]), I deem it significant that the aforementioned Beth-Shemesh-in-Naphtali occurs in the OT coupled with Beth-Anat (Jos. 19:38; Ju. 1:33). Though hitherto unidentified with certainty, *Beth-Anat* is well-known from Egyptian sources of the New Kingdom era. It was situated on a mountain to which it gave its name (ANET, 256), possibly identical with the goddess's sacred mountain *Inbb*. In any case, the concentration in the one tribal area (Naphtali) bordering on the Kinnereth of three sites named after some of the foremost deities of the Ugaritic pantheon (*Yrḫ, Šmš/Špš, Anat*) can hardly be attributed to coincidence.

[63]Ugaritic *ḏd*[// *a hlm*(plural!)] = "encampment" (lines 213-14). *Cf.* Dijkstra and de Moor (1975) 191f.; Margalit (1975) 294, and (1976) 295.

2.5.1	[*a<u>t</u>r*] [209]*ṣbi . nrt . ilm . špš*	4
	t]*r*[*tpš*] [210]*pǵt . minš . šdm*	4
	lm^{c}[*rb*] [211]*nrt . ilm . špš*	3
	mǵyt(.) [212]*pǵt . lahlm*	3

2.5.2 The text is less well preserved than one might have wished. However, even without the benefit of the restorations which we have suggested at the end of lines 208 and 209 respectively—in contrast to that of 210, admittedly conjectural—there is much to be learned from this passage, both negatively and positively.

2.6 Alone, the universally admitted restoration at the end of line 210 makes it abundantly clear that Pughat is proceeding in a westerly direction to *ablm*. Assuming, as we do, that *ablm* is the meadowland surrounding Khirbet Kerak and Tell el-Ubeidiyeh, then Pughat is self-evidently residing to the east of the sea. This conclusion is merely reinforced by our proposed reading in lines 208-9: "[In the wake of] the setting sun. . . ."[64]

2.7 The second inference of major importance is that Pughat is traveling alone and on foot. This inference is based on what the text relates as well as what it omits. In contrast to the description of Asherah's voyage to El (CTA 4:IV:4ff), or of Danel making the rounds on his estate (CTA 19:II:52ff; note that here too Pughat is on foot!), there is no mention of hitching an ass, or bridling a donkey.

2.7.1 But we need not be satisfied with this argument from silence. The image of a pedestrian Pughat is implicit in the phrase *minš . šdm*, a phrase which—with one exception—has eluded satisfactory interpretation.[65] The phrase is to be rendered—with Aistleitner[66]—"comrade of the fields."[67] There is little point to this characterization except to emphasize the fact that Pughat, traveling alone, is very much at home in the area and has no difficulty finding her way to *Ablm* as she traverses the fields which rim the Kinnereth.[68] The restoration at the end of line 209—a Gt

[64]*Cf.* KTU's three-sign lacuna (contrast CTA). Note the 'double-construct' as a result of which the five-word verse-line scans as a "4," rather than a "5"; *cf.* Margalit (1975) 295.

[65]Driver (1956) 67 [= Caquot *et al.* (1974) 457]: "the folk (?) in the fields"; Dijkstra and de Moor (1975) 212: "meeting place" (deleting *šdm*!). Ginsberg (ANET^2 155) left the phrase untranslated.

[66]*Cf.* Aisleitner (1964) 82, and (1967) *s.v.* 319.

[67]The root is √*ʾnš*, "be familiar (with)." The masculine gender of *minš* is no obstacle to this interpretation. The word *minš* (unlike *anšt*) is a pure *mqtl*-noun in apposition (with implied comparison) to the feminine subject.

[68]Pughat's familiarity with the fields is, of course, also the result of her occupational activities: *cf.* the women in the fields of Udm (CTA 14:III:112 & parallel). Note too that it is Pughat who first discerns the blight of the crops (CTA 19:I:28ff.) due to lack of rain. *Cf.* also Prov 31:16.

formation of $\sqrt{}$*rpš* "trudge" (*hapax legomenon*)[69]—merely makes explicit what is implicit in the phrase *minš . šdm.*

2.8 Immediately upon arrival at the Sutean camp in *Ablm*, Pughat-Anat is recognized by the sentries. This instantaneous recognition, perhaps even from a distance, combined with the consideration that people don't travel after dark in biblical times (*cf.* Judg 19:14), certainly not unescorted women in bedouin-infested regions[70]—suffice for us to conclude that Pughat has arrived before nightfall. Accordingly, all of the preceding activity ([*td*]*d . ttql . bym . . . trtḥṣ . . . tidm . . . t*[*mt*ᶜ(?)] . . . *t*]*r*[*tpš*])—the walk to the sea, the bathing, rouging, laundering, dressing, and the trek to *Ablm*—needs have transpired within the 12-16 daylight hours at Pughat's disposal.

3.1 Until quite recently, archaeological data from the eastern littoral of the Kinnereth were not conducive to a conclusion presupposing MB settlement in the area. The excavations at Ein-Gev (OT Afēq) and Mt. Susita (Hippos) carried out in the past pointed to the early Iron Age as the *terminus a quo.*[71]

3.1.1 This picture has changed dramatically following the surveys carried out after the Mideast war of June 1967, when the northeastern section of the Kinnereth littoral and part of the Golan heights passed into Israeli hands. Signs of MB and LB settlements were found at numerous points—named and unnamed—on the Golan slopes overlooking the sea.[72] Of particular interest to us is Tell Mašrafawi, situated just south of Wadi Shuqaif (co-ordinates 2135/2513). Forty dunams in size, and strategically located some 250 m. above the Kinnereth, it shows signs of settlement beginning with MB II (approx. 1900-1550), the most likely period for the composition of the *Aqht* tale as we know it.[73] The tell is situated less than three (aerial) kms. from the seashore at ed-Doqa

[69]Both CTA and KTU agree on the *r* as second letter. The initial *t* is self-evident from the context. The remaining letters are indicated alliteratively: *cf.* . . . *ŠPŠ trtPŠ*; *TrTPš PǵT*; and *nRT* . . . *TRTpš*. The root corresponds to OT *rpś*, used in connection with walking, or treading, on unclean surfaces. In Rabbinic Hebrew, $\sqrt{}$*rps* is used, *i.a.*, to denote the treading of grapes. *Cf.* now Dietrich-Loretz, "Die Ug. Feldbezeichnung *RPŠ* 'Schlamm, Sumpfeld,'" UF 10 (1979) 430 (citing KTV 4.348).

[70]*Cf. Pap. Anastasi* I xxiii 7ff.

[71]*Cf. Encyclopedia of Archaeological Excavations in the Holy Land* 422-23, 438-39 (Hebrew edition); *Encyclopedia Judaica*, vol. 3 175-77; vol. 15 535-36; and M. Dothan (1975) 63.

[72]*Cf.* Kochavi *et al.* (1962) section V, 244-98 (Hebrew).

[73]*Cf.* Margalit (1976) 186-88. Tell Mashrafawi also lies close to a Dolmen field dating to *ca.* 2100 B.C.E., and generally believed to represent secondary burial structures of nomadic peoples. *Cf.* Epstein (1974) 37-40. In our opinion, it is not unlikely that Ugaritic *skn* and *ztr* refer to such Dolmens, conceived as "storage-bins" (*skn*), and constructed as sun-discs (*ztr* = Hittite *sittari*).

(2100/2520).[74] From here it is a 20-25 km. journey over flat land to the vicinity of Ubeidiyeh. If Pughat set out on her mission at daybreak, spent one hour walking to, and another bathing in, the sea, she would still have at least ten hours of daylight to traverse the 20-25 km. stretch to *Ablm*.

3.2 The location of Danel's residence at or near Tell Mašrafawi (*e.g.*, the neighboring Lawiya, 2140/2503) not only answers to the requirements of the poetic narrative discussed above; it also casts additional and interesting light on the literary *raison-d'être* of one of the central motifs of the story.

3.2.1 The drama of the *Aqht* tale really begins with the present of the marvelous bow to the youthful *Aqht* by Kothar-Ḫasis (CTA 17:V). The drama shifts into high gear with the confrontation between *Aqht* and Anat at a party in Danel's house (CTA 17:VI). The marvelous bow kindles the envy of Anat who cannot rest until she has taken possession of it. The bow is thus the *casus belli* leading to Aqht's murder; and a planned hunting lesson[75] is apparently the pretext for luring Aqht to his death.[76] Finally, it may be observed that the plan chosen by Anat for liquidating Aqht combines the methods of the 'hired-gun' with that of the skilled fowler.[77]

3.2.2 The prominence of hunting elements in the story obviously speaks for an author and audience fond of, and familiar with, this sport.[78] It is thus of no little interest to learn that the northern littoral of the Kinnereth is even today renowned as a hunting-ground, and was undoubtedly more so in the past, before the introduction of modern highways and intensive land cultivation to the area.[79] Formerly, this renown gave Hellenistic Bethesda/Bethṣaida its name.[80] A Talmudic anecdote relates how the sage R. Joshua b. Ḥaninah brought to the Emperor Hadrian pheasant from—according to one tradition—Bethṣaida (Aramaic Ṣaydān) as testimony of Holy-Land bountifulness.[81] Now, the site of ancient Bethṣaida is in the immediate vicinity of Tell

[74]The survey map shows a relatively straight foot-path leading past Kafr Aqab (Aqabiah) to ed-Doqa, but owing to disuse over the past ten years, the path is today overgrown with shrubbery, and is not easily negotiated.

[75]In the vicinity of *mgdl* (Aramaic Magdala), north of Tiberias?

[76]CTA 18:I:23ff. Note especially lines 29 and 31.

[77]*Cf.* on the latter, Watson (1977) 69-75.

[78]*Cf.* Xella (1978) 78.

[79]*Cf.* also Baal ahunting in the Ḥuleh Valley (*aḫ šmk*) in CTA 10:II:4-9.

[80]Aramaic *bêt ṣayyad*, from √*ṣyd*, "hunt."

[81]*Kohelet Rabbah*, § II 8(2). A variant tradition gives Galilean Akbirin (near Safed) as the site. For the equation of *ṣaydān* with Bethṣaida (not Sidon!), *cf.* Press (1955) 4:795 (Hebrew).

Mashrafawi, both bordering on the Bateiḥa Valley, a distance of less than 10 (aerial) kms. from each other.

3.3 This concludes our discussion of the Kinnereth background of the *Aqht* story. We hope to have demonstrated that, in addition to the explicit references to the Sea of Kinnereth and its immediate vicinity which one finds in the poem, one can properly understand the epic narrative only by an intimate knowledge of the geographical and historical characteristics of the area. In this way alone can the conduct of the *dramatis personae* as well as the poet's choice of word and motif be elucidated. The identification of *ablm* and *mrrt tǵll bnr*; the presence and activity of Sutean nomads; the itineraries of Danel and Pughat; the contents of the curses; the prominence of hunting elements—all these are predicated on the Kinnereth and Central Jordan Valley as the locale of the drama that is *Aqht*.

IV. Implications and Ramifications

1.1 The demonstration of a Kinnereth setting for the *Aqht* story has important consequences for a number of problems in Ugaritic and OT research. We cannot hope to explore here all these consequences fully and in detail. We shall restrict ourselves accordingly to examining a single, yet central, problem in the light of the foregoing discussion.

2.1 The problem of the Ugaritic *rpum* and its relation to that of the OT Rephaim has been much discussed in recent years.[82] A major impetus to this renewed interest was provided by the publication of new textual materials; first, and foremost, RS 24.252 in *Ugaritica* V,[83] and (albeit in preliminary form) RS 34.126.[84]

2.2 Text RS 24.252 (=KTU 1.108) describes a banquet-feast attended by the gods (Anat, *Kṯr-Ḫss*, El, presumably also Baal) in honour of a personage—*i.e.*, one bearing a proper-name—named *rpu*, designated (formulaically) *mlk* . *ᶜlm*. To this personage are attributed qualities of 'strength' (*ᶜz; lan*), 'protection' (*ḏmr*), and 'patronymity' (*ḥtk*). The text concludes with an invocation of this figure to confer the aforenamed qualities as eternal blessings on the city of Ugarit and, in accordance with the commonly accepted restoration,[85] the *r*[*pi* .] *arṣ*, an expression

[82] *Cf.* L'Heureux (1974) 265-74; de Moor (1976) 323-45; and Caquot (1976) 295-304.

[83] Virolleaud (1968) 551-57.

[84] Caquot (1975) 427-29. The text (in transliteration only) has since been republished in KTU (1.161). The two publications differ considerably from each other at several points, a circumstance which impedes effective use of the material. The *editio princeps* is scheduled for publication in the (much-delayed) *Ugaritica* VII.

[85] *Cf.* however the recent dissent by M. H. Pope (citing G. A. Tuttle) in Pope (1977b) 181.

previously known from the *Krt* epic (CTA 15) where it is found in (seemingly) synonymous parallelism with the phrase *qbṣ . dtn*.

2.3 In a study of RS 24.252 published in 1970,[86] the writer suggested a connection between the Ugaritic *rpi arṣ* and the OT tradition of a giant race of people called Rephaim reputed to have inhabited the Bashan region of Transjordania in the mid-second millennium B.C.E. (Gen 14). A 'remnant' (*ytr*) of this people was said to have engaged the Israelites in battle at the time of the Exodus (Nu 21:31ff., & parallels). The link between the Ugaritic and OT texts was based not on the linguistic affinity of Ug. *rpu(m)* and OT *r*^{e}*p̄a*ᵓ*îm*, but rather on the nearly verbatim parallel furnished by the Ugaritic text to a biblical phrase recurring with formulaic regularity in exclusive association with the giant Og (Deut 3:11), king of the Rephaim people defeated by the Israelites in the aforesaid battle.[87] The OT phrase *yošēḇ b*^{e}ᶜ*aštarôt u-ḇ*^{e}ᵓ*edre*ᶜ*i(y)*—Josh 12:4 & parallels—corresponds, and virtually reproduces, Ugaritic (*wyqr*) *il . yṯb . b*ᶜ*ṯtrt / il . ṯpṭ . bhdr*ᶜ*y* (or: *bi!dr*ᶜ*y*) "(While the '*gravitas*' [Hebrew *kāḇôd*] of) El was seated in Ashtaroth / El was enthroned in Edrei" found in Obv. 2-3 of the Ugaritic text. In addition to striking verbal similarities, both texts, be it noted, share the peculiar presupposition (remaining to be clarified) that a personage (human or divine) could be seated (or resident) in two distinct places at one and the same time.

2.4 Whatever the precise signification of the Ugaritic couplet in the immediate context,[88] one thing seems clear and beyond equivocation, *viz.*, that the *mise-en-scène* of the narrative as a whole is Transjordanian Bashan (mod Golan/Jaulan) in the vicinity of Ashtaroth and Edrei, the very same area designated in the Hebrew Bible (Deut 3:13) "Land of the Rephaim."[89]

2.5 Although accepted in some quarters, the 'Bashan hypothesis' was received mostly with reserve, in some cases even outright denial.[90]

[86]Margulis (Margalit) (1970) 292-304.

[87]If the etymology suggested for the name ᶜOg by C. Rabin [(1971) 251-54] is correct, *viz.*, ᶜOg = (modern) South Arabic *ǵg*, "man," then we have a further tie-in with the Ugaritic tradition, which designates the Bashan-dwelling Danel *mt rpi*, "man-of-*rpu*."

[88]In Margulis (Margalit) (1970), we ventured the thought that the phrase *wyqr il yṯb* . . . presages the OT notion of an enthroned (√*yšb*) *k*^{e}*ḇ̇ôd* YHWH. We cited Ps 29:9-10 . . . *k*^{e}*ḇôd YHWH lmbwl* (read *lmš!l* ?) *yšb / wyšb YHWH mlk l*ᶜ*lm* (*cf. mlk* ᶜ*lm* of RS 24.252, though probably in slightly different meaning. *Cf.* below).

[89]Whether or not the geographical term 'Bashan' covers the slopes overlooking the Sea of Kinnereth, it is at least clear that the kingdom of the Rephaim in Bashan included this area, stretching to the Hermon in the north, and to Gilead/Argob in the south (*cf.* Deut 3:3ff., Jos 12:5). It was only in the Early Iron Age, with the coming of the Aramaeans, that the eastern littoral of the sea acquired a separate identity as Geshur (2 Sam 3:3; 13:37; and Josh 12:5).

[90]Unqualified acceptance was expressed by Pope and Tigay (1971) 120, and more recently by Pardee (1976) 245, n. 101). Rainey (1974) 187 considered the proposal "really

No truly decisive arguments were made against the interpretation.[91] Nevertheless, it was necessary to concede to the critics the bizarre circumstance of a text, written in Ugaritic and excavated at Ras Shamra, dealing with a mythic ritual alleged to transpire in the Bashan, a region several hundred kilometers away and, to judge by the administrative documents, completely beyond the economic and political orbits of the city-state kingdom of Ugarit.[92]

2.5.1 To be sure, attention was drawn in the JBL discussion to Danel's stock epithet *mt rpi* and to his connections with the Rephaim-texts (CTA 20-2). Also noted was the blessing bestowed on King Keret by the gods in CTA 15:III, a blessing which seems to imply the hero's affiliation to a group designated *rpi . arṣ.*, the same group which appears as petitioner of *rpu* in RS 24.252. Mention was also made of the place-name *nù-r-pê*, appearing as no. 29 in the list of Thutmosis III, immediately following *ᶜa-s-tá-r-tu* / Ashtaroth, and apparently identical with Hellenistic (I Mac 5:37) Raphon (modern er-Rafeh). Finally, the joint blessing asked at the end of RS 24.252 (Vs. 9-12) for the city Ugarit and the same *rpi arṣ* led us to surmise that the latter are "identical with the ruling circles at Ugarit... (and) with some type of family relationship, most probably 'ancestor' or 'patriarch' " to the one designated *rpu*.[93]

2.6 With the publication of RS 34.126 in 1975 surmise became certainty. The text is a royal genealogy of the dynastic House of Ugarit set within the framework of a ritual of ancestor worship. At least two of the deceased mentioned in the text—*nqmd* and *ᶜmṯtmr*—are well-known historical figures.[94] Along with others as yet unidentified (or even read with certainty), they are designated alternately *rpim qdmym*, *rpi arṣ*, and *qbṣ ddn*, the latter obviously a variant of the *qbṣ dtn* employed in poetic

---

interesting," but advised "caution ... in all such interpretations. Similar reserve can be found in Caquot (1976) 300, and Astour (1975) 282-83. Among the dissenters, see especially Parker (1972) 37-38; Görg (1974b) 474-75; Görg (1974a) 11-18; and de Moor (1976) 326-27, 337-40. The 'converts' now include S. Ribichini and P. Xella, in *Rivista di Studi Fenici* 7 (1979) 154-56.

[91]We intend to deal with the various criticisms in a future study of RS 24.252. Suffice it to note two points here: (1) the interpretation of *ᶜṯtrt* and *h/i!drᶜy* as place names is assured the moment it is conceded (a) that **yṯb b-* cannot mean "sits beside ..." in Ugaritic; and (b) that *ᶜṯtrt* and *h/i!drᶜy* are in poetic parallelism. (2) In the Egyptian transcriptions of Canaanite toponyms, the signs *-iw-* can correspond to West Semitic [ʾi] or [ʾa], as well as to [ʾu] (private communication of Mlle. N. Shupak, *apud* Professor Polotsky). *Cf.* (e.g.) Eg. *ʾu-bi-la* = Ug./Heb. *ʾa-b(i)l* (Helck, *Bezichungen*[2] [1971]:127; Eg. *la-wi-ša* = Can. *la-i-ša* (Rainey, IOS 2:395).

[92]*Cf.* Klengel (1975) 201-220, esp. 206.

[93]Margulis (Margalit) (1970) 301. Note also the recurrence of Ashtaroth (*ᶜṯtrt*) elsewhere in the RS 24 texts, *viz.*, 24.244 (=KTU 1.100):41, first identified by Astour (1968) 21.

[94]de Moor (1976) 343, and Kitchen (1977) 131-41, esp. 140ff.; now also J. F. Healey, UF 10 (1978) 83-91.

parallelism with *rpi arṣ* in the aforementioned *Krt* text (CTA 15:III). The initial phrase, *rpim qdmym*, occurring here for the first time, indicates that all three phrases refer not merely to timeless shades in the Netherworld, but to heroes of a bygone age assumed by their offspring (real or imagined) to have borne the epithet *rpu*(*m*).

2.6.1 The phrase **rpum qdmym* also sheds important light on the epithet *mlk . ᶜlm* found in RS 24.252 in formulaic conjunction with the personage designated *rpu*. This epithet, or title, has hitherto been taken to mean "eternal king," an interpretation inspired by biblical usage (*e.g.*, Jer 10:10; Gen 21:33), and an important argument for equating *rpu* with one of the well-known members of the Ugaritic pantheon, especially El.[95] But in light of the phrase *rpim qdmym*, it seems more sensible to understand *mlk ᶜlm* as "king of yore," with the vocable *ᶜlm* construed as a sort of synonymous variant of *qdm*.[96]

2.7 The data furnished by RS 34.126 also strengthen the case of those who argue that the blessing bestowed on Keret in CTA 15:III necessarily refers to *Krt*'s eminence among the living beings with whom he shared the affiliation of *rpi arṣ / qbṣ dtn* (in contradistinction to the *deceased rpi arṣ* who have become *rpum/ilnym*).[97] The designation *dtn* (or *ddn*)—known for some time to be a proper-name in the Amorite genealogies of Ḫammurapi of Babylon and Šamši-Adad I of Assyria[98]—points of course in the same direction. Combining the evidence of RS 34.126 and the Akkadian materials—both, interestingly enough, sharing a common '*Sitz-im-Leben*' as part of the cult of ancestor worship (Akkadian *kispu*)[99]—it is surely clear that Ditānu/Didānu is the ancestor—real or eponymous—of a West-Semitic tribal union (*qbṣ*) bearing his name. By the same token, the personage designated *rpu*/Rapiʾu stands in the relation of ancestor or patron—defined as *ḥtk* in RS 24.252—to a social or ethnic group known as *rpum/rpi arṣ*.[100]

[95]*Cf.* Parker (1970) 97-104, esp. 101-2; Cross (1973) 20-22; and de Moor (1976) 325-26.

[96]For *ᶜlm* and *qdm* as *membra synonyma* in OT poetry, *cf.*, *e.g.*, Mic 5:1; Mal 3:4; and Ps 77:6. *Cf.* already Caquot (1976) 299.

[97]*Cf.* L'Heureux (1974) 21; Margalit (1976) 182, n. 129; and de Moor (1976) 323ff. Contrast Astour (1975) section VIII 35; now also Pope (1977b) 167; Lipinski (1978) 97-98. The primary evidence for the *rpi arṣ* as (essentially) living beings (secondarily, deceased heroes) is still RS 24.252. It makes little sense for the *rpi arṣ* to invoke or receive the blessings of the deceased ancestor *rpu* if both are no longer among the living. *Cf.* now Healey (*loc. cit.* n. 94).

[98]Finkelstein (1966) 95-118; Lambert (1968) 1-2; Malamat (1968) 163-73; and Kitchen (1977) 141-42.

[99]*Cf.* de Moor (1976) 333, n. 72, and Lipinski (1978) 91ff.

[100]According to Kitchen (1977) 142, Didānu/Ditānu was "an early old-West Semitic princely ancestor in early Assyria *c.* 2160." However, both Kitchen and de Moor [(1976) 333, n. 72] fail to realize that what is true of Ditānu is necessarily true of *rpu*(*m*)!. This failure on de Moor's part leads him to some quite fantastic hypotheses, including the

2.8 What can we say about the nature of the human group known as *rpum / rpi arṣ*?

2.8.1 If the theory of M. Heltzer,[101] equating the *rpum*/Rephaim with the West-Semitic tribe of the "Rabbeans" known from Mari, should prove correct, then the question is easily answered: the *rpu* of RS 24.252 (and perhaps in Danel's stock epithet *mt rpi*)[102] would be an eponymous ancestor analogous to *dtn*/Ditānu. The two groups, Ditanites and Rabbeans/*rpum*, originally separate clans or tribes, would on this assumption have joined ranks to form the tribal union called *qbṣ . dtn*, similar presumably to the process whereby the 'sons of Abraham-Isaac' coalesced with the 'sons of Jacob-Israel' (itself a composite) to form the tribal confederation known as "(sons of) Israel."[103]

2.8.2 But there is another possibility, one which emerges from considering the Ugaritic text RS 24.272 (= KTU 1.124). The subject of this fragmentary and obscure text is an exchange between a personage designated *Dtn*, and a deity—probably El—referred to as "chief of the great gods" (*adn . ilm . rbm*). A proper understanding of this exchange still eludes us; nevertheless, the writer agrees with the conclusion reached by A. Caquot, that "*Dtn* joue un . . . role d'entremetteur entre celui qui l'a consulté . . . et un dieu qui connait et fixe les destins."[104]

2.8.3 What makes this characterization of the role of *Dtn* so interesting for us is that it comports well with the role of *rpu* in RS 24.252. The latter, as noted above, depicts the "great gods"—including El—at a banquet in honour of *rpu*. The human participants in this mythic-ritual affair are the *rpi arṣ*. The poet describes, to be sure, the wining and dining activities of the gods; but it is to *rpu*, presumably *qua* mediator between the *rpi arṣ* and the "great gods," that he addresses the petition for blessing and strength.

2.8.4 If this surmise is correct, then it seems not unlikely that the one designated *rpu* in RS 24.252, and the one called *dtn* in RS 24.272, are *one and the same*.[105] Supporting this inference would be the poetic

---

concoction of a NWS inscription allegedly misinterpreted by Israelite scribes (whose knowledge of Canaanite was presumably inferior to that of the 20th century Semitist . . .).

[101]Heltzer (1978b) 5-20. For further on the Rabbeans, see Astour (1978).

[102]There exists a possibility that *rpu* here is the toponym (*nù-*)*r-pê* (above, 2.5.1), in parallelism with *hrnmy*.

[103]*Cf.* Noth (1960) 124-27, and de Vaux (1971) 162, 167, 595.

[104]Caquot (1978) 1-6. Quotation from p. 3. *Cf.* already Caquot (1975) 429.

[105]The root √*rp*ᵓ means basically "heal, mend, repair" (certainly not "save"!). It seems unlikely that this is relevant for understanding *rpi arṣ* (*cf.* CTA 22:B:8-9 where *rpu* = (apparently) *mhr*. However, over time, and in the cultic context of ancestor worship, a secondary connotation of *rpu* = "mediator," deriving from √*rp*ᵓ, "heal," may have developed.

parallelism *rpi arṣ / qbṣ . dtn/ddn* in both CTA 15 and RS 34.126.[106] The expression *rpi arṣ* may have been a more specialized and/or honorific designation of the 'group of *Dtn*.'

2.9 In sum: the missing link between Ugarit and the Bashan is the evidence for the Raphaite/Rephaim origins of the dynasty founded around 1900 B.C. at Ugarit by a certain Yaqarum (= *mt . rpi* ?).[107] The Ugaritic Raphaites took with them—or in the course of time, received—the literary heirlooms of their brethren in Transjordania, including the epic tale of a Raphaite family residing on the lower Bashan/Golan Heights overlooking the Sea of Kinnereth, whose one-and-only son and divinely-ordained heir fell victim to the jealousy of a goddess and the treachery of neighboring Sutean nomads.

2.9.1 Despite their physical separation from the Bashan homeland, the Raphaites of Ugarit did not forget their origins, which they commemorated in prayer and ceremony. Attesting this devotion to the ancestral homeland is text RS 24.252. It need not be assumed that, for the purpose of *mrzḥ* (or *mrz*ᶜ)—the probable technical designation of the banquet-scene (RS 24.258:15)—and the related necromantic cult associated with ancestor worship (CTA 17:I:27-9; RS 34.126), the ruling Raphaite families of Ugarit betook themselves to the shores of the Kinnereth and the Bashan Heights. What we have in RS 24.252 is ritual make-believe: the participants reenact and relive the traditional anniversary of their ancestor's departure as if they themselves were still living in the Bashan region (as their brethren were as late as the 13th cent. B.C.E.).

2.10 The city of Ugarit vanished from the historical arena virtually overnight. At about the same time, the bastion of "Raphaite culture" in Transjordania was crumbling under the onslaught of new ethnic elements: Israelites, Ammonites, and Arameans. By the 12th-11th century, the Raphaites were but a memory. Their name and fame as men-of-arms lingered briefly on among sects of professional warriors specializing, it would appear, in the art of single-combat, and known as "offspring (Ugaritic *ḥtk*)[108] of the Rapha" (Hebrew *yᵉlîdê ha-rap̄a*ᵓ).[109] But the

[106]If the equation *dtn* = *rpu* proves correct, then the title *mlk* ᶜ*lm* applied to *rpu* in RS 24.252 might be considered an Ugaritic reflex of the old-Assyrian tradition about "kings who dwelt in tents." Healey (*loc. cit.* n. 94) has pointed out the affinity of the *MLKM/ma-li-kū* (RS 20.24 = *Ug*. V, 42-64) and the *rpum*.

[107]*Cf.* Kitchen (1977) 138. In the latest reports from the excavations at Ras Ibn Hani (CRAIBL, Jan.-Apr. 1978, 45-65; and UF 9 344) we are informed of a tablet (IH 77/21 B) wherein appears "le Rephaite Iaqar" [see also Bordreuil in this volume, p. 46-47, ed.]. Even if this should prove to be a different Yaqaru(m), as is most likely the case, this new piece of documentary evidence would be the first direct witness to the epithet *rpu* in relation to a (once-living) being.

[108]In Ugaritic, *ḥ-t-k* can mean either "sire" or "offspring," the differentiation probably made on the basis of different vocalic patterns. It thus seems to be by no means

memory of the Raphaites survived more lastingly in the cult of ancestor-worship: the word *rp*ʾ(*y*)*m* came to be synonymous, in Phoenician-Punic as well as in Hebrew, with the "shades" of the dead (Latin *manes*) generally, much as the head of the Amorite pantheon, El/Ilu, was destined to become a generic term for "deity."

3.1 The foregoing synthesis and reconstruction, if acceptable, take us a considerable way towards resolving what is perhaps the number-one crux posed by the Ugaritic literature, the poetry in particular: its unparalleled, at times even uncanny, resemblance to the (poetic) literature of the OT, especially in matters of structural form, poetic technique, and diction.

3.1.1 For the city of Ugarit receives no mention in the Hebrew Bible. It ceased to exist on the eve of Israel's birth as a nation. No patriarch ever came within 200 kms. of its city limits, as far as we can tell from the biblical account. During the last two hundred years of Ugarit's existence, most of the motley tribes destined to constitute the nation of Israel were living in servitude along the shores of the Nile. From the Ugaritic side, it is known that the city was never a part of the geographic entity called 'Canaan'; indeed, there is evidence to indicate that 'Canaanites'—*i.e.*, Phoenicians—were considered aliens in Ugarit.[110] Finally, there are reputable scholars who, on purely linguistic grounds, deny the label "Canaanite" to the Ugaritic language.[111] In short: there is a seemingly unbridgeable gap, both in time and in space, between Jerusalem and Ugarit alongside—as Cassuto and others have long recognized—a fundamental continuity in their respective literatures.

3.2 A Kinnereth background, and Raphaite-Bashan origin, for at least part of the Ugaritic literary corpus brings the latter into the heart of Canaan, at the very door-step of Jerusalem. For the area in question figures prominently both in the historical consciousness as well as on the geographical horizons of the Hebrew Bible. The patriarchs in particular are very much at home in Transjordania, and precisely at the time when the Raphaites/Rephaim are creating their poetic masterpieces.[112] And what the Hebrew patriarchs may have missed of this lore, their tribal "offspring" (Menasseh, Naphtali, and Gad in particular)

improbable that the Hebrew expression reflects an earlier Canaanite **ḥtk*(*y*) *rpi*. The *rpu* would be *ḥtk*, "father," and the devotees *ḥtk*, "offspring" (*cf.* RS 24.252).

[109] *Cf.* Margulis (Margalit) (1970) 300, and L'Heureux (1976) 83-86. To the OT data should be added the description of the *Retenu* champion in the Sinuhe story (ANET^2 20), pointing to a tradition of a thousand years.

[110] *Cf.* Rainey (1963) 43-45.

[111] *Cf.* Goetze (1941) 127-38; Friedrich (1949) 220-23; Blau, "On Problems of Polyphony and Archaism in Ugaritic Spelling," JAOS 88 (1968) 526.

[112] *Cf.* Noth (1948) 95ff., and de Vaux (1971) 165-69.

would presumably have been able to obtain some three or four centuries later. The same is likely true of the other Late-Bronze and Early-Iron settlers in the area (Ammonites and Arameans in particular).

3.2.1 Thus it may not be mere coincidence that, of all the major poetic compositions discovered at Ugarit, it is the story of *Aqht* which bears the closest affinities with the OT, whether it be the patriarchal bearing of the hero Danel as he receives the divine guest Kothar-Ḫasis for dinner (CTA 17:V; cp. Gen 18); or the theme of the well-to-do hero who lacks for nothing but a son-and-heir (a motif common to the *Krt* story as well); or the near verbatim phraseological parallels (*e.g.*, CTA 19:I:44ff = 2 Sam 2:21); or the explicit mention of Danel in the biblical corpus (Ezek 14:14, 20).

V. Conclusion

1.1 The hypothesis of a Kinnereth background for the Ugaritic epic literature was born early in the history of Ugaritic research, but it was a case of the wrong evidence culled from the wrong epic (de Vaux).[113] The attempt by Barton to demonstrate a Galilean background for *Aqht* was either ignored or dismissed as worthless fantasy by burgeoning Ugaritology.[114] In truth, there was much more chaff than grain in Barton's exposition. Ullendorff's short but important note in the early 60s was a call in the desert, lost in the winds of reaction to the historical and geographical hypotheses of an earlier era.

1.1.1 One is left to muse, how like the Jordan, runs the course of history, full of ironic twists and turns. . . .

[113]Nevertheless, the geographical background of the *Krt* epic remains, in our opinion, an open question. Khirbet ed-Damiyeh is still a contender (among others!) for identification with Udm, and if Astour's critique [(1974) 29ff.] of the Tyre-Sidon identifications in *Krt* is sound, then one may wish to consider the possibility of interpreting *ilt ṣrm / ṣdynm* in light of Josh 19:35! One notes, further, the explicit reference to Lake Semachonitis (Ḥuleh) adjacent to the Kinnereth and the Golan Heights, in CTA 10:II:9. (In III:12-13 restore perhaps *bǵ*[*r. lbnn*] . . . *bš*[*ryn*]. Cf. our forthcoming contribution in JNSL VIII [1980]).

[114]Mlle. Herdner, in her review of de Langhe (1945) [Herdner (1946) 131-38], refers to Barton's "hypotheses fantaistes," adding, "rien ne permet de supposer que *knrt* . . . *mgdl* . . . sont des noms propres" (135). For de Langhe's critique, *cf.* his (1945), vol. II 168ff. As noted above, de Vaux ignored Barton's contribution in renouncing his own adherence to the Kinnereth hypothesis [(1957)] 313-14. Ullendorf (1962) appears to have been unaware of Barton; and Astour of Ullendorff!

THE CULT OF THE DEAD AT UGARIT

MARVIN H. POPE

Yale University

This discourse will concentrate on two terms crucial for appreciation of the cult of the dead at Ugarit, the terms *rpum* and *mrzḥ*. Before turning attention to the aforementioned vocables, it may be expedient to consider summarily other evidences bearing on death.

It was the accidental discovery of a richly appointed tomb that led to the excavation of Ras Shamra and the recovery of the civilization, literature, and art of Ugarit. Under residential houses at Ugarit were well-built family vaults provided with installations for supplying the needs of the dead.[1] The care and feeding of the departed was here as elsewhere a major concern of the living and this responsibility fell mainly on the elder son who was called in Akkadian *pāqid* or *sāḫir*, "caretaker," *nāq mē*, "water-pourer," and *zākir šumi*, "name-caller."[2]

From the Ugaritic Epic concerning Aqhat we learn some of the duties of a son toward his father, living or dead, and the crucial importance of having a son. The hero Danel has no son and seeks divine aid through incubation rites. Baal answers the suppliant and intercedes with El who revives Danel's "soul" (*npš*)[3] so that he is able to sire the desired heir. The duties of the son are four times repeated with minor variations and it will suffice to give here a conflation of the lists in Danel's grateful response to the blessed birth:

[1]Cf. Schaeffer (1952) 49-56. Sukenik (1940) 59-65.

[2]Cf. Bayliss (1973) 115-25, and in particular pp. 116f. on the duty of the *pāqidu* to call the name of the deceased and pour water.

[3]The primitive sense of *napš* was apparently throat and thence developed a variety of senses subsumed under the sense "soul" as including all the life forces, not least the sexual urge. The sexual meaning of *nepeš* is patent in Prov 19:2, as recognized by Dahood (1962) 71.

In Sufi philosophy *nafs* was applied to the carnal instincts which the mystic sought to escape.

I will return and rest,
And my soul will repose in my breast,
For a son is born me like my brothers,
A root like my kindred,
One who will set up my ancestral stela,
In the sanctuary will supply thyme[4] to me,
To Earth send forth my spice,[5]
To the Dust sing toward me,
Counter insults of my enemies,
Repulse him who acts against me,
Hold my hand when I'm drunk,
Lift me when sated with wine,
Eat my piece in the house of Baal,
My portion in the house of El,
Smear my roof on a mud day,
Wash my clothes on a filth day.

[17(2 AQHT)1.12-23]

This list of filial duties presents a strange mixture of cultic and menial services.[6] We will emphasize those relating to mortuary matters, but in actuality all are so related through the obligations of son to father both in life and death. The phrase rendered "my ancestral stela" (*skn iliby*) is

[4]Thyme. This translation of the hapax legomenon *ztr* is conjecture based on the assumption of approximate synonymous parallelism with the following line which refers to *qṭr*, incense or spice. Appeal is made to Akkadian *zatēru*, Arabic *za^{c}tar*, "thyme," for a possible cognate; cf. Pope (1977b) 164. For a catalogue of other interpretations of the word, "summon," "genie," "enshrines," "inscription," "votive (sun) disk," cf. Healey (1979) 355. Healey himself surmises that the word may mean "protect, care for, honour" or possibly "invoke," following the Akkadian model of invoking the names of the dead. The form *ztr*, Healey suggests, n. 26, might be remotely connected with *ḏkr-zkr*, "mention, remember."

[5]References to incense in religious rites are too numerous to assemble. One biblical example may suffice, Isa 65:3b-4, the context being prophetic condemnation of funeral feasts:

Sacrificing in the gardens,
Burning incense on bricks,
Sitting in the tombs,
Spending the night in crypts,
Eating pig meat,
Carrion broth in their vessels.

The reading of the Qumran Isaiah scroll differs drastically from the Masoretic Text in verse 3d. The Qumran reading *wynqw ydym ^{c}l hbnym* is puzzling and difficult to correlate with the received text.

[6]The roof repair and laundry seem especially unlikely as cultic duties, unless the roof to be plastered belonged to a structure associated with the tomb and/or the funeral feast. The need for laundry might be occasioned by the orgiastic character of the celebration. Sumerian texts from Lagash dealing with the cult of the dead mention a certain "Saggalube the washer" and it may be that the funeral feast required postprandial clean-up operations. Cf. Bauer (1969) 107-14, and in particular p. 110, n. 8.

difficult because of the uncertainty of the exact meaning of the term *ilib*,[7] but the verb *nṣb* is related to the notorious *maṣṣēḇôṯ* of the Old Testament and the Arabic *naṣb*, 'idol,' 'statue' ('grave stone'). Whether the "soul" of the deceased was believed to be present in the grave is moot, but the grave marker, whether a crude stone or lifelike portrait, was apparently regarded as embodying or representing the person of the departed. It has been alleged that *npš* may designate the tomb in Ugaritic, but wrongly.[8] Nevertheless the term did later become a designation of the memorial stela or funerary monument, indicating that the stone itself was regarded as the essence or "soul" of the person, recalling Philo of Byblos' reference to "animated stones," *lithoi empsychoi*.

There is no reference in the passage cited above to pouring water or calling/ remembering the name of the dead, but the supplying of spice and incense which is mentioned was an important part of funerary offerings. Transmission of liquids into the grave through conduits or pipes was presumably common in Mesopotamian mortuary rites since there is a special term for the pipe or conduit, *arūtu*,[9] used for this purpose. Despite Jewish efforts to abolish or reform ancient rites regarded as idolatrous, the piping of wine and oil into the tomb is attested on the occasion of the visit of Rabban Gamliel's sons Judah and Hillel to the grave of Zakkai at Kabul (this Zakkai apparently liked wine and his mother bequeathed him 300 kegs and he left 3000 for his children). The Talmudic tractate on mourning condones this piping of wine to the dead and scouts the allegation that it smacks of the "ways of the Amorite."[10]

Singing to the dead is attested in Akkadian, but it may be that *ḏmr*[11] does not refer to singing but to protecting the grave and corpse against depredation. The following four lines referring to the protection of the father from insult and hostile acts and holding his hand or carrying him when drunk presumably apply to services during life.[12] One thinks of the

[7]For summary discussion of the problems and interpretations of Ugaritic *ilib*, cf. Margalit (1976) 145f.

[8]Cf. Pope (1978) 25-31.

[9]Cf. CAD, A/II, 324b, s.v. *arūtu*. The sun-god Šamaš in the netherworld is the caretaker (*pāqidu*) of the *arūtu* through which the deceased drinks. Accordingly a curse on the corpse asks that Šamaš never let his (the ghost's) pipe receive cool water below.

[10]Cf. Zlotnich (1966) 58 and 136.

[11]Cf. CAD Z s.v. *zumāru*, 154b: "the king makes food portions for the Lisikūtu-spirits (possibly ancestral spirits) (while) the singer sings (the song indicated), when he (the singer) has reached the refrain, he (the king) throws (the pieces of meat) into the opening (of a conduit through which previously, . . . blood, honey, oil, beer and wine were poured)."

[12]Mother, too, would need help when in her cups. Jerusalem forsaken is depicted as a besotted mother—drunk, however, with the cup of the Lord's wrath—with none to hold her hand of all the children she has borne and reared, Isaiah 51:17-18.

dereliction of Noah's son Ham in this duty.[13] In the *mrzḥ* it was apparently obligatory to drink beyond mere inebriation, to delirium and oblivion. The eating of the deceased's "piece" or "portion" in the house of Baal or El presumably refers to representation of the deceased by his son in sacrificial meals, but it is not excluded that the piece or portion eaten may be that of the dead since the eating of the dead in what anthropologists call "morbid affection" persists to this day.[14] There is a Ugaritic mythological fragment which relates that the goddess Anat ate her brother's flesh without a knife and drank his blood without a cup because he was beautiful. Whether her brother (Baal) was alive or dead we are not told.[15] The references to roof repair and laundry would seem mundane and menial chores, but they could be cultic in connection with funerary praxis.

The notion of immortality for a mortal is broached once in the Ugaritic poems and summarily dismissed.[16] When the goddess Anat attempted to get the coveted composite bow from the young hero Aqhat, she offered him immortality (*blmt*, non death) and the high life of the gods:

Ask life, O Hero Aqhat,
Ask life and I will give it,
Immortality and I will bestow it.
I will make you count years with Baal,
With El's sons you will count months.
Like Baal, when he revives, prepares,
Revives, prepares, and serves him drink.
One sings and chants before him
Sweetly [and they] respond.
So will I revive Aqhat the hero.

[17(2 AQHT)6.26-33]

To which Aqhat replied:

Don't lie to me, O Virgin.
To a hero your lies are rot.

[13]Cf. Cohen (1974).

[14]A few years ago the Nobel Prize in medicine was awarded for research sparked by the circumstance that the Fore tribe of New Guinea still eat their dead and rub themselves with their juices, frequently resulting in viral infection. Study of this problem led to discoveries useful in treating infectious hepatitis.

[15]Astour (1965a) 180, related Anat's cannibalism to the raw flesh feasts of the Dionysiac and Orphic orgies.

[16]For the bearing of this passage on the effort to date the Book of Job on the basis of the history of the idea of immortality, cf. Pope (1966b) 527f.

Man, what fate gets he?
What lot gets a mortal?
Glaze they will pour on my head,
Lime on top of my pate.
The common death I'll die.
I will surely die.

[17(2 AQHT)6.34-39]

When one dies, the soul (*npš*)[17] goes out from the nostrils like a breeze or vapor. Anat gave instructions to her henchman for the murder of Aqhat:

I will put you like an eagle in my girdle,
Like a falcon in my sheath,
Aqhat, when he sits to eat,
Danel's son to dine,
Over him eagles will hover,
A flock of falcons watch.
Among the eagles I'll hover.
Over Aqhat I'll release you.
Strike him twice on the pate,
Thrice over the ear.
Pour out blood like a hunter(?),
Like a butcher to his knees.
Let his soul go forth like a wind,
Like a breeze his spirit,
Like vapor from his nostril.

[18(3 AQHT)4.17-26]

The next line *bap mp!rh ank laḥwy* is difficult. The phrase *bap mhrh*, "from the nostrils of his/her warrior(s)" yields little sense. Whether the following clause *ank laḥwy* means "I will revive (him)" or "I will not revive (him)" is an important issue, but impossible to decide.

The problem of mortality or immortality of an ailing king who, as a son of El, is divine confronts us in the Keret Epic. Keret's son weeps as he addresses his sick sire:

In your life, our father, we rejoice(d)
In your immortality we exult(ed).

[16.2(125)98-99]

[17]The regular synonym of *npš* is *brlt* which has long eluded efforts to find an etymology or cognate. Cf., e.g., the proposal to connect the word with Akkadian *erēšu*, "desire," from *mērištu* > *mēriltu* with change of *m* to *b*, Cutler, *et al.* (1973) 67. The present writer has proposed (in a note to appear in Ugarit-Forschungen) connection with Arabic *bur(ʾ)ula-t* applied to the neck-feathers (*ʿufra-t*) of male birds when excited, analogous to the primitive sense of *napš* as "throat."

He goes on to say:

Shall gods die?
Progeny of the Beneficent One not live?

[16.2(125)105-6]

According to W. G. Lambert,[18] "The gods could not die in Sumero-Babylonian thought in the sense of getting old and eventually dying of natural causes. But they could die a violent death. There are three kinds of causes for divine deaths. Younger gods could kill off the old in a succession struggle, or rebels could be made to pay the ultimate penalty, or in monster-slaying the distinction between dragon and god could be blurred so that here too a god could die." Two of these causes of divine death are well attested at Ugarit. The question whether the senior god is displaced by a junior (El and Baal) is disputed.[19]

Another mooted matter is whether old gods, like men, were thought to suffer senility and loss of sexual power. On this there are two opinions.[20]

The gods are not immune or insensitive to death (though they have superhuman recuperative powers) and they mourn for one another in human fashion. When it was reported to El,

"Mighty Baal is dead,
Perished the Prince, Lord of Earth,"

Then beneficent El, benign,
Descended from the throne, sat on the footstool,
From footstool he sat on the ground.
He strewed straw of mourning on his head,
Dust of wallowing on his pate.
For clothing he donned loincloth.
Skin with stone he scraped,
Flint (he used) for rasp,
Plucked cheek and chin,
Harrowed upper arm,
Ploughed like a garden (his) chest,
Like a valley harrowed his body.
He lifted his voice and cried:
"Baal is dead! What of the people?
Dagan's Son! What of the multitudes?"

[5(67)6.9-24]

[18]Lambert (1980) 64.

[19]Cf. L'Heureux (1979).

[20]Cf. Pope (1955) 35-42, "El as Bull; His Marital Relations." Van Selms (1954). Løkkegaard (1953) 219-23. Cross (1973) 20-24. Oldenburg (1969). L'Heureux (1979). Pope (1979) 705ff.

Baal's sister/consort Anat similarly lacerated herself, spoke of going down to the netherworld after Baal, drank tears like wine. She took Baal's body on her back up to his mountain and buried him with a series of sacrifices of seventy beasts at a time [6(62)1.1-29].

The opposition between Baal and Mot has to be viewed in the light of the climate of Syria-Palestine and the crucial importance of the rain.[21] Baal as the god of the rain represents life and fertility and his foe Mot or Death the opposite. In the ritual portion of the poem called the Birth of the Beautiful Gods it is said:

Mot the Prince sits,[22]
In his hand the scepter of bereavement,
In his hand the scepter of widowhood.
The vine pruners prune him,
The vine binders bind him,
They fell his vintage like a vine.[23]

[23(52)8-11]

It appears that Prince Death is here subjected to pruning, binding, and felling under viticultural figures. The pruning and felling of the god reminds one of the Ndembu ritual wounding and killing of the god Kavula by chopping a cassava root.[24]

In another act of mayhem on Mot the goddess Anat puts him through the mill as cereal when he failed to deliver Baal whom he had mangled.

She seizes divine Mot,
With sword she cleaves him,
With sieve she sifts him,
With fire she burns him,
With millstones she grinds him,
In the field she scatters him.
His flesh the birds eat,
His parts the sparrows consume.
Flesh to flesh cries.

[6(49)2.30-37]

This reaping, sifting, burning, grinding, and sowing of Mot as if he were grain, and the subsequent resurrection of Baal with return of fertility to earth, has been related to a variety of myths and rituals in the

[21] Cf. de Moor (1971).

[22] Cf. Tsumura (1974) 407-13. On the term *šdmt* here rendered "vintage" cf. p. 412.

[23] Cf. Kosmala (1964) 147-51.

[24] Turner (1975), especially Chapter 3, "Some White Symbols in Literature and Religion."

ancient Near East and elsewhere,[25] to the Seth-Horus-Osiris myth of Egypt, the Adonis-Attis myth of Syria, the Mesopotamian myths of Nergal-Ereshkigal-Enmešarra, Dumuzi/Tammuz, the Hittite-Hurrian myths of Teshub and Telepinu, and the Greek myth of Pluto-Demeter-Kore. Particular attention has been called to the treatment of Tammuz in the grain ritual of the Sabaeans of Harrân and the cereal offering briefly prescribed in Leviticus 2:14-16 (crushed new grain parched and burnt as a memorial fire offering) and described in little more detail by Philo[26] and Josephus[27] and in the Mishnah.[28] Striking comparison is also made with the East and Central European rite of Spring in which an effigy of Death is carried out of town and demolished, but the remains distributed and believed to have fecundating powers.[29]

Whether Mot was a god of fertility as well as of sterility and death in the Ugaritic mythological poems remains moot. The immediate sequel to Anat's reaping, threshing, and sowing of Mot as grain was Baal's return to life signaled by the restoration of fertility to earth. The death of Death brings Baal to life. The rabbis drew a parallel between the grain of wheat (which is buried naked, stripped of its garments, and emerges clothed in its husk) and the resurrection of the righteous in their own clothes (Ketubbot IIIb). Similarly the death and resurrection of Jesus in John 12:24 is related to the sprouting of wheat. "Unless a grain of wheat falls into the ground and dies, it remains alone; but if it dies, it bears much fruit." This view of the bond of life and death in the processes of nature lies at the heart of so-called fertility religions, especially the cult of Baal in Syria-Palestine and of Osiris in Egypt.

There is a passage in the Baal-Mot cycle which may be, and has been, taken to mean that Mot considers himself a competitor with Baal not simply as destroyer but as life-giver. When Baal had built his house on Mount Ṣapān, he turned his thoughts to his arch enemy and rival, Mot, imagining that:

> Mot says to himself,
> The Beloved communes within:
> 'I alone am he who rules over the gods,
> Who fattens gods and men,
> Who satisfies the multitudes of earth.'
>
> [4(51)7.47-52]

The verb here rendered "fatten" (*ymru*) might mean "command," as parallel to *mlk* ᶜ*l* "be king over," but it might also be in synonymous

[25] Jacobs and Jacobs (1945) 77-109; Worden (1953) 273-97; Gray (1965) 68ff.

[26] De Septenario II, 20.

[27] Antiquities III, 250 (Whiston's Translation) Book III, Chap. X.5.

[28] Menahoth X, 3-4.

[29] Frazer, *The Golden Bough*, one-volume ed., 351, 357-72. Cf. Astour (1980) 231, n. 42.

parallelism with *yšb*ᶜ, "satisfy, sate," of the following line. Unfortunately, there is no sure way to determine which possibility was intended.

Both Baal and Mot die and come back to life. Just how Mot manages to accumulate himself after being dismembered by Anat, we are not told. After Mot receives Baal's gloating message about the building of his house, Mot sends back Baal's messengers with a striking communiqué of his own in which he speaks of his voracious appetite, complains of short rations, and invites Baal to a banquet in which he (Baal) is to be both guest and pièce de résistance. The proximate cause of Mot's desire to devour Baal appears to be the charge that Baal's smiting of *ltn* (=Leviathan) occasioned the deterioration of the heavens:[30]

Message of divine Mot,
Word of the Beloved {son} of El, the Hero:
"My craving is the lions' in the desert,
The appetite of the dolphin in the sea,
Buffalo (that) rush to the pond,
Hinds that haste to the fountain,
How long will my gullet lack red/mud?
When with both my hands will I eat?
My seven portions in a bowl,
A river mixed as a cup?
We invite Baal with my brothers,
We call Hadd with my kin.
'Eat with my brothers food,
Drink with my kin wine.'
Let us drink, O Baal;
I will surely pierce you."

[5(67)1.12-26]

There is a broken line with only three legible letters, and the text continues fragmentary for several more lines, but enough is preserved to show that the first eight lines of the column rehearsing the latter part of Mot's message, are repeated by the messengers:

Since you smote Leviathan, the swift serpent,
The slant one with seven heads,
The heavens withered and drooped.
The tripe of your torso I'll eat
In ruddy two-ell bites.

[30]This passage remains troublesome and consensus with respect to details has not yet been reached. For divergent interpretations cf. Pope (1966a) 236f.; Emerton (1972), 50-71; Emerton (1978) 73-77; Pope (1978) 25-31. It is generally recognized that Mot here speaks of his hunger and thirst in terms reminiscent of Psalm 42:1-2; Margalit (1980) 87-106, differs radically from all other interpretations in viewing the speech as addressed by Baal to Mot.

You will go down the throat of divine Mot,
Into the gullet of El's Beloved Hero.

[5(67)1.1-9, 27-35]

The insatiable appetite of Death and Hell is a common poetic theme, as in Isaiah 5:14. Mot's epithet, Beloved of El, or sometimes just plain Beloved, is presumably antiphrastic since pure affection for death is rare. Invitation to dinner is generally a friendly gesture, but hardly so when the guest is also the menu. The actual smiting of Leviathan (projected for future agenda by Yahweh in Isaiah 27:1) is not related in extant Ugaritic poems. Moreover, that accomplishment is claimed by Anat among her boasts of doughty deeds done in defense of her consort.[31] The demolition of the heavens is a feature of the day of divine wrath (Isaiah 13:13, 34:4; Haggai 2:6; 2 Peter 3:12). The implication that Baal is somehow responsible for the celestial withering evokes the cliché used to describe the situation that obtains while Baal is dead and Mot is in the ascendancy. Translations and interpretations vary, as with many crucial Ugaritic passages, but the following rendering seems most reasonable:

The Lamp of the Gods, Šapš,
The glowing orb of Sky,
Is in the power of divine Mot.

[3(ᶜNT VI)5.25-26; 4(51)8.21-25; 6(49)2.24-25]

In the dry season of Syria-Palestine one may well imagine that the Rain-god is defunct and that sun and sky are under control of Death.

Baal's response to Mot's invitation is abject fear and submission:

Welcome, O divine Mot!
Your slave am I forever.

[5(67)2.11, 19]

Baal had given his divine errand boys, Gapn and Ugar, instructions for going to the Netherworld to deliver a message to Mot, whose abode's entry was blocked by twin mountains with strange names, apparently non-Semitic. These mountains have to be lifted (like plugs or lids) in order to gain access to the netherworld below.

Then set face
Toward Mount *trǵzz*,
Toward Mount *ṯrmg*,
Toward the (twin) mounds that plug Earth.
Raise the mountain on the hands,
The hill on top of the palms,

[31]Cf. Ginsberg (1941) 12-14.

And descend to the infernal "freedom" house,
Be counted among those who descend into Earth.
[4(51)8.1-9]

After the initial entry, there is still a way to go before reaching Mot's infernal, watery see:[32]

Then set face
Toward his city Slushy.
Low the throne he sits on,
Infernal filth his heritage.
[4(51)8.10-14]

The messengers are warned to keep a safe distance between themselves and Mot:

Beware, divine lackeys!
Do not get near divine Mot,
Lest he make you like a lamb in his mouth,
Like a kid in the breach of his gullet you be lost.
[4(54)8.14-20]

There follows the cliché depicting the glowing sun as subject to the power of Death, and then the messengers are advised to do their obeisance from a distance of a thousand fields, a myriad acres and then deliver their message, presumably without getting closer. The soggy state of Mot's city (*qrt*) is suggested by the appellation "Slushy" (*hmry*). A cognate form *mhmrt* is applied to Mot's moist gullet which Baal must descend. The same word is used in Psalm 140:11 of (slimy) pits impossible to escape.[33]

We turn now to the crucial terms *rpum* and *mrzḥ*, both long known from the Bible, rabbinic literature, and North Semitic inscriptions. It was recognized from the first that the Rephaim of the Old Testament are the dead, their spirits or ghosts, as is clear from the poetic parallelism in Isaiah 26:14 and Psalm 88:11. The abode of the Rephaim is the netherworld (Proverbs 9:18). Tabnit, king of Sidon, curses the prospective despoiler of his tomb thus: "Let there be no . . . resting place for you with the Rephaim" (KAI 13:7-8). King Eshmunazar adds to a similar curse against grave robbers, "and may they not be buried in a grave" (KAI 14:8). A neo-Punic-Latin bilingual tomb inscription renders *lol* [*nm*]*arapam*, "to the divine Rephaim," with *D*(*is*) *M*(*anibus*) *SAC*(*rum*)

[32]On the vastness of the netherworld, cf. Pope (1964) 276, n. 22.

[33]Further on the miry character of the netherworld, cf. the article just cited, *passim*, and Tromp (1969) 54-71. On *hmry* and *mhmrt*, cf. Held (1973) 173-90 and Pope (1978) 25-31.

(KAI 117:1). These and more evidences, which need not be fully rehearsed here, establish the equation of the Rephaim and the Latin *manes*, the shades.

An apparent complication in the biblical data is the fact that the term Rephaim is used as a gentilic for aboriginal denizens of the promised land. In Genesis 14:5 we are told that Chedorlaomer and his cohorts smote the Rephaim in Ashtaroth-karnaim along with other shady sorts called Zuzim (which the LXX renders "strong peoples," *ethnē ischyra*), the Emim ("fearsome ones"), and the Horites. Deuteronomy 2:10 informs us that the Emim formerly lived in Moab, were tall as the Anakim (another shadowy breed of giants [Numbers 13:33]), also known as Rephaim, but called Emim by the Moabites. Deuteronomy 2:20 further relates that the territory of Ammon, like that of Moab, was known as the land of Rephaim, that Rephaim formerly lived there, but the Ammonites called them Zamzumim. These Zamzumim also were tall like the Anakim, but the Lord dispossessed and destroyed them for Israel. The designation Zamzumim is probably to be related to Arabic *zamzam* which is used onomatopoetically of buzzing or humming noise but also for a troop of people, both senses being appropriate to the dead, the not-so-silent majority[34] who chirp, mutter, and whisper from the dust (Isaiah 8:19, 29:4).[35]

The Rephaim are also listed in Genesis 15:20 along with sundry "ethnic" groups that once inhabited areas between the Nile and the Euphrates—Kenites, Kenizzites, Kadmonites, Hittites, Perizzites, Rephaim, Amorites, Canaanites, Girgashites, Jebusites. These Kadmonites are probably not "easterners," as commonly supposed, but "ancient ones," as in the Ugaritic designation of the Rephaim as ancient, "invite the ancient Rephaim" (*qra rpim qdmym*; RS 34.126, line 9). Note that the Rephaim in the list of Genesis 15:20 is the only item lacking the gentilic afformative. All these diverse peoples of yore, including the Kadmonites (whether "easterners" or "oldlies") had manifestly been long defunct. Notable among these ancient giants was Og, king of Bashan, who already in Moses' day was the last survivor of the "remnant of the Rephaim" (Deuteronomy 3:11). Og's domain, Bashan, and his cities Ashtaroth and Edrei (Joshua 12:4, 13:12), have interesting connections. The cosmic associations of Bashan are hinted in Psalm 68:15-23. Bashan is the mighty mountain which God//Yahweh coveted for his

[34]The realization that the millions who tread the earth are but a handful to the tribes that slumber in its bosom is quite ancient. Ishtar, both in the Gilgamesh Epic and in the Descent to the Netherworld, threatened to raise up the dead outnumbering the living. The netherworld in Ezekiel 39:16 is called "Crowd Town" and the "multitudes, multitudes, in the Valley of Decision" on the Day of the Lord, Joel 3:14, are the citizens of that same infernal metropolis.

[35]Cf. Ebach (1977) 57-70, especially 57, n. 3 for bibliography.

eternal abode (Psalm 68:16), and in verses 21-23 of the same Psalm it is said that God will shatter the heads of Israel's enemies and bring them back from the depths of the Sea so that Israel may plunge feet in the blood of their enemies and their dogs' tongues will partake of the same (the text seems slightly garbled). The collocation of Bashan and the depths of the Sea suggests that Bashan has cosmic, chthonic connections. In Jeremiah 22:20 there is the call to ascend Lebanon, Bashan, and Abarim to cry out for the destruction of Jerusalem's lovers. All three of these eminences have connections with the cult of the dead. In CTA 22.2 (Gordon's text 124) the Rephaim are wined and dined in "a refectory at the summit," *bt ikl bpr*^{c}, "in the heart of Lebanon," *birt lbnn*. The "mountains of Abarim" in Moab (Numbers 33:47), include Moses' burial spot, Mount Nebo. The connection of Abarim with the Rephaim and the cult of the ancestors has already been perceived by J. Ratosh, who correctly divined that the term means "the departed," defunct ancestors. In Israel's wandering in the wilderness they camped at Oboth (="ghosts") and then moved on to Iye-Abarim, "stone-heaps of the departed" (Numbers 21:10-11). In Ezekiel 39:11-21, the burial place for Gog is called "Vale of the Departed" and "Vale of Gog's Mob," alias "Crowd Town." The funeral banquet there, following massive burial operations, will consist of flesh and blood of the fallen mighty ones, variously called bucks, rams, he-goats, bullocks, all terms for high-ranking nobles, summarily called "Bashan fatlings all."

The "cows of Bashan" in Amos 4:1, applied to the luxurious women of Samaria, and not excluding those of Jerusalem, means that they are "Hell bent," for they will be taken with hooks through the breaches of the city wall and cast into Harmon. The term Harmon has never been explained and I have ventured to suggest connection with biblical Hinnom and Ugaritic *hrnm* in the regular epithet of the Hero Danel, *mt rpi//mt hrnmy*, "*rpa* man" and "Harnamite man."[36] The term *hrnmy* has been connected with the place name Hermel[37] in Lebanon, rightly or wrongly, but this does not exclude relation with Hinnom through the meaning of Arabic *harmal, hirmil*, connected with *harim*, "be old, weak, decrepit," which comports with the ambivalent attitude toward the dead as weak and torpid shades needing care and sustenance as well as powerful gods who can bestow blessing, weal or woe on the living.

To return to Og of Bashan, it is his abode in Ashtaroth and Edrei that makes a striking connection with the Ugaritic *rpu mlk* ^{c}*lm* who has the same address. In RS 24.252 the lines following *rpu mlk* ^{c}*lm, il yṯb* b^{c}*ṯrt // il ṯpṭ bh/idr*^{c}*y*, do not mean "El sits with Ashtart" and "El

[36]Cf. Pope (1977b) 173, n. 58.
[37]Albright (1953) 27f.

judges with Hadd the Shepherd."[38] In the first place the expression *yṯb b-*, like Hebrew *yšb b-*, means "dwell in," not "sit with." In Ugaritic the sense "sit with" occurs once and the preposition is *tḥt* used like German *unter* in the sense "among."[39] The element *hdrʿy* or *idrʿy* can hardly mean "Hadd the Shepherd" since *hd* as a cognomen of Baal is used only as a B-word in poetic parallelism following mention of Baal. The element *il* in *il yṯb* and *il ṯpṭ* is not the proper name but is used here in the generic sense "god" in asyndetic relative construction, "the god (who) dwells," "the god (who) rules" in Ashtaroth and in Edrei.[40] The relative construction is confirmed by the following use of the relative particle *d* before the verb "sings" (*d yšr*):

> Then drank *rpu*, king of Eternity,
> Then drank [the god] strong and noble,
> The god (who) dwells in Ashtaroth,
> The god (who) rules in Edrei,
> Who sings and chants to lute and flute,
> To drum and cymbal, to castanets of ivory,
> With the goodly colleagues of Kothar.
>
> [UT 5.2.1.1-5]

There is nothing to suggest that this musical virtuoso, *rpu mlk ʿlm*, is either El or Baal. Alan Cooper[41] has proposed identification of this *rpu*

[38]So Virolleaud (1968) 553, followed by many others, notably F. M. Cross and his pupils. Cf. L'Heureux (1979) 43.

[39]The passage in question is 17 (2 Aqht) 5.6-7:

ytšu yṯb bap ṯǵr	He rose and sat in the entry of the gate,
tḥt adrm dbgrn	Among the dignitaries on the threshing-floor.

Note that *yṯb b-* here means "sit *in*"; one would hardly sit *with* a gate. The circumstance is transparent, Danel sits among the dignitaries. Dijkstra and de Moor render "before the dignitaries," (1975) 181, but there is nothing to indicate that Danel was a king or in any way exalted above his peers. In the latest published *rpum* text, RS 34.126, lines 22-25, *tḥt* is five times repeated before the titles and names of various denizens of the netherworld, including the kings Ammištamru and Niqmad, following the imperatives *rd* and *špl*, "descend" and "below." The crucial problem here is the entity *ksh/i* to which or to whom the imperatives are addressed. Healey (1978) 84, 87, renders "chair(?)" and explains that "The chair/throne is to be ritually sent down into the netherworld for the benefit of Niqmaddu and other kings in the netherworld." The word *tḥt* Healey construes as a noun, "seat," in all five instances.

[40]The proposal of Margulis (1970) 293f. equating *ʿṯtrt* and *h/idrʿy* with the biblical Ashtaroth and Edrei, the abode of Og of Bashan, Deut 1:4; Josh 9:10, 12:4, 13:12, has not gained general acceptance. Cf., e.g., the counter arguments of Dietrich, Loretz, and Sanmartín (1975) 117. The similarity, *mutatis mutandis*, seems to me too striking to be discounted.

[41]In an article entitled "*MLK ʿLM*: 'Eternal King' or 'King of Eternity'?" to be published in the volume *Love and Death in the Ancient Near East*, ed. Marks and Good.

mlk ᶜ*lm* with Reshep on the basis of all three elements of his title, *rpu* as healer, and *mlk* ᶜ*lm* as King of Eternity (i.e., the Netherworld) which corresponds to the Egyptian titles of Osiris and Reshep, *ḥqꜣ ḏ.t* and *nb nḥḥ*, "Lord of Eternity," and of his Mesopotamian counterpart Nergal as *šar erṣeti*, "King of the Netherworld." The only apparent impediment to this identification is the consideration that in the summons to the gods in hierarchical order with mention of their respective abodes in the Snake Text, RS 24.244, a god called simply *mlk* whose abode is ᶜ*ṯtrt*, i.e., Ashtaroth, is listed in eighth place while Reshep is in sixth place and his abode is given as *bbt*, perhaps *bābāt*, "gates," since elsewhere (RS 12.61) Reshep is called *tǵr*, "gatekeeper," of the sun-goddess, *špš*. There is, however, an addition on the margin of the bottom left side of the Snake Text which joins Reshep with ᶜ*ṯtrt*, either the goddess or the city, or both. This marginal reading is *aṯr ršp* ᶜ*ṯtrt* ᶜ*m* ᶜ*ṯtrt mrh* followed by the words *mnt nṯk nḥš*, "incantation (for) snake-bite," which in all other instances in the text follow immediately the designation of the abode of the deity. Virolleaud[42] rendered the lines preceding the reference to snake bite "(C'est) le lieu (sacrée) de Rešep (et) ᶜAštart avec (=associés à) ᶜAštart, (tournée) vers Mr." Virolleaud noted that Reshep and Ashtart are not encountered elsewhere joined, as they seem to be here. Further Virolleaud observed that the association of Reshep-Ashtart (or of Ashtart alone) with (another) Ashtart oriented toward *mr* (=Mari?) recalls nothing known from the mythology of Ugarit. This suggests that Virolleaud's dubious rendering of the lines should be reconsidered in light of the forms of designation of deities and their abodes in the other eleven sections of the text in which the name of the deity is preceded by the preposition ᶜ*m*, "toward" and the name of the abode follows immediately either in the adverbial accusative without preposition or with the directive suffix *h*, "toward deity X at place Y." In this light, *aṯr ršp* ᶜ*ṯtrt* could mean "toward Reshep at Ashtaroth," but Reshep is already listed as residing at *bbt*. In keeping with the usual form in this text, ᶜ*m* ᶜ*ṯtrt mrh* would mean "toward Ashtart at *mr* (Mari?)," but Ashtart was already listed in fourth place joined with Anat at the place *inbb*. The problem is further complicated by the fact that *mlk*, the eighth in the list, also lives at Ashtaroth. It is, of course, possible that more than one deity could reside in the same town or even in the same house. It is unfortunate that the connection of *ršp* and ᶜ*ṯtrt* was not incorporated into the text and accorded the same treatment as other deities and their abodes.

As we have seen, Og of Bashan who, like *rpu* King of Eternity lived in Ashtaroth and Edrei, also belonged to the Rephaim (as does everyone eventually). In spite of the apparent confusion in holy writ, the Rephaim were not a particular ethnic group like the Jebusites, Amorites, or

[42]Virolleaud (1968) 574.

Hittites, but the ghosts of deceased, aboriginal denizens who still haunted the land. Jewish folklore about Og casts doubt on the historicity of the Israelites' encounters with him. Og was an antediluvian who survived because the flood reached only to his ankles. Moses who was himself no runt, standing about 15 feet, jumped his full height into the air with an axe handle of the same length to reach Og's ankles and destroy him.[43] A Phoenician tomb inscription seems to invoke the Mighty Og as a bogy to pursue the grave robber.[44]

The notion that the term *rpum, rpim* at Ugarit, beside the clear application to the dead, also designated a living group of chariot warriors, like the Mesopotamian *maryannu,* has played havoc with the understanding of their nature and role in the texts in which they figure.[45] The basis for the mistaken view that the Rephaim are living chariot warriors is found in fragments relating to the Aqhat Text. Danel, presumably after the death of his son Aqhat, invites the *rpum,* who are also called gods (*ilynm*), to come and eat and drink at a *mrz*^{c} at his place (*a<u>t</u>r*), house and palace. The *rpum* harness horses (*asr sswm*) and mount their chariots (*t*^{c}*ln lmrkbthm*) and proceed to Danel's threshing floor (*grnt*) and plantation (*mṭ*^{c}*t*). For six days the Rephaim eat and drink in a refectory on the (mountain) summit—in the heart of Lebanon (*tlḥmn rpum tštyn bt ikl bpr*^{c} ... *birt lbnn*). On the seventh day something happens involving Mighty Baal, but the text breaks off at that point. The horses and chariots which convey the Rephaim to the banquet do not compel the conclusion that the riders must be the quick rather than the dead. The Rephaim as spirits of the deified ancestors presumably could elect any mode of transportation they might fancy. By way of parallel, the Dioscuri as the house-gods of the Spartan kings, corresponding to the Rephaim, are depicted on a funerary stela coming on horseback to partake of the *theoxenia.*[46] With the problem of chivalry of the Rephaim dispelled, there is nothing to suggest that the Ugaritic Rephaim are anything but the spirits, ghosts, or shades of the departed deified ancestors who are wined and dined in communal meals with the family, the revered ancestors and the great gods. This funeral feast, corresponding to the Mesopotamian *kispu,* was, as already indicated, the

[43]Cf. Ginzberg (1909) vol. 3, 346.

[44]Cf. Starcky (1969) 262. Line 2 . . . *lptḥ* ^{c}[*lt*] *arn zn lrgz* ^{c}*ṣmy h*^{c}*g ytbqšn hadr* Starcky translated ". . . pour ouvrir ce sarcophage et pour troubler mes os, le Ug me cher chera, le Puissant."

[45]Cf. L'Heureux (1979) chapters 4, 5, 6.

[46]Cf. Nilsson (1940) 69 and fig. 32. Horowitz (1979) appropriately compares the Rephaim with the Iranian Fravashis, the ancestor-spirits who were represented as mounted warriors in the conflict of good against evil.

Marzeaḥ of the Bible, the Ugaritic Rephaim Texts, and Phoenician and Aramaic inscriptions.[47]

It has been supposed that the reference to Rephaim of Earth in El's blessing of Keret on the occasion of his second marriage, following the loss of his first wife and children, confirms the notion that there was a class of living, flesh and blood, terrestrial Rephaim.[48] Earth in this connection, however, refers to the netherworld which is the abode of the Rephaim. El in his blessing vouchsafes for Keret numerous progeny which will insure his welfare both in life and death and bring him honor when he joins his ancestors.[49] Between enumerations of the children Keret will father, El addresses Keret:

> Greatly exalted be Keret
> Mid the Rephaim of Earth,
> In the assembly of the departed of Ditan.
>
> [15(128)3.3, 14]

Keret's ancestry as well as that of the kings of Ugarit and of the First Dynasty of Babylon was connected with the Amorite tribe of Ditān/Didan. Ditanu is sixth among the list of twenty-seven generations of royal ancestors of Ammi-Ṣaduqa, son of Ammi-Ditana, of the Amorite First Dynasty of Babylon.[50] In a new Rephaim Text from Ugarit, RS 34.126,[51] the *qbṣ ddn,* spelled with middle *d* as in the Assyrian King List, is invited to a seven-day feast along with other ancient Rephaim (*rpim qdmym*) including the more recently defunct kings of Ugarit, Ammištamru and Niqmad, in order to assure health/peace (*šlm*), to the reigning king Ammurapi, his sons, his house, and to the city and gates of Ugarit. The exaltation of Keret among the Rephaim of Earth and among his Did/tanite ancestors by means of plentiful progeny evokes the Arabic blessing for newlyweds, "with *rpa* and (with) children," *biʾr-rifāʾi waʾl-banîna.* Numerous progeny was the coveted blessing insuring survival of the family and clan. The name H/Ammurapi, composed of *ᶜamm,* "people" and *rpʾ*, related to healing and fertility, is explained as meaning "extensive family," *kimta-rapaštum.*[52]

[47] Cf. Porten (1968) 177-86. Pope (1972) 170-203. Pope (1977a) 210-229.

[48] L'Heureux (1979) 201-4.

[49] Cf. Astour (1980) 233 and 238, n. 78.

[50] Finkelstein (1966) 95-118.

[51] Cf. Caquot (1975) 426-31. Pope (1977b) 177-81. Healey (1978) 83-88. Pitard (1978) 65-75.

[52] CAD K 377b s.v. *kimtu.*

Despite unfounded scepticism in some quarters, there is scant reason to doubt that the West Semitic Marzeaḥ was a feast for and with the departed ancestors, corresponding to the Mesopotamian *kispu*. The first known Rephaim Texts at Ugarit present the Rephaim as guests at a *mrz*ᶜ at Danel's place, but it was not realized until the discovery of texts containing the correct form, *mrzḥ*, that the variants represent the same affair. The two biblical references to the Marzeaḥ may seem discrepant at first blush, but actually are not. In Amos 6:7 the term occurs in the context of luxury, wine, food and song, and RSV accordingly rendered "revelry." In Jeremiah 16:5-9 it is clear that Marzeaḥ-house is the locus of a funeral feast, for it occurs in a context of mass death by sword, disease, and famine with corpses spread like dung on the ground, eaten by bird and beast. Here RSV rendered "the house of mourning." The passage is quasi-poetic and should be treated such:

Do not enter the Marzeaḥ-house,
Or go to lament and mourn them,
For I have taken my peace from this people,
My mercy and compassion.
Small and great shall die in the land.
They shall not be buried.
None shall lament for them,
Nor gash or make themselves bald.
They shall supply no mourner's meal
To comfort him for the dead.
They shall not make them drink the consolation cup
For father or for mother.

The following verses speak of the banquet house and I have argued elsewhere[53] that the Marzeaḥ-house, the banquet (drinking) house, and the wine-house are essentially synonymous.

Do not enter the drinking house
To sit, eat and tope with them.
For thus says the Lord of Hosts, the God of Israel:
Behold, I am stopping in this place,
Before your eyes, and in your days,
The sound of mirth, the sound of joy,
The sound of groom and bride.

The mention of groom and bride does not necessarily indicate a monogamous affair. One of the persistent charges is that cult feasts with wine and song also included ritual incest otherwise called "sacred marriage."[54]

[53]Pope (1977a) 216.

[54]*Ibid.*, pp. 210-29. The term "incest" is used both in the primitive sense of "unchastity" (from Latin *castus*, "chaste") and the technical sense of sexual relations forbidden

The nuptial language also does not rule out the funeral feast. Even in post-biblical Jewish mourning the dead were called "groom" or "bride." A *ḥuppāh* or wedding canopy was spread over the grave and nuts, pomegranates, strips of purple, flasks of myrrh, fish, and such were suspended from the canopy or scattered on the grave.[55] It was even permitted to pipe wine and oil into the tomb. Such practices were considered acceptable and exempt from the charge of following the "ways of the Amorite."[56] Nevertheless it is patent that such were indeed survivals of pre-Jewish practices. The use of nuptial terminology in connection with death is a striking phenomenon deserving special study.[57]

A main feature of the Marzeaḥ[58] was the imbibing of wine or other intoxicating beverage. Inebriation to satiety or beyond that to oblivion was often the result, if not the purpose, of the ceremonial bibbing. We have a Ugaritic text which illustrates this rather graphically:

El sacrificed in his house,
Provided game in the midst of his palace.
He invited the gods to mess.
The gods ate and drank,
Drank wine to satiety,
Must to inebriation.

There is an enigmatic episode involving a rebuke of El by the gatekeeper or porter of El's house and reference to cuts of meat for the dog, after which

El sat [in] [his pl]ace,
El sat in his *mrzḥ*.
He drank wine to satiety,
Must to inebriation.
. . . .
An apparition accosted him,
With horns and a tail.
He floundered in his excrement and urine;
El collapsed, like those who descend into Earth.

The goddesses Anat and Ashtart go roaming or hunting as the obverse of the text peters out. The reverse mentions the return of the goddesses and

because of consanguinity. Unchastity would cover incest and a lot more.

[55]Cf. Zlotnick (1966) 14, 15, 37, 58, 77, 106, 108, 126, 135-37, 142.

[56]*Ibid.*, pp. 58, 136. See above n. 9.

[57]Cf. Toynbee (1971) 95ff. Ms. Toynbee is puzzled at parents' dedication of a tomb for their ten year old son and later for themselves as an "eternal bridal chamber" (*aiōnion nymphōna*) in a "garden tomb" (*kēpotafion*).

[58]Porten (1968). Eissfeldt (1969a) 212-27. Eissfeldt (1969b) 187-95. Loewenstamm (1969) 71-77. de Moor (1969) 167-75. Rüger (1969) 203-6. Margulis (1970b) 131-38.

administration of various medicines, including green olive juice, apparently to relieve crapulence. The reference to a dog and cuts of meat recalls the alleged mode of putting out the lights at the beginning of the orgies which early Christians were accused of carrying on, including drunkenness, incest and ingestion of an infant's flesh and blood.[59] Only gods attend the present feast and Baal is not among the few that are named; in view of the funerary connections of the Marzeaḥ, one may surmise that this may be a wake for Baal. El as the host of the feast corresponds to the *rb mrzḥ*a or the symposiarch of the Palmyrene texts relating to the Marzeaḥ. The gods collectively drink to satiety and inebriation, but El goes beyond this to delirium, diarrhea and enuresis, and loss of consciousness. Dignity does not appear to be a concern of the father of the gods, and it may be assumed that the other gods follow the leader. The explicit mention of excrement and urine is reminiscent of the biblical animadversion against the drunkards of Ephraim (Isaiah 28:7-9):

> These, too, reel with wine,
> With drink they stagger.
> Priest and prophet stagger with drink,
> Dazed with wine, reeling with drink.
> They stagger in . . . ,
> Totter in . . . .
> All the tables are full,
> Vomit and excrement all about.

The mention of excrement in connection with sacred inebriation recalls a rabbinic anecdote which alleges ritual defecation as the mode of worship of Baal Peor. According to Numbers 25 Israel's sin at Baal Peor featured ritual incest. At least one nameless Israelite brought a woman before his family and all the people while they were weeping at the door of the tent of meeting and proceeded to perform an act with her in an alcove or arched structure which made it possible for Aaron's grandson Phinehas to skewer both the man and the woman at once. The plague visited on Israel as punishment claimed twenty-four thousand lives, presumably not all of them innocent of the great sin which produced rumblings and repercussions through the centuries (Num 31:6, Deut 4:3, Josh 22:17, Hos 9:10, Ps 106:28) into Christian times (1 Cor 10:8). Psalm 106:28 tells us something about the episode which the earlier narrator neglected to mention, either because it was assumed that everyone knew or else because it was deemed unspeakable, namely that the affair was a funeral feast:

[59]Cf. Hennrichs (1970) 18-35. Pope (1977a) 211-14.

They were joined with Baal Peor,
And ate sacrifices for the dead.

Further, we learn from rabbinic sources that the Baal Peor affair was a Marzeaḥ and that wife-swapping was a feature of the celebration.[60] The Marzeaḥ is associated with a later festival of ill repute called Mayumas[61] which was so rank the Romans were constrained to ban it. The implicit equation of Marzeaḥ and Mayumas is made on the sixth century mosaic map at Madeba which labels the area in Transjordan where the Baal-Peor incident took place as Betomarseas (i.e., Beth Marzeaḥ) alias Maioumas.[62]

From Palmyra there is a great deal of information about the Marzeaḥ which has been treated in detail in a monograph by J. T. Milik[63] without hint or inkling of its connections with the cult of the dead which are indicated by the association with the Rephaim in the Ugaritic Texts. There is a doctoral dissertation on the Marzeaḥ[64] which assembles and discusses virtually all the relevant data, but with hyper-caution on the crucial issue of its primary significance as a feast for and with the dead. When the history[65] of the Marzeaḥ festival comes to be written, correlated with parallel phenomena which the anthropologists and historians of religion of the nineteenth century so assiduously gathered, and with the ever increasing data being recovered by archaeologists, it will be the story of the primary preoccupations of mankind through the ages, love and death, and concern for survival in communion with the departed and hope for generations to come. The tracing of connections of the Marzeaḥ with the central Christian rite, the Eucharist as communion sacrifice and memorial, will require special scholarly sensitivity and daring.

[60]Sifre Numbers 131.

[61]Midrash Leviticus Rabbah 5:3, Numbers Rabbah 10:3, 7.

[62]Cf. Pope (1972) 190f., nn. 34, 35.

[63]Milik (1972).

[64] Bryan (1973).

[65]The Marzeaḥ may now be attested at Ebla in text 46 of the administrative documents published by Pettinato (1980) 309. Three women receive variegated dresses on the occasion of a *Mar-za-u*$_9$ which Dahood suggested may be a Marzeah. If so, this extends attestation of the institution several centuries earlier than the Ugaritic data.

Part Three

UGARIT IN RETROSPECT AND PROSPECT

What follows is a slightly edited transcript of the tape recording of the concluding session of the symposium. All remarks were extemporaneous, and the symposium was fortunate in having Professor Gordon, himself a pioneer in the study of Ugarit, Ugaritic, and their impact, accept the role of chairman and main speaker. As indicated by the title, the purpose of the session was an examination of the day's proceedings, to assess the contributions of the symposium's speakers, and to look forward to what future excavations and textual studies might hold in store for Ugarit, its civilization, and the many fields and areas affected by the site. Assisting Professor Gordon were Professors Astour, Dornemann, Pardee, and Pope, each of whom addressed areas of their own special competency. Following their remarks, questions and observations from the floor concluded the program of the symposium.

UGARIT IN RETROSPECT AND PROSPECT

CYRUS H. GORDON

I'm not going to comment on the various papers in the order they have been given, but I've rather strung them together in an order that would provide me with some sequence.

I want to start with Jack Sasson's paper. He stressed that you have to know what category of text you are dealing with before you can begin analysis and comparisons. If you are dealing with a literary text, it's a literary text; it's not a historic annal. And, of course, this is very fundamental. There are, however, kernels of historic facts imbedded in texts which are not at all historical. I don't think any of us take the Gilgamesh epic as a historical document. But the plain fact is that Gilgamesh has turned up in the king lists. Menes some time ago used to be considered a legend if not a myth, and now we have his own contemporary inscriptions—brief, but accepted as contemporary, as well as genuine, by Egyptologists. And perhaps most remarkable of all, Utnapishtim, old Ziusudra, the son of Ubara-tutu, is not only historical in the sense that his papa appears in historical lists, but there's an archaeological control to the flood and to the date of this flood, because the silt, not at places like Ur, but precisely at Shuruppak, his home town according to the epic, ties in best with the chronology of the king lists. So we mustn't despair of extracting history from legend, and even from myth.

Professor Dornemann pointed out much of interest at sites other than Ugarit, and, of course, even the Ugaritic texts deal with other sites. I'm not just referring to the historic documents, the economic documents or the administrative texts dealing with the outliers—the various towns in the kingdom. But Ḫubur is certainly not a part of the Ugaritic kingdom. There is no reason for thinking that Kret or Danel were Ugaritians. It's interesting to note that even there we have some controls. Kothar-wa-Ḫasis is based in Crete, at least in Caphtor. It is interesting to note that the architecture that he sponsors, according to the text, has Cretan analogies—Cretan contacts. For instance, when he advocates the window, we know that in early architecture, if there is any civilization that stresses windows, it is Crete. And it is not only in the architecture itself, but—what is it—in the Town Mosaic, I think they call it, in the Herakleion museum, windows are exceedingly prominent. But there is something else about it. You know, in the Danel and Aqhat epic, when a deity flies in at low level, he can be seen—he can be spotted—from the place where the king is holding court. This is distinctly Minoan; there are no city walls; if you have a high city wall you are not going to spot an airplane, or a deity, coming in at low level! In other words, even here there is a kind of architecture built into the story which rings true.

Now this, of course, takes us to this very important aspect that Elisha Linder stressed in his excellent and comprehensive paper—a paper which reflects long concern with that particular side of the story—that is, Ugarit as the center of a kind of thalassocracy, where the sea was very important to almost everything that went on. And, of course, here is a good example of where mythology and administrative texts tie in. You have this Sinarana, who is plying his trade by ship with Caphtor, the land of Kothar-wa-Ḫasis, so that when we speak of the diffusion of culture we are not talking about something mysterious which somehow or other blew across the Mediterranean, but it's something that goes hand in hand with actual contact via ships.

I was very much interested in Dr. Margalit's paper. He made the striking statement that Ugarit is nowhere mentioned in the Old Testament. Well, this is true; but David Owen has told us of a Ugaritic tablet sent from Ugarit to Aphek in Palestine, and we have to get used to enhancing the corpus of material in the Bible with extra-biblical materials. I think all of us are familiar with this. For example, there was a great King of Israel named Omri, and his greatest conquest was the subjugation of Moab. Well, we don't know of that from the Bible; we only know that from the Mesha stone which was discovered in the last century. So the fact that something appears in the Bible, or that it is absent, is really not the only criterion. The first time I took an active interest in materials that must have been in the Bible worlds, but somehow or other received no mention, was with Baruch Levine's doctoral dissertation, where we singled out elements that appear in Ugarit, but don't appear in the Bible, and then surface again in the Rabbinic period. After all, the Bible is only a fragment of Hebrew literary and cultural activity.

Dr. Margalit is doing something which has to be done. You know, sometimes we cast aside old hypotheses because someone very prominent has attacked them, or they just fall out of favor. Often they have to be revived with modifications. I want to point out, though, that in the case of the Aqhat epic, or the Kret and Aqhat epics, we don't have to depend only on topography and what one particular tribe may have been involved with. The tribe of Levi must have known something about

Danel and Aqhat, because there is a member, one of the patriarchs, a son of Levi who is named Qahat, [a name] which all of us take to be identical with Aqhat, the son of Danel.

So we come to Marvin Pope's paper. His studies on the death cult and the problems of death and life and death and love have reached a very mature stage, as you can see from his presentation. I look forward to his further research on the subject. But I want to suggest that in "death and life" we have a kind of merism, a sort of totality, such as we have in "heaven and earth," which was mentioned in another context. Baal, the god of life-giving forces and fertility, wouldn't be complete without his counterpart, Mot, and in monotheism, such as we have in the Old Testament, all necessary functions must be attributed to the one god. So God has the epithet, *mēmîtim ḥayyeh*. He takes away life and gives life. He kills and he revives. So this is sort of inevitable in the very nature of things that we should have problems of this kind. Of course they have to be worked out, and they couldn't possibly be in better hands than in Marvin Pope's. A little detail: I'm just wondering about the dog that appears in connection with death, if he doesn't have something to do with Anubis. Well, he's a jackal, but almost a dog, and yet no Egyptian burial could possibly be complete without being under the loving care of Anubis.

Dr. Giveon's talk reminds me, in this connection, of something that I think is fundamental. Of all the major aspects of the Bible world, I think the one that is most sinned against, because it's in isolation, is Egypt. There is a tremendous amount of material, and for reasons that I needn't go into, Semitists who are biblical scholars have studied, at least in the past, Akkadian, and now Ugaritic, but we tend to neglect the Egyptian side. Dr. Giveon mentioned that there were no doctors, according to one text, in Ugarit. May I call your attention to something which is rather curious, and I trust not without interest. In text 2050 of the *Ugaritic Textbook*, you have a list of infirmary or medical supplies. You've got the bed; the covers; the knives; the scalpels; the scales for weighing drugs and ingredients; you have a number of very fine surgical instruments; and, quaintly enough, a pair of cups for the cupping operation—for stimulation. Have a look at that text if you are interested. It's true we don't have medical texts as such, but I assure you that a town that had good hippic texts, for the care of horses, probably had someone around to take care of people, even though horses were worth a lot more than people at that time.

I was very much interested in Professor Pardee's presentation. If I understood him correctly, parallelism is fundamental, and I think what has been called metrics, and shouldn't be called metrics, is the corollary. That is to say, if you have a juxtaposition of parallel statements such as "dogs like meat, cats eat fish," it may not sound very poetic, but on the other hand the parallelism brings a kind of metric approximation in its wake. And bulk; I don't want to use the word meter, but bulk, the number of syllables, or the amount of time it takes to say something must be a consideration or else we wouldn't have the phenomenon of ballast variants. So this was a factor. I agree entirely with Professor Pardee, although I may be a little prejudiced here, that G. D. Young—you know, we not only, as scholars, like our own publications, but we like our student's publications—G. D. Young, as his doctoral dissertation took the nature of Biblical and Ugaritic prosody, and he digested the best parts of his dissertation and expressed them in an article in the *Journal of Near Eastern Studies*, which Dr. Pardee has quoted. I think this was an exceedingly sound principle. It is something which, at that time, was rather unpopular, but at last we're coming around to it.

Now, as for this element of what's not predictable: you know when you scan a Homer or a Virgil, there are certain limitations, certain variations; but on the other hand you know there are going to be six feet—six poetic feet to the line. This is not so in Hebrew poetry. I'm going to suggest something, and I hope it doesn't sound too vague, but I know it's a problem that remains to be solved. May I suggest to you that the Hebrew poets, unlike the Greek, Latin, or pre-Modern poets of the West, have something which I can call a bag of tricks, by which I mean that there are a lot of alternatives. You could have different lines of different lengths and all kinds of chiasms—you know the kind of thing that I am referring to. I would suggest that we collect the different units that we have. I don't want anything hypothetical or theoretical; we need to take samples of the actual strophes and groupings of verses, list them, and then treat these as a bag of tricks that the poet very creatively could draw on. And after we list the repertoire, we can try to determine if there are tolerated and non-tolerated sequences. I think this is going to be very productive, and I've had the feeling for a long while that it's along these lines that we're going to make notable progess in the future.

David Owen's paper was very significant, not only because of Taǵuǵlina and the tablet—I pronounced the word with a *ǵayin* rather than with a *ḫa* because that's the way it's actually written in Ugaritic alphabetic spelling. We get the vowels from David Owen's tablet, but we get the consonants in their most correct form from the Ugaritic tablet. It wasn't only that he brought to light this very, very important document showing that Palestine was indeed linked rather directly, at least by the mail service, to Ugarit, but there is something else which struck me as very significant: he controls the archaeology *and* the epigraphy. You know, we're getting into an age with a knowledge explosion that forces us into more and more narrow specialization. Now this is a necessity. I'm not knocking it. But if you can control different aspects of the subject, this is a tremendous asset.

David Owen mentioned that Aphek was a literary and translation center. It's the kind of place where we may hope to find archives. And you know, this business of Genesis 14 and the archives of Ebla at this very early date raises a problem. How on earth did something from the middle of the Early Bronze Age find its way into Genesis, because no matter how early you want to put father Abraham, no one has ever placed him in the middle of the Early Bronze Age. May I suggest to you that the nature of the detailed comparisons—and they are very familiar to you—but it's particularly that pentapolis—you know, Sodom, Gomorrah, Admah, Ṣeboim, and Zoar—that pentapolis which appears twice in Genesis 14 and occurs in the same order at Ebla—perhaps it is to be explained in that Genesis 14 is based on some archive, perhaps going back to the Ebla period—but kept in Jerusalem or perhaps some other archive, still buried and undiscovered in the Holy Land. This may have surfaced, and when it surfaced, the Hebrews were interested in preserving it because it had to do with a figure named Abraham, and specifically Abraham, the Hebrew. In any case, these are the vistas which are being opened up, and we have to think about these things in order to be prepared, because I'm very much an optimist. Sooner or later I think these dreams are going to come true. If there is anything that I have learned during my career as a scholar, it is that not only do the most amazing things happen, but things more amazing than what we ever dreamed of take place.

I want to come now to Dr. Bordreuil's presentation, particularly his work and discoveries and publications of the material from Ras Ibn Ḫani. Now you know there are many outlying sites mentioned in the Ugaritic tablets—in the administrative texts. There were scribes at the other end to take care of the correspondence. A lot of activity went on. These places must have had archives, if not as great as those at Ugarit, at least they would be the branch libraries, if not the central library. And this reminds us of something that we have to bear in mind. No one is going to be doing definitive work in our lifetime, even in the lifetimes of the youngest here. The material is going to keep increasing, and we will have to update our knowledge and enlarge the corpus from year to year during the years to come.

I want also to mention something—I don't want to go into great detail here—but Prof. Bordreuil will know what I mean. It's not enough to put out new editions. There are some new editions appearing, and they serve a useful purpose. *The texts have to be collated from the originals before it's worth putting new editions out,* and I was very much encouraged by his statement that they are correcting the errors in collating the tablets of PRU 2 and 5. This is the only way to do it.

Now coming to Prof. Craigie's presentation. He's absolutely right: we have to have more rigid controls. One thing I have noticed in the field is that the impressionistic approach is a thing of the past. Even when I first got into Ugaritic studies, I was very impatient at the work of a great pioneer—Rene Dussaud—because his phonetics were sloppy. He was saying all kinds of things, and I had been trained well enough to know that this was impossible, or many, many instances of what he put out were impossible. We have to have more and more rigid controls, otherwise the progress would be meaningless; but in demanding these rigid controls, we have to be careful not to intimidate students so that they are forced into an attitude of stagnation. We don't want to scare them into a feeling that, even if they do their best, it's not good enough. This is a very, very important thing—we must stress the positive.

Now I've been reading about pan-Ugaritism, and my friend Mitchell Dahood has been capable of overshooting his mark. On the other hand, let me tell you that Father Dahood knows this. This wouldn't surprise him. What I like to do—this is my own predilection—if I find 40 or 50 examples of a phenomenon, this satisfies me. I want to go on to the next thing. If, for instance, I find *ba* or *la* in the Hebrew in the meaning of "from" and I have 40 or 50 of each, this is plenty. I don't have to overkill. Father Dahood likes to get the last drop out of the lemon when he squeezes it. His work is of inestimable value, but something will have to be done. What is the term they used to use in Washington? Sanitized. That is, to clean up a little bit of the mess, and then we're going to have something refined and excellent. But, quite seriously, I don't think there is any danger of pan-Ugaritism. There is a danger of *not enough* emphasis on Ugarit. We should try to avoid mistakes, but they will be corrected. We have lots of critics around.

May I point out to you that the prototype of Pan-Ugaritism is Pan-Babylonianism. In all seriousness, the Pan-Babylonians did not go far enough. If they knew of the archives at places like Ugarit, places like Ebla, sites even like Aphek that are just opening up, they would have had much more ammunition. It's true they were unbalanced, and they often exaggerated, and they could lapse into error, but they understated. They didn't overstate the case. The corrective for pan-this and pan-that is not to be too narrow in our approaches. If we know a little bit more about Crete, the Hittites, and the Egyptians, and the other significant elements in the area, then we'll know that it isn't all Ugarit, or it isn't all Babylonian, but the importance of Ugarit has not been exhausted by a long shot, and tremendous strides remain in the future.

Our French colleague, Prof. Margueron, is operating in the field, and we need this. We need precious work of this kind, because this is the source of our new material. Moreover, his meticulous concern with method and detail goes hand-in-hand with the best of the current stage of Ugaritic studies. This has to go in tandem with another approach. Both approaches are necessary, and they don't have to be fostered by the same people. I'm referring to Prof. Astour, whose wide perspective is also necessary, because when you deal with a phenomenon like Ugarit, you're dealing with contacts in every direction—North, East, South, and West. And for this reason, we have to have perspective. So it's just as well, you know, that all of us are not cast in the same mold. Deep, meticulous and detailed study must go forward along with broad historic horizons.

Panel

Now, ladies and gentlemen, I've already said more than I should—not more than I wanted to say, but more than I should—and I'm going to call on my panel colleagues to say something if they wish to, and in any case all of us will be very glad to take your questions and answer them to the best of our ability. Dr. Pardee.

DR. PARDEE. I have a few remarks grouped under retrospects and prospects that I will try to get through as briefly as possible. The first remark is that I don't see how we can agree on all kinds of very deep things when we can't even agree how to pronounce the name of the city we are talking about. Peter Daniels, sitting beside me at the table, came up with six different pronunciations—*Ū́-ga-rit, U-gā́r-it, U-ga-rī́t*—and those three with a "Y" in front of each one. Plus, there were a couple more where we couldn't decide where to put the tonic accent because it was pitch instead of stress, or something.

For the present, for the retrospects of the presentation of the material from Ugarit, I think we have to say frankly that in the past the presentation of epigraphic materials has been far better than the presentation of archaeological materials. Everyone agrees pretty much that Virolleaud was good, that Nougayrol was excellent, but as far as the archaeological materials are concerned, we've seen very little of them, and most of us, I suppose, have heard horror stories about how the archaeological excavations were carried on, at least during the early years. As far as the treatment of the material from Ugarit is concerned, here I think we should pay attention to Prof. Craigie's paper. I think that on the whole we have more positive features about our treatment of the Ugaritic materials than negative features. According to his *bilan* at least, there is more progress being made than backsliding.

Quickly on to prospects: let me change immediately what I said a moment ago about the presentation of the archaeological materials. I think the prospects are for an excellent presentation of the archaeological materials by an improved archaeological method, not only from the perspective of stratigraphy, but also from the perspective of how they are going about it. It was obvious from Prof. Margueron's remarks that they are going about it from a more anthropological perspective. They're bringing in more points of view on the archaeology, and I think that's excellent, and I think we have excellent prospects for the future.

The second point I would make is—repeating one of Prof. Gordon's—I think we have more prospects from more reliable texts, in the future, on the basis of what Prof. Bordreuil and others are doing. He was rather kind with *KTU* when he was up here. When I spoke to him after the session, he was a bit less kind (between the two of us). Perhaps I shouldn't be tattling on him, but according to Prof. Bordreuil, the texts in *KTU*, especially those excavated after 1948, are quite faulty and have to be used with a great deal of care. All we can hope for is that Prof. Bordreuil is more careful, and a presentation of these texts will be made available to the scholarly community before too long.

A third point that I would make is that an increased number of texts will permit more formal analysis of the type seen in Prof. Levine's paper. We've been working with very few texts in several of our categories in the past. As more and more texts come out, I believe we will be able to do more and more formal analysis and thus be able to pin down what words should mean from a purely philological perspective, and when we know what they should mean, then we could do some more philology and find out what they really *do* mean.

A fourth point, under which I have three main categories, is responsibilities to the scholarly community. I suppose retrospect and prospect come together here. The first one I would mention is methodology. And speaking of Pan-Ugaritism again, I agree that 33% of Dahood's suggestions might be right. Prof. Andersen, in a recent review, suggested that maybe 25% of someone's contributions might turn out to be correct. My question is: who is going to weed out the 67% or the 75%? It seems to me that it is putting an undue burden on the scholarly community to spend a good deal of its time weeding out unacceptable material, and perhaps instead of doing that work, we should be training our students to weed out the unacceptable material themselves, so that the dissertations they publish are maybe 50% correct, or 60% correct, or 70% correct, rather than 25% to 33% correct.

A second point under this main heading is terminology. I think we have a responsibility to the scholarly community to use terminology which someone coming from another discipline, for example, can understand. Here I cite some terms that I myself am acquainted with, having worked on them. For example, the use of "ambivalent" vs. "ambiguous" in describing the prepositional system, and describing the Hebrew and Ugaritic poetic systems as metrical or nonmetrical—a burden of my paper today was that I would like to see us using the terms in the sense that scholars in the other language disciplines are using them, etc.

The final point is that of making the material available to the scholarly community: I think we must applaud the scholars of the past, such as Driver, Ginsberg, Gibson in his new addition of Driver's translations, and especially Prof. Gordon and his well known *Ugaritic Literature*, which I understand is supposed to be coming out in a new addition. I think that we have acquitted ourselves quite well in providing good translations of the texts for the scholarly community. As a final prospect, however, I would like to suggest that the next step that we owe the scholarly community is reasoned commentaries of the Ugaritic texts—somewhat like the biblical commentaries. There is a long tradition of commenting on the biblical text, and someone can easily sit down and write a 700-page commentary on the Song of Songs, for example. I think we are getting to the point now where we need 300- or 400-page commentaries on the *Aqht* legend, or the Baal-ᶜAnat cycle. Thank you.

DR. GORDON. Dr. Astour, would you like to make some comments?

DR. ASTOUR. Well, my wishes are, for instance, that special studies in Ugaritic society, like the one we heard from Prof. Linder, be continued. This is very important. Not only the literature—the mythology—but also the social, economic, military side of Ugarit, as part of the ancient Near East, is very important, and collecting and classifying all this information can give us a great deal of insight in the workings of ancient societies.

Second, the role of geography—the study of geography of the ancient Near East and of the area of Ugarit especially. Here Prof. Giveon said that for him the assonance between Akuty and Akurita is more important than whether it was possible or not to cover this much of the mountains. Well, this is not the realistic approach. Geography dominates history, you see. If Hannibal wanted to go to Italy, he had to go over the Alps. And they had to conquer great difficulties. And we cannot ignore it. One of the bad habits of philologists, *especially* philologists, is that they work on small-scale school maps in books, which don't show any relief of the country, and they seldom consult the scale, you know, so it is all very approximate. For me, for instance, the terrain decides the direction of the roads—of the commercial roads, of the international connections, and of strategical roads—and we know that armies have to use roads that are accessible to them. Therefore, for me, the distance between Nii and Ugarit, and the terrain between them, is of such nature that it excludes the possibility that Ugarit was the goal of the side expedition of Amenhotep or Amenophis II. For all Egyptologists, Assyriologists, Romanists, Hellenists—everyone who works in a special field tends to exaggerate the importance of his particular civilization or state. So for Egyptologists, who are used to the great bombastic boasts of the Egyptian pharaohs, they seem to be the strongest people in the world. How could it be Thutmosis II or III did not dominate Ugarit? Well, we see that there is a strange conspiracy of silence for 100 years about all of this territory, and then the record starts again. There is a certain system in this kind of ignorance. All the domination of Thutmosis III over North Syria—I omitted it all from my paper—lasted, with two interruptions, only six years. He could not conquer Halab for long after he fought in Nuḫašše, then here in Halab, then already he had to fight again for Qidšu, or Qinza, far south. So this power was not so overwhelming. It is very possible that the Ugaritic navy was really as strong as Prof. Linder told us. Maybe he didn't want to engage in naval struggle; maybe to go on this narrow sea coast all the way to Ugarit was dangerous. Maybe it would distract his forces from the main theater of warfare against Mitanni, which was very strong and very influential in this area and had the sympathy of the local population on their side. Well, there are all kinds of ways, but I cannot accept the idea that Ugarit had been conquered by Egypt and had remained totally unknown, unregistered, unlisted in any records for so long. So I believe that geography and chronology should play a greater role in history than we expected up to now.

Now my wishes for future exploration. Of course there is a great deal to be uncovered in Ras Shamra itself. I had the privilege of being there and driving over the mountains, too, so I know them firsthand, on good asphalt roads, not as the Egyptians had to go, God knows, on what kind of goat trails. Well, anyway, the thing is that there remains a lot to be excavated in Ugarit, and you see that everytime we find something new—something new architecturally, or seals, and also tablets—but there are also many very interesting objects *around* Ugarit, and it would be worthwhile to diversify a little bit of this exploration to start soundings, or possibly large-scale excavation, in a few selected points of this part of Syria, and in particular in Siyannu. There is a huge mound which is still called Siyannu, with a village next to it. It was a capitol of a state about which we know from its relation with Ugarit, and we later know about it from a Syrian text that it was a little kingdom, and I am almost sure that excavation there would discover the royal palace of the bronze age, and certainly archives. You see, I am not sure whether in any town of the Ugaritic kingdom there were scribes and archives. Perhaps not. But in royal cities, and in capitols of big provinces, quite certainly. So, therefore, it would be a good thing if the French archaeologists together with the Syrian, maybe some others, would take care of this trial excavation in Siyannu and maybe a few more of the larger mounds which probably had walls in earlier times in the plain of Ugarit and Jablon. These things could bring more material; you see, we have discovered very interesting tablets in Ras Ibn Hani, and it is quite possible that such things also may be found in Siyannu, or in this mound here: Tell Busireh—which everybody believes to be a Phoenician harbor, an old Phoenician harbor which Forrer has plausibly identified with Ušnatu. Again I haven't seen any reports, not only about excavations, but even about surface surveys of it. These things should be continued because all of that also belongs to the sphere of interest of Ugarit.

And now about the Aphek tablet about which Prof. Owen told us. Well, it confirmed brilliantly what we could have already seen from PRU VI about the Palestinian, South Canaanite cities with which Ugarit was in very close relations. We knew earlier about Ashdod, and then we have Ashqelon, we have Acco, we have a few more places, and then, of course, Tyre, Sidon. We see then that the greatest intensity of the commercial relations was with the South, with Egypt, with Egyptian possessions. There is also a place called Halānu there. It is interesting to know where it is located. It could have been in Bashan, or maybe somewhere on the sea coast. In this way, archaeological excavations which find texts confirm, corroborate, the information, the data of Ugaritic commercial and administrative texts. In this way, by combining archaeology, study of the texts, and economic studies about commercial connections, we can work out quite a fine picture of international life, commercial, political, diplomatic relations in the international period *par excellence*, in the 14th and 13th centuries B.C.

DR. GORDON. Thank you, Dr. Astour. I happen to note that in the few points that I jotted down, my eye skipped, in two instances, something I just want to mention very briefly.

You know, before we can tackle tablets, and see what's distinctive in them, we have to know the formulas. For instance, in epistles, once you are relieved of figuring out what the introduction, and conclusions, and other things are, then you can get down to business. I want to commend Baruch Levine on defining the formulas in the texts that he has been describing to us, because it's only when we have this rigidly defined that we'll be able to make full use of these documents. The other point that has to be mentioned is that something I always look forward to, and benefit from without exception, is Dr. Craigie's *Ugaritic Newsletter*. This fills a tremendous need, and I know all of us feel, rightly so, that we are beholden to him for this.

Marvin Pope, would you like to say something to us?

DR. POPE. Well, I thought I would pretend to be a philosopher and keep quiet, but I can't resist. There are so many things I'd like to talk about. My beginning with Ugaritic way back about 1939 has been a constant discovering the errors of yesterday and recanting and also rejecting some of the foibles of my own teachers. Who can discern error? *šuggiyôt mî yābîn*?

But I was particularly interested in Peter Craigie's talk on progression/regression; this is the problem of sifting. If I may quote Jonas Greenfield on the numbers game, the question is not what the percentage of Dahood's ideas are right, the question is which 10%! This is the problem we have among ourselves. I'm continuing recanting, but as for the charge of Pan-Ugaritism or Pan-Biblicism and so forth, I would emphatically deny the allegation and rebuke the allegator, in respect to that. I'm an incurable comparativist and would compare anything that seems comparable, and some of the most exciting things that I have learned have resulted from sticking my nose in other people's business and asking questions of people across other fields. I have some very helpful informants in other areas. I've roamed as far away as India, in which I don't pretend to have any competence, but I have tried to rely on the best opinion I can get as to what is relevant and what isn't, and I would think it would be a mistake not to do it. Ugaritic has much more to contribute to biblical studies still, in terms of correcting past errors, and finding new things, even into the New Testament. The doxology on the end of the Lord's Prayer, now it seems to me, has a parallel in that Ugaritic Rephaim prayer with the Kingdom and the Power and the Glory; it seems to me to be striking enough to call to attention. It is well known that Ugaritic confirms Beelzebul, rather than Beelzebub of the New Testament—little things of that sort.

There are even items in current events worth thinking about. Mr. Carter has suggested that we form a commission to study Muslim sectarianism and Shiʾite Islam. We've gotten some rude jolts out of ignorance in this area. Ugaritic has a contribution there, which I called to the attention of a specialist—we have an Israeli Arabist visiting with us [at Yale] this year, and he's a specialist in Shiʾite Islam. I called to his attention the relevance of *ʿAli* in Ugaritic. It was Nyberg who discovered the God, ʿAl/ʿAli, and Sellin said it was a *Hirngespinst*—a phantom of his brain—which stung Nyberg into writing a long article with more examples of ʿAl/ʿAli, almost all of which were *wrong*. But, Ugaritic confirmed the correctness of his identification with that "sweet" and H. L. Ginsburg was the one who saw it: "sweet to the field was the rain of Baʿal, and to the field, the rain of ʿAli," and this of course explains the Muslim poet who said he has eschewed those who, when they mentioned ʿAli, worshiped the clouds. That's what started Nyberg on this recognition that in the passage where *ʿal*, the preposition, made no sense in Hosea and in Samuel, it turned out to be a divine name; Dahood added a few more, I added a few more in Job, and people are still finding ʿAlis, rightly or wrongly, in the Bible. But this explains, you see, why the Shiʾite Muslims and the Alanite Muslims around Ras

Shamra deified the Caliph Ali, because he was already the old weather god.

There is a great temptation here to get off on the dog, and go on to the dogs. There is a lot more material there than I could even hint at. There is in Milik's book on *Dédicaces faites par des dieux et des thiases sémitiques* a very striking thing—Nergal-*kalba*—in these texts, and he doesn't know quite what to make of that, and I don't either. But the dog is all over the place in the Parsee religion. You can't bury a corpse without having a four-eyed dog look at it. Now it's kind of hard to get four-eyed dogs, but I suppose those that have the markings may be easy enough. This may be Cerberus who, with two heads, had four eyes. But this goes all the way up into the inquisition and the rebuke of Christian artists for introducing dogs into Christian art. I think I may have mentioned this.

Now about the *marzeaḥ*, there's a great deal more to be said, too. I hope at the AOS meeting in St. Louis to show that this new, if provocative, religious center excavated on the Sinai border by Zeev Meshel, at Kuntillat Ajrud, which he calls a religious center of the Judean monarchy, was none other than a *marzeah*, and to show the connections with all the characters, including the art, which is extremely interesting and provocative. Not only did YHWH have a consort, but some of the scenes that are there—the Tree of Life, tying in with the *Song of Songs*, and also that scene that is called "Praying Figures." This is à propos, Jack, of part of my answer to you about when we get a text that tells us all these things [Sasson: marvellous!]. We are overlooking some stuff that we've already got that I think is relevant to it. Well, here again I'd better stop.

I want to say something about the use of Arabic, but this didn't come up. This has been a controversial issue. I make no apology for the appeal to Arabic for lexicographical material. There's a great danger, but there's a still greater danger in not using Arabic. Jonas Greenfield's dissertation showed us that there are many words that occur in Mishnaic Hebrew that don't occur in Biblical Hebrew, that also occur in Akkadian that occur in Colloquial Arabic, and these words have been part of the *Wortschatz* of Syria-Palestine for millennia. I just now found, I believe, the etymology of that word *BRLT*, in a word which the Arabic lexicographers had trouble with. It has the same history as *nepeš* in the meaning of "throat" and "appetite," and while some of my students expurgated it from one of my own articles, I'm going to reassert it. I think they'll maybe allow me to [do so].

Now, I suppose this is no time, with a captive audience—there are a lot, a list, of things I'd like to argue about with a number of scholars here—but I think the thing that is most encouraging is Prof. Bordreuil's paper. We certainly are not going to run out of new material, and I don't suppose I'll live to vex myself with Eblaite, but I would certainly like to get my hands on some of this new material that is coming out shortly.

DR. GORDON. I'm glad that the last person on the panel represents the discipline that gives us our material—archaeology. Dr. Dornemann.

DR. DORNEMANN. I don't want to say very much. I think we've cut into the discussion quite already, but I do want to make just a couple of comments. I think the others have mentioned quite a bit the material we still need in the way of archaeological evidence, basically publication—hopefully getting back into some of the older works of Schaeffer to find out where some of these tablets were actually found in the temple areas, what is the stratigraphical context—the actual location in position of much of this material? Hopefully, some of that will be resurrected and be available to us to guide the analysis and the ideas on the tablet information. I don't want to say too much or to take up very much time, but I do want to make the point of trying to keep our minds open as far as what archaeological material is available and what we should expect in the future, so that when someone sees the business of the mention of the doctor being needed at Ugarit, what happens when next season we dig up a doctor's residence and we have a whole archive of materials dealing with his profession. Let's keep that in mind when we make our conclusions, and I think maybe we can cut down on the percentages of what extraneous material should be culled out by later generations.

One of the major things I think we have to consider is, is Ugarit really representative of Syria? Certainly geographically Ugarit is placed in Syria itself, but can we really generalize from Ugarit to the inland areas, to the north central areas, the Aleppo Plateau, on the basis of what is found at Ugarit? I think that the tremendous influence of Egypt on Ugarit has been demonstrated amply, and also, of course, in the Hittite period, the control of the area within the Hittite empire organization. In that respect, I think the institutions and much of the cultural materials from Ugarit are obviously heavily influenced by the trade and the political situation, and I think that has to be examined in each period of Ugarit's history. We cannot at this point generalize to other areas, say to the Aleppo district, or to central Syria (the Homs district) on the basis of what we have at Ugarit. Basically, because Ugarit has the very strong coastal connections, and the trade connections along the coast have influenced not only the cultural materials, but also probably the ideas that are reflected in the texts—in the mythological texts, and other texts. This is a word of caution more than anything else with regard to what we have; it may not be thoroughly representative of what we can expect with further excavation in some of the other major sites, and excavation is continuing now in some of these major sites. Many of the excavators in the Euphrates Valley have now broken off to other parts of Syria and have taken up excavation. I think in the next decade the amount of information that we will have available to us will probably revolutionize our thinking in many respects. You can see what Ibla has done in shaking up the world as far as the third millennium is concerned. It would be sort of interesting to see every time something new like this comes up everyone shaken up again rather than taking some forethought as to what is missing and what is logically to be expected from one area. Let's not carry our theorization too far on the basis of just isolated material that is available from one site without realizing its limitations. Thank you.

DR. GORDON. Thank you, Dr. Dornemann. Now, I think we have, well, not more than ten minutes, but we do have that much time if you wish to address questions to any members of the panel.

FLOOR. We heard today three different interpretations of *Repāʾîm*, and I wonder if you'd like to fight it out.

GORDON. Ten minutes isn't enough to fight it out. Any other points?

FLOOR. This is a rather small detail, but Prof. Astour said that some of the small city-states preferred Mitannian overlordship, or *probably* preferred Mitannian overlordship to some of the other alternatives. I wonder if you could suggest any reasons for that?

ASTOUR. How could I know any reasons? What about modern states which are in the same kind of quandry? They find the preferable alternative, the lesser evil. Probably the Mitannian rule was less oppressive. Maybe they asked for less tribute, and so on. That's all I can say. I don't know the reasons and in general, a historian should not think what people thought at that time—not to put in their minds his own thoughts. You just have to register what happened, and what *they* thought—that we cannot tell. I only know that when, for instance, the kings of Halab fought against the aggression of the Hittites of Hattusilis I, immediately the Hurrians of Hanigalbat also attacked the Hittites, and for a long time they were allies. Later, they imposed on them their sovereignty, and they finally accepted it. You see, they had an Egyptian orientation, and they had Hittites—they had help—finally they accepted this one. And another thing, we note the descendants of the Mitannian governors that they established all along the great road from the Euphrates all the way to Palestine, so that even in the Amarna Age, the little kinglets of these places still had Indo-Aryan and Hurrian names. Well, that means that probably they were quite popular with their subjects. The Egyptians didn't remove them, and they stayed there. All that speaks rather about a certain benign rule. That's the impression, at least. And again, the colossal influence of the Hurrian civilization, let's say, in Alalah, and Tunip, and Qatna—colossal!—and of the Hittites—very little. In Egypt —I haven't read the entirety of my paper—but [at Ugarit], for instance, it is extraordinary: they had been for 150 years at least under Hittite domination, but not one single tablet in Hittite has been discovered. Not a Hittite-Ugaritic dictionary, but Hurrian-Ugaritic—yes. Hurrian-Sumerian-Akkadian-Ugaritic—these things we find, but Hittite—no. They were not interested in the Hittite civilization at all, but considerably more in Hurrian civilization. They had Hurrian texts written in syllabic and in alphabetic, all of them religious. They were very much interested in Hurrian rituals, but in Hittite—no, not at all. Only political or commercial links, not civilization.

GORDON. Did you want to add to that, Dr. Dornemann?

DORNEMANN. Yes, I have just been working on the materials from Hadidi, which fall basically—the tablet materials—into the Mitannian period. I have a very strong suspicion, though it is just suspicion at this point, that what we attribute as the Mitannian contribution to the Near East may not be so much Mitannian as a *local* tradition fostering a continuation of the tradition which I think you could trace back at least into Ibla and possibly earlier than that eventually. What the Mitannians have allowed, basically, is the fostering and reworking of the old traditions, continuing those, and this is really the first—with the Egyptian influence and Hurrian forces from the south, and the Hittite influences from the north and west—this is the first time the orientation is basically toward the Central Syrian area, Aleppo district, and Jezira, as opposed to influences from the other areas. So it may be that many of the things we attribute to the Mitannians are not Mitannian at all, but are a long-standing Central-Syrian tradition. I have a suspicion that we may find with more excavation that this is much more the case.

GORDON. We have time for another question or two. Yes, Baruch [Levine].

FLOOR [Levine]. On the question of comparative methods, I have always felt that the best definition of comparativism is conveyed by the story wherein one man asks another, "How is your wife?" and the answer is, "Compared to what?" It seems to me that what has happened in Ugaritic studies and in many other areas, off and on, is that we misunderstand what the comparative method is supposed to do. A person starts out with a question. The question is, "What does this word mean?" "What does this poem mean?" "When did this event happen?"

"What was this law?" "This institution?" "Where did something happen?" The comparative person is going to try to look wherever he can, to bring anything to bear that he can, in order to answer that question. But he started from a certain point. What happens, and has happened, it seems to me to a great extent, is that we are zigzagging a great deal—some of us. We start with Question A and we look around and we see that in trying to answer Question A we've gotten onto this and that and the other thing. Before we know it, we're not really answering Question A anymore; we're off on a tangent answering all other kinds of things, and then we are being circular, in other words. And some of the confusion that has come in, especially in linguistics, philology, textual studies, literary studies, religion, and so forth—these areas of comparison between Ugarit and the biblical world, for instance—I think some of the confusion comes from the fact that we don't stick with the question we started out to ask, at least at that time. We move on, and don't realize we're moving on, to ask a different question. So, "compared to what" is the key word for the problem of the labels that we have. Somebody asked me the other day whether I thought comp[arative] lit[erature] departments were any good, and I said, "Generally speaking, I don't believe in the whole business, because I can't understand any person who devotes his life to English literature who is not a comparative student of literature." If you have to be called by some special name in order to do it, you're already in trouble. I think the same thing applies to us. I don't see *how* we can possibly understand Ugaritic without Hebrew, Hebrew without Ugaritic, but one has to know what station you're starting from, and then we can stay out of trouble.

GORDON. You have to have at least two things before you can engage in any comparison and sometimes one compares without having this *or* that. So, we have to beware. Yes?

FLOOR. Sort of along this line, do you think that the time may come when we will have enough agreement among the people who study Ugaritic to know how it was vocalized and be able to do more in that area?

GORDON. Well, I think we know a great deal *now*. This doesn't mean that if one of us were transported back to ancient Ugarit, they would accept their accent as normal. But I think for our purposes, we know pretty much what we have to know. We're always going to be learning more and we're never going to know the last word. But I don't think that's one of the real problems—the pronunciation—because we're dealing with written records, and that isn't one of the stumblingblocks.

FLOOR. I just was wondering whether the character of the writing was mnemonic enough that it does not necessarily reflect, let's say, dialectial differences that may occur in the language. . . ?

GORDON. I want to call your attention to something rather curious. When a Semitic language like Hebrew or Aramaic is found spelled out in Latin or Greek letters—by the ancients—it's harder to read than it is with the consonants, *lacking* all the vowels. If you don't believe me, you can try some of these North African inscriptions written in Punic and Neo-Punic. They're *easier* to read in the familiar scripts.

Anyway, there's time for one more point. Yes, Jack [Sasson].

FLOOR [Sasson]. Mr. Chairman, I just hope that in your perspective, you might also want to say that in the past 50 years, Ugaritic studies have prospered despite the many difficulties that have been going on in the world; perhaps we might see the day when many things will happen in peace and everyone will be able to travel everywhere, see everything, and discuss many things, and just throw barbs at each other that are scholarly and nothing else. I think that will be a wonderful thing, in the future.

GORDON. *Inshaᶜallah.*

Bibliography

Abrahams, R. D., and Foss, G.

1968 *Anglo-American Folksong Cycle.* Englewood Cliffs, NJ.

Aharoni, Y.

1947 *The Settlement of the Israelite Tribes in Upper Galilee.* Jerusalem.

1967 *The Land of the Bible.* Trans. A. F. Rainey. Philadelphia.

Aistleitner, J.

1964 *Die mythologischen und kultischen Texte aus Ras-Shamra.* Budapest.

1967 *Wörterbuch der Ugaritischen Sprache.* Berlin.

Albright, W. F.

1936 New Canaanite Historical and Mythological Data. *Bulletin of the American Schools of Oriental Research* 63: 23-32.

1938 Recent Progress in North-Canaanite Research. *Bulletin of the American Schools of Oriental Research* 70: 18-24.

1940a L'hypothèse négebite des origines cananéennes. Pp. 253-56 in *Actes du XXe Congres Internationale des Orientalistes, Brussels, 1938.* Louvain.

1940b New Light on the History of Western Asia in the Second Millennium B.C., I. *Bulletin of the American Schools of Oriental Research* 77: 20-32.

1940c New Light on the History of Western Asia in the Second Millennium B.C., II. *Bulletin of the American Schools of Oriental Research* 78: 23-31.

1944 An Unrecognized Amarna Letter from Ugarit. *Bulletin of the American Schools of Oriental Research* 95: 30-33.

1953 The Traditional Home of the Syrian Daniel. *Bulletin of the American Schools of Oriental Research* 130: 26-27.

1961 The Old Testament and the Archeology of the Ancient East. Pp. 27-47 in H. H. Rowley, ed., *The Old Testament and Modern Study.* Oxford.

1965 The Role of the Canaanites in the History of Civilization. Pp. 328-62 in G. E. Wright, ed., *The Bible and the Ancient Near East.* New York.

1966 The Amarna Letters from Palestine, Syria, the Philistines, and Phoenecia. *Cambridge Ancient History*^{2}, fasc. 51 = *Cambridge Ancient History II*^{3}, 2, 98-116, 507-36.

1968 *Yahweh and the Gods of Canaan: A Historical Analysis of Two Contrasting Faiths.* London.

Albright, W. F., and Lambdin, T. O.

1954 New Material for the Egyptian Syllabic Orthography. *Journal of Semitic Studies* 2: 113-27.

Alfred, C.

1971 Egypt: The Amarna Period and the End of the Eighteenth Dynasty. *Cambridge Ancient History III*^{2}, fasc. 71 = *Cambridge Ancient History II*^{3}, 2, 49-97.

Alonso-Schökel, L.
1965 *The Inspired Word.* New York.

Alt, A.
1914 Herren und Herrensitze Palästinas im Anfang des zweiten Jahrtausends v. Chr. *Zeitschrift des deutschen Palästina-Vereins* 64: 21-39.
1926 Zür geschichte von Beth-Sean 1500-1000 v. Chr. *Palästina Jahrbuch* 22: 108-20.

Amiran, R.
1970 *Ancient Pottery of the Holy Land.* New Brunswick, NJ.

Arnaud, D.
1975 Les textes d'Emar et la chronologie de la fin du Bronze récent. *Syria* 52: 87-92.

Artzi, M., et al.
1976 Alašiya of the Amarna Letters. *Journal of Near Eastern Studies* 35: 171-82.

Astour, M. C.
1963 Place-Names from the Kingdom of Alalaḫ in the North Syrian List of Thutmose III: A Study in Historical Topography. *Journal of Near Eastern Studies* 22: 220-41, map.
1965a *Hellenosemitica.* Leiden.
1965b New Evidence on the Last Days of Ugarit. *American Journal of Archaeology* 69: 253-58.
1968 Two Ugaritic Serpent Charms. *Journal of Near Eastern Studies* 27: 13-36.
1969a Les étrangers à Ugarit et la statut juridique des Ḫabiru. *Revue d'assyriologie et d'archéologie orientale* 53: 70-76.
1969b The Partition of the Confederacy of Mukiš-Nuḫašše-Nii by Šuppiluliuma: A Study in Political Geography of the Amarna Age. *Orientalia* 38: 381-414.
1970 Maʾḫadu, the Harbor of Ugarit. *Journal of the Economic and Social History of the Orient* 13: 113-27.
1972a Ḫattušiliš, Ḫalab, and Ḫanigalbat. *Journal of Near Eastern Studies* 31: 102-9.
1972b The Merchant Class of Ugarit. Pp. 11-26 in *Gesellschaftsklassen im Alten Zweistromland und in den Angrenzenden Gebieten.* XVIII Recontre Assyriologique Internationale. Munich.
1973a A North-Mesopotamian Locale of the Krt Epic? *Ugarit-Forschungen* 5: 29-39.
1973b Ugarit and the Aegean: A Brief Summary of Archaeological and Epigraphic Evidence. Pp. 17-27 in H. Hoffner, ed., *Orient and Occident: Essays Presented to Cyrus H. Gordon* (Alter Orient und Altes Testament 22). Neukirchen-Vluyn.
1975 Place Names. Pp. 249-369 in *Ras Shamra Parallels* II. Arranged by Duane E. Smith. Rome.
1977 Tunip-Hamath and Its Region: A Contribution to the Historical Geography of Central Syria. *Orientalia* 46: 51-64.

1978 The Rabbeans: A Tribal Society on the Euphrates from Yahdun-Lim to Julius Caesar. Syro-Mesopotamian Studies 2/1: 1-12.

1980 The Netherworld and Its Denizens at Ugarit. Pp. 227-38 in B. Alster, ed., *Death in Mesopotamia*. Mesopotamia 8. Copenhagen.

Atkins, H. G.

1923 *A History of German Versification*. London.

Avishur, Y., and Blau, J., eds.

1978 *Studies in the Bible and Ancient Near East Presented to Samuel E. Loewenstamm on his Seventieth Birthday*. Jerusalem.

Barnett, R. D.

1969 ᵓAnath, Baᶜal and Pasargadae. *Mélanges de l'Université Saint-Joseph* 45: 405-22.

1978 The Earliest Representation of ᶜAnath. *Eretz-Israel* 14: 28-31.

Barton, G.

1940 Danel: A Pre-Israelite Hero of Galilee. In *Memorial Lagrange*. Paris: Ecole Biblique. = *Journal of Biblical Literature* 60: 213-25.

Bascom, W. R.

1965 Four Functions of Folklore. Pp. 279-98 in A. Dundes, *The Study of Folklore*. Englewood Cliffs, NJ.

Bass, G. E.

1967 Cape Gelidonya: A Bronze Age Shipwreck. *Transactions of the American Philosophical Society*, 57.

Bauer, J.

1969 Zum Totenkult in altsumerichen Lagash. *Zeitschrift der deutschen morgenländischen Gesellschaft*, Supplements 1:XVII. Deutscher Orientalistentag. Teil I, 107-14.

Baumgartner, W.

1940 Ras Schamra und das Alte Testament. *Theologische Rundschau* (NF) 12: 163-88.

1941 Ras Schamra und das Alte Testament, II. *Theologische Rundschau* (NF) 13: 1-20; 85-102; 157-83.

1947 Ugaritische Probleme und ihre Tragweite für das Alte Testament. *Theologische Zeitschrift* 3: 81-100.

Baumgartner, W., et al.

1967 *Hebräisches und Aramäisches Lexicon zum Alten Testament*. 3rd edition. Leiden.

Bayliss, M.

1973 The Cult of the Dead Kin in Assyria and in Babylonia. *Iraq* 35: 115-25.

Bee, R. E.

1978a The Textual Analysis of Psalm 132: A Response to Cornelius B. Houk. *Journal for the Study of the Old Testament* 6: 49-53.

1978b The Mode of Composition and Statistical Scansion. *Journal for the Study of the Old Testament* 6: 58-68.

Ben-Aryeh, Y.

1956 *The Central Jordan Valley*. Jerusalem.

Bennett, W.

1963 *German Verse in Classical Meters*. Anglica Germanica 6. The Hague.

Bordreuil, P.
1975 Nouveaux textes économiques en cunéiformes alphabétiques de Ras Shamra-Ougárit (34e campagne 1973). *Semitica* 25: 19-29.

Borger, R.
1956 *Die Inschriften Asarḫaddons König von Assyria.* Archiv für Orientforschung Beiheft 9. Graz.

Bostico, S.
1965 Museo Archeologico di Firenze: I. I stele Egiziani dall Antico al Nuovo Regno. II. Florence.

Bounni, A.; Lagarce, E. and J., and Saliby, N.
1926 Rapport préliminaire sur la première campagne de fouilles (1975) à-Ibn Hani (Syrie). *Syria* 52: 233-79.
1978 Rapport préliminaire sur la deuxième campagne de fouilles (1976) à Ibn Hani (Syrie). *Syria* 55: 233-301.

Bowra, C. M.
1962 *Primitive Song.* Cleveland.

Bryan, D. B.
1973 *Texts Relating to the Marzeaḥ: A Study of an Ancient Semitic Institution.* Dissertation. Johns Hopkins University.

Burns, T. A.
1977 Folkloristics: A Conception of Theory. *Western Folklore* 36: 109-34.

Cagni, L.
1977 *The Poem of Erra.* Sources from the Ancient Near East I/3. Malibu, CA.

Caquot, A.
Remarques sur la tablette alphabétique R.S. 24.272. Pp. 1-6 in Y. Avishur and J. Blau, eds., *Studies in the Bible and Ancient Near East. Presented to Samuel E. Loewenstamm on his Seventieth Birthday.* Jerusalem.
1975 Resumé des Cours de 1974-75. *L'Annuaire du Collège de France* 75: 426-31.
1976 La Tablette R.S. 24.252 et la question des Rephaim Ougaritiques. *Syria* 53: 295-304.
1977-78 Hébrew et Araméen. *L'Annuaire du Collège de France* 79: 465-91. ["Nouveaux textes ougaritiques de Ras Ibn Hani," pp. 481-91].

Caquot, A.; Sznycer, M., and Herdner, A.
1974 *Textes ougaritiques. Tome I: Mythes et Légendes.* Paris.

Cassuto, U.
1971 *The Goddess Anath.* Jerusalem.

Cathcart, K. J.
1973 *Nahum in the Light of Northwest Semitic.* Biblica et Orientalia 26. Rome.

Ceresko, A. R.
1976 The Chiastic Word Pattern in Hebrew. *Catholic Biblical Quarterly* 38: 303-11.
1978 The Function of Chiasmus in Hebrew Poetry. *Catholic Biblical Quarterly* 40: 1-10.

Civil, M.
1967 Šū-Sîn's Historical Inscriptions: Collection B. *Journal of Cuneiform Studies* 21: 24-38.

Clines, D. J. A.
1976 KRT 111-114 (I iii 7-10): Gatherers of Wood and Drawers of Water. *Ugarit-Forschungen* 8: 23-26.

Cohen, E. E.
1973 *Ancient Athenian Maritime Courts.* Princeton.

Cohen, H. H.
1974 *The Drunkenness of Noah.* Birmingham, AL.

Cornelius, F.
1973 *Geschichte der Hethiter, mit besonderer Berücksichtigung der geographischen Verhältnisse und der Rechtsgeschichte.* Darmstadt.

Craigie, P. C.
1971 The Poetry of Ugarit and Israel. *Tyndale Bulletin* 22: 3-31.
1973 Helel, Athtar and Phaethon. *Zeitschrift für die Alttestamentliche Wissenschaft* 85: 223-25.
1974 The Comparison of Hebrew Poetry: Psalm 104 in the Light of Egyptian and Ugaritic Poetry. *Semitics* 4: 10-21.
1977a Three Ugaritic Notes on the Song of Deborah. *Journal for the Study of the Old Testament* 2: 33-49.
1977b The Problem of Parallel Word Pairs in Ugaritic and Hebrew Poetry. *Semitics* 5: 48-58.
1978 Deborah and Anat: A Study of Poetic Imagery (Judges 5). *Zeitschrift für die Alttestamentliche Wissenschaft* 90: 374-81.
1979a Deuteronomy and Ugaritic Studies. *Tyndale Bulletin* 28: 155-69.
1979b Parallel Word Pairs in Ugaritic Poetry: A Critical Evaluation of Their Relevance for Psalm 29. *Ugarit-Forschungen* 11: 135-40.

Cross, F. M.
1973 *Canaanite Myth and Hebrew Epic: Essays in the History of the Religion of Israel.* Cambridge, MA.

Culley, R. C.
1978 Review of Douglas K. Stuart, *Studies in Early Hebrew Meter* (Harvard Semitic Monographs 13, Missoula, MT) in *Catholic Biblical Quarterly* 40: 255-56.

Cutler, B., and MacDonald, J.
1973 An Akkadian Cognate to Ugaritic BRLT. *Ugarit-Forschungen* 5: 67-70.

Dahood, M.
1962 Ugaritic Studies and the Bible. *Gregorianum* 43: 55-79.
1965 *Ugaritic-Hebrew Philology.* Rome.
1966-70 *The Psalms.* 3 vols. Anchor Bible, 16, 17, 17a. New York.
1972 Ugaritic-Hebrew Parallel Pairs. *Ras Shamra Parallels* I: 71-382. Collaboration by Tadeusz Penar.
1975 Ugaritic-Hebrew Parallel Pairs, and Ugaritic-Hebrew Parallel Pairs, Supplement. *Ras Shamra Parallels* II: 1-33, 34-39.

Danchin, P.
n.d. *An Introduction to English Metre*. Nancy.

de Contenson, H.
1970 Sondage ouvert en 1962 sur l'acropole de Ras Shamra. Rapport préliminaire sur les résultats obtenus de 1962 à 1968. *Syria* 47: 1-23.
1973 Le niveau Halafien de Ras Shamra. Rapport préliminaire sur les campagnes 1968-1972 dans le sondage préhistorique. *Syria* 50: 13-33.
1977 Le néolethique de Ras Shamra V d'après les campagnes 1972-1976 dan le sondage S.H. *Syria* 54: 1-23.

de Contenson, et al.
1972 de Contenson, H.; Lagarce, E.; Lagarce, J., and Stucky, R. Rapport préliminaire sur la XXXIIe campagne de fouilles (1971) à Ras Shamra. *Syria* 49: 1-25.
1973 de Contenson, H.; Courtois, J. C.; Lagarce, E.; Lagarce, J., and Stucky, R. La XXXIIIe campagne de fouilles à Ras Shamra en 1972, rapport préliminaire. *Syria* 50: 283-309.
1974 de Contenson, H.; Courtois, J-C.; Lagarce, E.; Lagarce, J., and Stucky, R. La XXXIVe campagne de fouilles à Ras Shamra en 1973, rapport préliminaire. *Syria* 51: 1-29.

de Langhe, R.
1945d *Les textes de Ras Shamra-Ugarit et leurs rapports avec le milieu biblique de l'Ancien Testament*. 2 vols. Gembloux/Paris.
1958 Myth, Ritual and Kingship in the Ras Shamra Texts. Pp. 122-48 in S. H. Hooke, ed. *Myth, Ritual and Kingship*. Oxford.

Deloffre, F.
1973 *Le Vers Française*. Paris.

de Moor, J. C.
1968 Murices in Ugaritic Mythology. *Orientalia* 37: 212-15.
1969 Studies in the New Alphabetic Texts from Ras Shamra I. *Ugarit-Forschungen* 1: 167-75.
1971 *The Seasonal Pattern in the Ugaritic Myth of Ba*ᶜ*lu According to the Version of Ilimilku* (Alter Orient und Altes Testament 16). Neukirchen-Vluyn.
1976 Rāpi'ūma-Rephaim. *Zeitschrift für die Alttestamentliche Wissenschaft* 88: 323-45.

de Moor, J. C., and Vander Lugt, P.
1974 The Spectre of Pan-Ugaritism. *Bibliotheca Orientalis* 31: 3-26.

Desroches-Noblecourt, Ch.
1956 Interprétation et datation d'une scène gravée sur les fragments de récipient en albâtre provenant des fouilles du palais d'Ugarit. Pp. 179-220 in Schaeffer, C. *Ugaritica III*. Mission de Ras Shamra 8.

de Vaux, R.
1937 Le cadre geographique du Poème de Krt. *Revue Biblique* 46: 262-72.
1937b Les textes de Ras Shamra et l'Ancien Testament. *Revue Biblique* 46: 526-55.
1957 Review of J. Gray, *The Krt Text in the Literature of Ras Shamra* (Leiden). *Revue Biblique* 64: 313-14.

1971 *Historie Ancienne d'Israel: des origines à l'installation en Canaan.* Paris.

Dietrich, M.; and Loretz, O.

1966 Der Vertrag zwischen Šuppiluliuma und Niqmandu: Eine Philologische und Kulturhistorische Studie. *Die Welt des Orients* 3: 206-45.

1969 Die Soziale Struktur von Alalaḫ und Ugarit (V). Die Weingärten des Gebietes von Alalaḫ in 15. Jahrhundert. *Ugarit-Forschungen* 1: 37-64.

1972a *Konkordanz der Ugaritischen Textzählungen.* Alter Orient und Altes Testament 19. Neukirchen-Vluyn.

1972b Zur Ugaritischen Lexicographie (V). *Ugarit-Forschungen* 4: 27-35.

Dietrich, M.; Loretz, O., and Sanmartín, J.

1976 *Keilalphabetische Texte aus Ugarit.* Alter Orient und Altes Testament 24. Neukirchen-Vluyn.

Dijkstra, M., and de Moor, J. C.

1975 Problematic Passages in the Legend of *Aqhâtu. Ugarit-Forschungen* 7: 171-215.

Dinçol, A. M.

1974 Über die Hydronomie und Oronomie Anatoliens zur Zeit der Hethiter. *Berytus* 23: 29-40.

Donner, H.

1967 Ugaritismen in der Psalmenforschung. *Zeitschrift für die Alttestamentliche Wissenschaft* 79: 322-50.

Dornemann, R.

1970 *The Cultural and Archaeological History of the Transjordan in the Bronze and Iron Ages.* Dissertation. University of Chicago.

1978 Tell Hadidi: A Bronze Age City on the Euphrates. *Archaeology* 31: 20-26.

1979 Tell Hadidi: A Millennium of Bronze Age City Occupation. *Annual of the American Schools of Oriental Research* 44: 113-51.

Dorson, R.

1963 Current Folklore Theories. *Current Anthropology* 4: 93-110.

Dossin, G.

1938 Les archives épistolaires du palais de Mari. *Syria* 19: 105-26.

1956 Une lettre de Iarîm-Lim, roi d'Alep, à Iašûb-Iaḫad, roi de Dî. *Syria* 33:63-69.

1970 La route de l'étain en Mésopotamie au temps de Zimri-Lim. *Revue d'assyriologie et d'archéologie orientale* 64: 97-106.

Dothan, M.

1975 Aphek on the Israel-Aram Border and Aphek on the Amorite border. *Eretz-Israel* 12: 63-65.

Dozy, R.

Supplément aux Dictionnaires Arabes 2 vols. Leiden.

Driotin, É. and Vandier, J.

1962 *Les peuples de l'Orient Mediterranéen II: L'Égypte.* 4th ed. (Clio I). Paris.

Driver, G. R.

1956 *Canaanite Myths and Legends*. Edinburgh.

1965a Review of M. Dahood, *Proverbs and Northwest Semitic Philology* (Rome, 1963). *Journal of Semitic Studies* 10: 112-17.

1965b Ugaritic Problems. Pp. 95-110 in *Studia Semitica . . . Ioanni Bakoš Dicata*. Bratislava.

Drower, M. S.

1968 Ugarit. *Cambridge Ancient History*, fasc. 63 (*Cambridge Ancient History* II^3, 2, 130-60).

1970 Syria c. 1550-1400 B.C. *Cambridge Ancient History*, fasc. 55 = *Cambridge Ancient History* II^3, 1: 417-525.

Drower, M. S. and Bottero, J.

1968 Syria Before 2200 B.C. *Cambridge Ancient History*, fasc. 55 = *Cambridge Ancient History* II^3, 2: 315-62.

du Mesnil du Buisson, R.

1935 *Le site archaeologique des Mishrifé-Qaṭna*. Paris.

Dundes, Alan

1965 *The Study of Folklore*. Englewood Cliffs, NJ.

Dussaud, R.

1927 *Topographie historique de la Syrie antique et mediévale*. Bibliothèque Archéologique et Historique 4. Paris.

1933 Les Phéniciens au Negeb et en Arabie d'après un texte de Ras Shamra. *Revue de l'histoire des religions* 108: 5-49.

1935 Deux stèles de Ras Shamra portant une dédicace au dieu Dagon. *Syria* 16: 177-80.

1937 *Les découvertes de Ras Shamra (Ugarit) et l'Ancien Testament*. Paris. (Revised, 1941).

Ebach, J.

1977 Unterweltsbeschwörung in Alten Testament. *Ugarit-Forschungen* 9: 57-70.

Edel, E.

1953 Die Stelen Amenophis II aus Karnak und Memphis mit Bericht den asiatischen Feldzüge des Königs. *Zeitschrift des Deutschen Palästina-Vereins* 69: 97-176.

1966 *Die Ortsnamenlisten aus dem Totentempel Amenophis III*. Bonn.

1979 Zwei Ägyptische Ortsbezeichungen. *Orientalia* 48: 82-90.

Edwards, I. E. S., et al.

1970-75 Edwards, I. E. S.; Gadd, C. J., and Hammond,N. G. L., eds. *The Cambridge Ancient History*. 2 vols. in 4 parts. Cambridge.

Eissfeldt, O.

1969a Neue Belege für nabatäische Kultgenossenschaften. *Mitteilungen des Instituts für Orient-forschungen* 15: 217-27.

1969b Kultvereine in Ugarit. Pp. 187-95 in *Ugaritica* IV.

Eliade, M.

1965 *Myth and Reality*. New York.

Elwert, W. T.

1965 *Traité de versification française*. Paris. (Trans. from *Französische Metrik*, Ismening-Munich, 1967.)

Emerton, J. A.
1972 A Difficult Part of Mot's Message to Baal in the Ugaritic Texts. *Australian Journal of Biblical Archaeology* 2/1: 50-71.
1978 A Further Note on CTA 5 I 4-6. *Ugarit-Forschungen* 10: 73-77.
Epstein, C.
1974 The Dolmens in the Golan. *Qadmoniot* 7: 37-40 (Hebrew).
Ertem, H.
1973 Boğazköy *Metinlerinde Geçen Cografya Adlari Dizini.* Ankara. (A List of Geographical Names in the Boğazköy Texts.)
Finet, A.
1964 Iawi-Ilâ, roi de Talḫayûm. *Syria* 41: 117-42.
Finkelstein, J. J.
1966 The Genealogy of the Hammurapi Dynasty. *Journal of Cuneiform Studies* 20: 95-118.
Finley, T. J.
1979 *Word Order in the Clause Structure of Syrian Akkadian.* Dissertation. University of California at Los Angeles.
Finnegan, R.
1977 *Oral Poetry: Its Nature, Significance, and Social Context.* Cambridge.
Fischer, J. L.
1963 The Sociopsychological Analysis of Folktales. *Current Anthropology* 4: 235-92.
Fisher, L., et al.
1972 Fisher, L. R., Knutson, F. B., and Morgan, D. F., eds. *Ras Shamra Parallels: The Texts from Ugarit and the Hebrew Bible,* Vol. I (Analecta Orientalia 49). Rome.
1975 Fisher, L. R.; Smith, D. E., and Rummel, S., eds. *Ras Shamra Parallels: The Texts from Ugarit and the Hebrew Bible,* Vol. II (Analecta Orientalia 50). Rome.
Fisher, L. R., and Knudson, F. B.
1969 An Enthronement Ritual at Ugarit. *Journal of Near Eastern Studies* 28: 157-67.
Forrer, E.
1929 *Forschungen* I, 2. Berlin.
Freedman, D. N.
1972 Acrostics and Metrics in Hebrew Poetry. *Harvard Theological Review* 65: 367-92.
1974 Strophe and Meter in Exodus 15. Pp. 163-203 in H. N. Bream; R. D. Heim, and C. A. Moores, eds., *A Light Unto My Path: Old Testament Studies in Honor of Jacob M. Myers.* Philadelphia.
1977 Pottery, Poetry, and Prophecy: An Essay on Biblical Poetry. *Journal of Biblical Literature* 96: 5-26.
Friedrich, J.
1949 Kanaanäisch und Westsemitisch. *Scientia* 84: 220-23.
Frost, H.
1957 The Stone Anchors of Ugarit. *Ugaritica* 4: 235-45.
Frye, N.
1957 *Anatomy of Criticism.* Princeton.

Gardiner, A. H.
1947 *Ancient Egyptian Onomastica.* Oxford.
1961 *Egypt of the Pharaohs: An Introduction.* Oxford.

Garelli, P.
1969 Le Proche-Orient asiatique: Des origines aux invasions des Peuples de la Mer. Paris.

Gaster, T. H.
1938 A Phoenician Naval Gazette. *Palestine Exploration Fund, Quarterly Statement* 70: 105-12.
1961 *Thespis: Ritual, Myth, and Drama in the Ancient Near East.* Rev. ed. Garden City, NY.

Gese, H.; Höfner, M., and Rudolf, K.
1970 *Die Religionen Altsyriens, Altarabiens und die Mandäer.* Stuttgart.

Gibson, J. C. L.
1975 Myth, Legend, and Folk-lore in the Ugaritic Keret and Aqhat Texts. *Congress Volume, Edinburgh, 1974* = Vetus Testamentum Supplements 28: 60-68.
1978 Note on the Phonology of Ugaritic. I. P. 140 in J. C. L. Gibson, ed., *Canaanite Myths and Legends.* Edinburgh. Originally ed. by G. R. Driver.

Ginsberg, H. L.
1935 Notes on 'The Birth of the Gracious and Beautiful Gods.' *Journal of the Royal Asiatic Society* 1935: 45-72.
1941 Did Anath Fight the Dragon? *Bulletin of the American Schools of Oriental Reserach* 84: 12-14.
1955 Ugaritic Myths, Epics and Legends. In J. B. Pritchard, ed., *Ancient Near Eastern Texts Relating to the Old Testament.* 2nd rev. ed. Princeton.

Ginzberg, L.
1909 *The Legends of the Jews.* 7 vols. Philadelphia.

Gitay, Y.
1978 *Rhetorical Analysis of Isaiah 40-48: A Study of the Art of Persuasion.* Dissertation. Emory University.

Giveon, R.
1964 Toponymes Ouest-Asiatiques à Soleb. *Vetus Testamentum* 14: 240-55.
1967 Royal Seals of the XIIth Dynasty. *Revue d'Égyptologie* 19: 29-37.
1978 Two Unique Egyptian Inscriptions from Tel Aphek. *Tel Aviv* 5: 188-91. (Reprinted in Kochavi, 1978c, 30-33.)
1979 Remarks on Some Egyptian Toponym Lists Concerning Canaan. Pp. 135-41 in M. Görg and E. Pusch, eds., *Festschrift Elmar Edel.*

Goetze, A.
1941 Is Ugaritic a Canaanite Dialect? *Language* 17: 127-38.
1957 *Kleinasien* (Handbuch der Altertumswissenschaft, 3 Abt., 1 Teil, 3. Band, 3. Abschnitt, 1. Unterabschnitt), 2nd ed. Munich.
1956 The Struggle for the Domination of Syria (1400-1300 B.C.); Anatolia from Shuppiluliumash to the Egyptian War of Muwatallis; The

Hittites and Syria (1300-1200 B.C.). *Cambridge Ancient History*, fasc. 37 = *Cambridge Ancient History II*[3], 2: 1-20, 117-29, 252-73.

Gonda, J.

1968 *Stylistic Repetition in the Veda*. Amsterdam.

Gonnet, H.

1968 Les montagnes d'Asie Mineure d'après les textes Hittites. *Revue hittite et asianique* 26: 95-171.

Good, E. M.

1978a Review of D. K. Stuart, *Early Hebrew Meter* (Missoula, MT, 1976), in *Journal of Biblical Literature* 97: 273-74.

1978b Review of W. R. Watters, *Formula Criticism and the Poetry of the Old Testament* (Beihefte zur Zeitschrift für die Alttestamentliche Wissenschaft 138, Berlin, 1976) in *Journal of Biblical Literature* 97: 274-75.

Gordon, C. H.

1958 Abraham and the Merchants of Ura. *Journal of Near Eastern Studies* 17: 28-31.

1965 *Ugaritic Textbook*. Analecta Orientalia 38. Rome.

1966 *Ugarit and Minoan Crete*. New York.

1977 Poetic Legends and Myths from Ugarit. *Berytus* 25: 5-133.

Görg, M.

1974a *Untersuchungen zur Hieroglyphischen Wiedergabe Palästinischer Ortsnamen*.

1974b Die Gattung des Sogenannten Tempelweihespruchs (I Kgs 8,12f.). *Ugarit-Forschungen* 6: 55-63.

Gray, G. B.

1972 *The Forms of Hebrew Poetry*. New York (Reprint of the 1915 edition).

Gray, J.

1957 *The Legacy of Canaan*. Vetus Testamentum Supplements 5. Leiden. (Second edition, 1965).

Grayson, A. K.

1972-76 *Assyrian Royal Inscriptions*. 2 vols. Wiesbaden.

Gröndahl, F.

1967 *Die Personennamen der Texte aus Ugarit*. Studia Pohl 1. Rome.

Gurney, O. R.

1966 Anatolia *c.* 1600-1380 B.C. *Cambridge Ancient History*, fasc. 44 = *Cambridge Ancient History II*[3], 1: 659-83.

Güterbock, H. G.

1956 The Deeds of Suppiluliuma as Told by His Son, Mursili II. *Journal of Cuneiform Studies* 10: 41-68, 75-98, 107-30.

1967 The Hittite Conquest of Cyprus Reconsidered. *Journal of Near Eastern Studies* 26: 73-81.

1970 The Predecessors of Šuppiluliuma Again. *Journal of Near Eastern Studies* 29: 73-77.

Hall, V., Jr.

1963 *A Short History of Literary Criticism*. New York.

Hallo, W. W.

1980 A Letter Fragment from Tel Aphek. *Tel Aviv* 7. In press.

Halporn, J. W., Ostwald, M., and Rosenmeyer, T. G.

1963 *The Meters of Greek and Latin Poetry*. London.

Hava, J. G.

1970 *Al-Farāᶜid al-Duriyyah Arabī-Inklīzī*. Beirut. (First published 1899.)

Healey, J. F.

1978 Ritual Text KTU 1.161—Translation and Notes. *Ugarit-Forschungen* 10: 83-88.

1979a Ups and Downs in El's Amours. *Ugarit-Forschungen* 11: 701-8.

1979b The *Pietas* of an Ideal Son in Ugarit. *Ugarit-Forschungen* 11: 353-56.

Helck, W.

1955 *Urkunden der 18. Dynastie*. Berlin.

1960 Die Ägyptische Verwaltung in den Syrischen Besitzungen. *Mitteilungen der Deutschen·Orient-Gesellschaft* 92: 1-13.

1962 *Beziehungen Ägyptens zu Vorderasien im Dritte und Zweite Jahrtausend v. Chr.* Wiesbaden. (2nd ed., rev., in 1971.)

1969 Überlegungen zur Geschichte der 18. Dynastie. *Oriens Antiquus* 8: 281-327.

1971 Second edition, revised, of (1962).

1976 Ägyptische Statuen im Ausland. *Ugaritica* 8: 101-15.

Held, M.

1973 Pits and Pitfalls in Akkadian and Biblical Hebrew. *Journal of the Ancient Near Eastern Society* 5: 173-90.

Heltzer, M.

1977 The Metal Trade of Ugarit and the Problem of Transportation of Commercial Goods. *Iraq* 39: 203-11.

1978a *Goods, Prices and the Organization of Trade in Ugarit*. Wiesbaden.

1978b The *Rabbᵓum* in Mari and the RPI(M) in Ugarit. *Orientalia Lovaniensia Periodica* 9: 1-20.

Hennrichs, A.

1970 Pagan Ritual and the Alleged Crimes of the Early Christians. Pp. 18-35 in P. Greenfield and J. A. Jungemann, eds. *Kyriakon: Festschrift J. Quasten*, I (Münster).

Herdner, A.

1946 Review of R. de Langhe, *Les textes de Ras Shamra-Ugarit et leurs rapports avec le milieu Biblique de l'Ancien Testament* (Paris, 1945) in *Syria* 25: 131-38.

1963 *Corpus des tablettes Cunéiforms alphabétiques découvertes à Ras Shamra-Ugarit de 1929 à 1939*. 2 vols. Paris.

Hillers, D. H., and McCall, M. H.

1976 Homeric Dictated Texts: A Reexamination of Some Near Eastern Evidence. *Harvard Studies in Classical Philology* 80: 19-23.

Hirsch, H.

1963 Die Inschriften der Könige von Agade. *Archiv für Orientforschung* 20: 1-82.

Holmes, Y. L.
1975 The Messengers of the Amarna Letters. *Journal of the American Oriental Society* 95: 376-81.
Hooke, S. H.
1958 *Myth, Ritual and Kingship*. Oxford.
Horowitz, W. J.
1972 *Graphemic Representation of Word Boundary: The Small Vertical Wedge in Ugaritic*. Ann Arbor, MI.
1979 Our Ugaritic Mythological Texts: Copied or Dictated? *Ugarit-Forschungen* 9: 123-30.
1979 The Significance of the Rephaim. *Journal of the Northwest Semitic Languages* 7: 37-43.
Houwink ten Cate, P. H. J.
1973 Anatolian Evidence for Relations with the West in the Late Bronze Age. Pp. 141-55 in R. A. Crossland and A. Birchall, eds., *Bronze Age Migrations in the Aegean: Archaeological and Linguistic Problems in Greek Prehistory*. London.
Hrouda, B.
1957 *Die Bemalte Keramik des Zweiten Jahrtausends in Nordmesopotamien und Nordsyrien*. Berlin.
1962 *Tel Halaf*, vol. 4. Berlin.
Hunger, H.
1968 *Babylonische und Assyrische Kolophone*. Alter Orient und Altes Testament 2. Neukirchen-Vluyn.
Jack, J. W.
1935 *The Ras Shamra Tablets. Their Bearing on the Old Testament*. Edinburgh.
Jackson, J. A., and Kessler, M., eds.
1974 *Rhetorical Criticism: Essays in Honor of James Muilenberg*. Pittsburgh.
Jacob, E.
1969 *Ras Shamra et l'Ancien Testament*. Neuchâtel.
Jacobs, V., and Jacobs, I. R.
1945 The Myth of Mot and ʾAlʾeyan Baʿal. *Harvard Theological Review* 38: 77-109.
James, W. F.
1966 *The Iron Age at Beth Shan*. Philadelphia.
Jason, H., and Segal, D.
1979 *Patterns in Oral Literature*. Chicago.
Jean, C.-F.
1939a *Biḫrum* dans les lettres de Mari. *Revue d'assyriologie et d'archéologie orientale* 36: 112.
1939b Excerpta de la correspondence de Mari, II. *Répertoire d'épigraphie sémitique* 1939: 62-69.
Jirku, A.
1933 Kanaʿanäische Psalmenfragmente in der Vorisraelitischen Zeit Palästinas un Syriens. *Journal of Biblical Literature* 52: 108-20.

Kapelrud, A. S.
1965 *The Ras Shamra Discoveries and the Old Testament.* Oxford.
Kelley-Buccellati, M., and Shelby, W. R.
1977 *Terqa Preliminary Reports, No. 4: A Typology of Ceramic Vessels of Third and Second Millennia from the First Two Seasons.* Syro-Mesopotamian Studies 1/6. Malibu, CA.
Kirby, W. F., trans.
1907 *Kalevala, The Land of the Heroes.* London.
Kirk, G. S.
1970 *Myth, Its Meaning and Functions in Ancient and Other Cultures.* Berkeley/Los Angeles.
Kitchen, K. A.
1962 *Suppiluliuma and the Amarna Pharaohs: A Study in Relative Chronology.* Liverpool.
1966 Suppiluliuma. Pp. 251-82 in *I Protagonisti della Storia Universale,* no. 66. Milan.
1969 Interrelations of Egypt and Syria. Pp. 77-95 in M. Liverani, ed. *La Siria nel Tardo Bronzo.* Orienis Antiqui Collectio 9. Rome.
1977 The King List of Ugarit. *Ugarit-Forschungen* 9:131-42.
1979 Ramesside Inscriptions, Historical and Biographical, II, 4. Oxford.
Klengel, H.
1963 Der Schiedsspruch des Muršili II. Hinsichtlich Barqa und seine Übeneinkunft mit Duppi Tešup von Amurru (KBo III 3). *Orientalia* 32: 32-55.
1965-70 *Geschichte Syriens im 2. Jahrtausend v. u.Z.* 3 vols. Berlin.
1975 Condizioni ed Effetti del Commercio Siriano nell'Età del Bronzo. *Studi Micenei ed Egeo-Anatolici* 16, 201-20.
Kluckholn, C.
1942 Myths and Rituals: A General Theory. *Harvard Theological Review* 35: 45-79.
Knudtzon, Jörgen Alexander
1907-15 *Die El-Amarna Tafeln.* 2 vols. Aalen.
Kochavi, M.
1975 The First Two Seasons of Excavations at Aphek-Antipatras. *Tel Aviv* 2: 17-42. (Reprinted in Kochavi and Beck, 1976).
1967-69 *Judaea, Samaria, and the Golan: Archaeological Survey 1967-68.*
1977 Aphek-Antipatris, Five Seasons of Excavations at Tel Aphek-Antipatris (1972-76). Tel Aviv.
1978a Canaanite Aphek, Its Acropolis and Inscriptions. *Expedition* 20: 12-17.
1978b The Archaeological Context of the Aphek Inscriptions. Pp. 1-7 in Kochavi (1978c).
1978c *Aphek-Antipatris 1974-77: The Inscriptions.* Reprint Series, No. 2. Tel Aviv.
Kochavi, M., and Beck, P.
1976 *Aphek-Antipatras 1972-73, Preliminary Report.* Reprint Series Number 1. Tel Aviv.

Kochavi, M. *et al.*
1972 *Judea, Samaria, and the Golan: Archaeological Survey 1967-68.* Jerusalem.
Kosmala, H.
1964 Mot and the Vine: The Time of the Ugaritic Fertility Rite. *Annual of the Swedish Theological Institute* 3: 147-51.
Kuentz, C.
1928 *La Bataille de Qadesh.* Cairo.
Kühne, C.
1973 *Die Chronologie der Internationalen Korrespondenz von El-Amarna.* Alter Orient und Altes Testament 17. Kevelaer/Neukirchen-Vluyn.
Kühne, C., and Otten, H.
1971 *Šaušgamuwa-Vertrag.* Studien zu den Bogazköy-Texten 16. Wiesbaden.
Kühne, H.
1978 West German Archaeologists Hit the Jackpot at Tell Sheikh Hamad, Syria. *Jordan Times,* June 11-12, 4.
Kuhnigk, W.
1974 *Nordwestsemitische Studien zum Hoseabuch.* Biblica et Orientalia 27. Rome.
Kurylowicz, J.
1972 *Studies in Semitic Grammar and Metrics.* Warsaw.
Laessøe, Jørgen
1959 A Statue of Shalmaneser III from Nimrud. *Iraq* 21: 147-57, pls. XL-XLII.
Lambdin, T.
1953 The *mi-ši* People of the Byblian Amarna Letters. *Journal of Cuneiform Studies* 7: 75-77.
Lambert, W. G.
1968 Another Look at Hammurabi's Ancestors. *Journal of Cuneiform Studies* 22: 1-2.
1980 The Theology of Death. Pp. 53-66 in B. Alster, ed., *Death in Mesopotamia.* Mesopotamia 8. Copenhagen.
Lane, E. W.
1968 *An Arabic-English Lexicon.* 8 vols. Madd-al-Qamus. 1st ed. 1863-93.
Laroche, E.
1966 *Les Nomades Hittites.* Paris.
Lehmann, W. P.
1956 *The Development of Germanic Verse Form.* Austin, TX.
Levine, B.
1974 *In the Presence of the Lord.* Studies in Judaism in Late Antiquity. Leiden.
L'Heureux, C.
1974 The Ugaritic and Biblical Rephaim. *Harvard Theological Review* 67: 265-74.
1976 The *y*^{e}*lîdê hārāpā*: A Cultic Association of Warriors. *Bulletin of the American Schools of Oriental Research* 221: 83-85.

1979 *Rank Among the Canaanite Gods: El, Ba^c al, and the Repha^{\supset} im.* Harvard Semitic Monographs 21. Cambridge.

Linder, E.

1970 *The Maritime Texts of Ugarit: A Study in Late Bronze Age Shipping.* Dissertation. Brandeis University.

1972 A Seafaring Merchant Smith from Ugarit, and the Cape Gelidonya Wreck. *International Journal of Nautical Archaeology and Underwater Exploration* 1: 163-64.

1973 Naval Warfare in the El-amarna Age. Pp. 163-73 in D. J. Blackman, ed., *Marine Archaeology: Proceedings of the 23rd Symposium of the Colston Research Society, University of Bristol, April 4-8, 1971.*

Lipinsky, E.

1978 Ditanee. Pp. 91-100 in Y. Avishur and J. Blau, eds., *Studies on the Bible and the Ancient Near East Presented to Samuel E. Loewenstamm.*

1977 An Ugarit Letter to Amenophis III Concerning Trade with Alašiya. *Iraq* 39: 213-17.

Liverani, M.

1962 *Storia di Ugarit nell'età degli archivi politici.* Studi Semitici 6. Rome.

1974 The *kumānu* Measure as 1/4 of 1 *ikū*. Assur 1/1, 11.

Loewenstamm, S. E.

1969 Eine Lehrhafte Ugaritische Trinkburleske. *Ugarit-Forschungen* 1: 71-77.

1975 Ugarit and the Bible, I. *Biblica* 56: 103-19.

Løkkegaard, F.

1953 A Plea for El, the Bull, and the Other Ugaritic Miscellanies. Pp. 219-23 in *Studia Orientalia Ioanni Pedersen Dicata.* Copenhagen.

Lord, A. B.

1965 *The Singer of Tales.* New York.

Lüthi, M.

1976 Aspects of the Märchen and the Legend. Pp. 14-33 in D. Ben-Amos, ed., *Folklore Genres.* Austin, TX.

McKnight, E. V.

1978 *Meaning in Texts. The Historical Shaping of a Narrative Hermeneutic.* Philadelphia.

Malamat, A.

1968 King Lists of the Old Babylonian Period and Biblical Genealogies. *Journal of the American Oriental Society* 88: 168-73.

Mallowan, M. E. L.

1939 White-Painted Subartu Pottery. Pp. 887-94 in *Mélanges Syriens offerts à Monsieur René Dussaud,* II. Paris.

1947 Excavations at Brak and Chagar-Bazar. *Iraq* 9: 1-259.

Margalit, B.

1975 Studia Ugaritica I: Introduction to Ugaritic Prosody. *Ugarit-Forschungen* 7: 289-313.

1976 Studia Ugaritica II: Studies in KRT and AQHT. *Ugarit-Forschungen* 8: 137-92.

1980 *A Matter of Life and Death*. Alter Orient und Altes Testament 206. Neukirchen-Vluyn.

Margolis, B.

1972 The Kôšārôt/Kṯrt: Patroness-Saints of Women. *Journal of the Ancient Near Eastern Society* 4: 52-61.

Margueron, J.

1975 Quatre compagnes de fouilles à Emar (1972-74): un bilan provisoire. *Syria* 52: 53-85.

1977 Ras Shamra 1975 et 1976: Rapport préliminarie sur les campagnes d'automne. *Syria* 54: 151-88.

Margulis, B.

1970a A Ugaritic Psalm (RS 24.252). *Journal of Biblical Literature* 89: 292-304.

1970b A New Ugaritic Farce (RS 24.258). *Ugarit-Forschungen* 2: 131-38.

Martinez, E. R.

1967 *Hebrew-Ugaritic Index to the Writings of Mitchell J. Dahood*. Rome.

Matthiae, P.

1970 Mission archéologique de l'Université de Rome à Tell Mardikh. *Annales Archéologiques Arabes Syriennes* 20: 55-71.

1977 *Ebla: Un impero ritrovato*. Turin.

Mazar, B.

1946 Canaan and the Canaanites. *Bulletin of the American Schools of Oriental Research* 102: 7-12.

Milik, J. T.

1972 *Dédicaces failes par des dieux (Palmyre, Hatra, Tyr) et des thiases sémitiques à l'époque romaine*. Recherches d'epigraphie proche-Orientale 1. Paris.

Moortgat, A.

1957 Archäologische Forschungen der Max Freiherr von Oppenheim-Stiftung im Nördlichen Mesopotamien 1955. *Veröffentlichungen der Arbeitsgemeinschaft für Forschung des Landes Nordrein-Westfalen* 62: 1-24.

Muhly, J. D.

1977 The Copper Ox-Hide Ingots and the Bronze Age Metals Trade. *Iraq* 39: 73-82.

Muilenberg, J.

1969 Form Criticism and Beyond. *Journal of Biblical Literature* 82: 1-18.

Munn-Rankin, J. M.

1967 Assyrian Military Power 1300-1200 B.C. *Cambridge Ancient History*, fasc. 49 = *Cambridge Ancient History* II^3, 2: 274-306.

Newberry, P. E.

1907 *The Timins Collection*. London.

Newman, L. I., and Popper, W.

1918 *Studies in Biblical Parallelism*. Semitic Philology, Vol. I. Berkeley.

Nilsson, M. P.

1940 *Greek Popular Religion*. New York.

Noth, M.
1948 *Überlieferunggeschichte des Pentateuch.*
1960 *The History of Israel.* 2nd English ed. New York.

Nougayrol, J.
1955 *Le palais royal d'Ugarit,* 3: *Textes Accadiens des Archives Sud.* Mission de Ras Shamra 6. Paris.
1956 *Le palais royal d'Ugarit,* 4: *Textes Accadiens des Archives Sud.* Mission de Ras Shamra 9. Paris.
1968 *Ugaritica* 5: *Textes Suméro-Accadiens des Archives et Bibliothèques Privées d'Ugarit.* Mission de Ras Shamra 16. Paris.
1970 *Le palais royal d'Ugarit,* 6: *Textes Accadiens des Achives Sud.* Mission de Ras Shamra 6. Paris.

Oded, B.
1971 Darb el-Hawarneh: An Ancient Route. *Eretz-Israel* 10: 191-92 (Hebrew).

Oldenburg, U.
1969 *The Conflict Between El and Baᶜal in Canaanite Religion.* Leiden.

Oppenheim, A. L.
1954 The Seafaring Merchants of Ur. *Journal of the American Oriental Society* 74: 6-17.

Otten, H.
1968 *Die Hethitischen Historischen Quellen und die Altorientalische Chronologie.* Mainz/Wiesbaden.
1969 Die Berg- und Flusslisten im Ḫišuwa-Festritual. *Zeitschrift für Assyriologie* 59: 247-60.
1976 Zum Ende des Hithiterreiches Aufgrund der Boğazköy-Texte. Pp. 27-29 in *Jahresbericht des Instituts für Vorgeschichte der Universität Frankfurt A.M.* Munich.

Owen, D. I.
1980 An Akkadian Letter from Ugarit at Tel Aphek. *Tel Aviv* 7, in press.

Pardee, D. G.
1976 The Preposition in Ugaritic. *Ugarit-Forschungen* 8: 214-322.
1977 Review of *Ras Shamra Parallels I* in *Journal of Near Eastern Studies* 36: 65-68.

Parker, S. B.
1970 The Feast of *Rāpiʾu. Ugarit-Forschungen* 2: 243-49.
1972 The Ugaritic Deity *Rāpiu. Ugarit-Forschungen* 4: 97-104.

Parrot, A.
1940 Les fouilles de Mari, sixième campagne (automne 1938). *Syria* 21: 1-28.

Patton, J. H.
1944 *Canaanite Parallels in the Book of Psalms.* Baltimore.

Perdu, O.
1977 Khenemet-Nefer-Hedjet. *Revue d'Égyptologie* 29: 68-95.

Pettinato, Giovanni
1976 The Royal Archives of Tell Mardikh-Ebla. *Biblical Archeologist* 39: 44-52.

1977a Relations entre les royaumes d'Ebla et de Mari au troisième millénaire, d'après les archives royales de Tell Mardikh-Ebla. *Akkadica* 2: 20-28.

1977b Gli archivi relai di Tell Mardikh-Ebla. *Rivista Biblica* 25: 225-43.

1978 L'Atlante Geogratico del Vicino Oriente Antico attestato ad Ella ead Abū Ṣalābīkh (I). *Orientalia* 47: 50-73.

1980 *Testi Amministrativi della Biblioteca L 2679, Parte I.* Materiali Epigrafici di Ebla 2. Naples. Universitario Orientali di Napoli, Seminario di Studi Asiatici, Series Maior II.

Pfeiffer, C. F.

1962 *Ras Shamra and the Bible.* Grand Rapids, MI.

Pitard, W. T.

1978 The Ugaritic Funerary Text RS 34.126. *Bulletin of the American Schools of Oriental Research* 232: 65-75.

Poebel, A.

1914 *Historical Texts.* Publications of the Babylonian Sec. IV, no. 1. Philadelphia.

Pope, M. H.

1955 *El in the Ugaritic Texts.* Vetus Testamentum Supplements 2. Leiden.

1964 The word *šaḥa̱t* in Job 9:31. *Journal of Biblical Literature* 83: 269-78.

1966a Review of John Gray, *The Legacy of Canaan. Journal of Semitic Studies* 11: 228-41.

1966b Review of R. Gordis, *The Book of God and Man. Journal of Biblical Literature* 85: 526-29.

1972 A Divine Banquet at Ugarit. Pp. 170-203 in J. M. Efird, ed. *The Use of the Old Testament in the New and Other Essays: Studies in Honor of William Franklin Stinespring.* Durham, NC.

1977a *Song of Songs.* Anchor Bible 7C. Garden City, NY.

1977b Notes on the Rephaim Texts from Ugarit. Pp. 164-82 in M. de J. Ellis, ed. *Essays on the Ancient Near East in Memory of Jacob Joel Finkelstein.* Memoirs of the Connecticut Academy of Arts and Sciences 14. New Haven.

1978 A Little Soul-Searching. *Maarav* 1: 25-31.

1979 Ups and Downs in El's Amours. *Ugarit-Forschungen* 11: 701-8.

Pope, M. H., and Tigay, J. H.

1971 A Description of Baal. *Ugarit-Forschungen* 3: 117-30.

Porten, B.

1968 *The Archives from Elphantine.* Berkeley and Los Angeles.

Porter, B., and Moss, R. L. B.

1962 *Topographical Bibliography of Ancient Egyptian Hieroglyphic Texts, Reliefs and Painting,* vol. 7. Oxford.

Press, Y.

1955 *A Topographical-Historical Encyclopedia of Palestine.* Vol. 4. (Hebrew).

Quicherat, L.

1850 *Traité de Versification Française.* Paris.

Rabin, C.
1967 Og. *Eretz-Israel* 8: 251-54. (Hebrew).

Rainey, A. F.
1963 A Canaanite at Ugarit. *Israel Exploration Journal* 13: 43-45.
1967 *A Social Structure of Ugarit.* Jerusalem.
1971 A Front Line Report from Amurru. *Ugarit-Forschungen* 3: 131-49.
1974 The Ugaritic Texts in Ugaritica 5. *Journal of the American Oriental Society* 94: 184-94.
1975 Two Cuneiform Fragments from Tel Aphek. *Tel Aviv* 2: 125-29. (Reprinted in Kochavi, 1978c, 8-12).
1976 A Tri-lingual Cuneiform Fragment from Tel Aphek. *Tel Aviv* 3: 137-40. (Reprinted in Kochavi, 1978c, 13-16.)

Richardson, M. E. J.
1978 Ugaritic Place Names with Final *-Y*. *Journal of Semitic Studies* 23: 298-315.

Richter, W.
1971 *Exegese als Literaturwissenschaft.* Göttingen.

Riis, P. J.
1960 L'Activité de la mission archéologique danoise sur la côte phénicienne en 1959. *Annales Archéologiques Arabes Syrienne* 10: 111-32.

Rosenthal, F.
1939 Die Parallelstellen in den Texten von Ugarit. *Orientalia* 8: 213-37.

Rüger, H. P.
1969 Zu RS 24.258. *Ugarit-Forschungen* 1: 203-6.

Saarisalo, A.
1927 *The Boundary Between Issachar and Naphtali: An Archaeological and Literary Study of Israel's Settlement in Canaan.* Helsinki.

Sasson, J. M.
1966 Canaanite Maritime Involvement in the Second Millennium B.C. *Journal of the American Oriental Society* 86: 126-38.
1979 *Ruth: A New Translation, with a Philological Commentary and a Formalist-Folklorist Interpretation.* Baltimore.

Schaeffer, C. F.-A.
1931 Les fouilles de Minet-el-Beida et de Ras Shamra, deuxième campagne (Printemps 1930). *Syria* 12: 1-14.
1935 Les fouilles de Ras Shamra-Ugarit, septième campagne (Printemps 1934) rapport sommaire. *Syria* 16: 141-76.
1936 Les fouilles de Ras Shamra-Ugarit septième campagne (Printemps 1935) rapport sommaire. *Syria* 17: 105-49.
1939 *Ugaritica I: Études relatives aux découvertes de Ras Shamra. Première série.* Mission de Ras Shamra 2. Paris.
1948 *Stratigraphie comparée et chronologie de l'Asie Occidental.* London.
1949 *Ugaritica II.* Mission de Ras Shamra 3. Paris.
1956 *Ugaritica III.* Mission de Ras Shamra 8. Paris.
1959 *The Cuneiform Texts of Ras Shamra-Ugarit.* Paris.
1962 *Ugaritica IV.* Mission de Ras Shamra 9. Paris.

1970 Recherches archéologiques nouvelles à Ras Shamra-Ugarit: Découverte d'un troisième palais: Rapport préliminaire des fouilles 1968-1969 (XXXe et XXXIe campagnes). *Syria* 47: 209-13.

1972 Note additionelle sur les fouilles dans le Palais Nord d'Ugarit. *Syria* 49: 27-33.

Scholes, R.

1974 *Structuralism in Literature*. New Haven.

Schoors, A.

1972 Literary Phrases. Pp. 1-71 in *Ras Shamra Parallels* I.

Segert, S.

1958 Die Schreibfehler in den Ugaritischen Literarischen Keilschrifttexten. Pp. 193-212 in *Von Ugarit Nach Qumran* (Eissfeldt Festschrift). Berlin.

1959 Die Schreibfehler in den Ugaritischen Nicht-Literarischen Keilschrifttexten. *Zeitschrift für die Alttestamentliche Wissenschaft* 71: 23-32.

Simons, J.

1937 *Handbook for the Study of Egyptian Topographical Lists Relating to Western Asia*. Leiden.

Singer, I.

1977 A Hittite Hieroglyphic Seal Impression from Tel Aphek. *Tel Aviv* 4: 178-90. (Reprinted in Kochavi, 1978c, 17-29.)

Smith, S.

1940 *Alalakh and Chronology*. London.

1949 *The Statue of Idrimi*. Occasional Publications of the British Institute of Archaeology in Ankara, No. 1. London.

Starcky, J.

1969 Une inscription Phénicienne de Byblos. *Mélanges de l'université Saint-Joseph* 45: 260-73.

Starr, R. F. S.

1937-39 *Nuzi: Report on the Excavations at Yorgan Tepe: 1927-1931*. 2 vols. Cambridge.

Stuart, D. K.

1976 *Studies in Early Hebrew Meter*. Harvard Semitic Monographs 13. Missoula, MT.

Sukenik, E. L.

1940 Arrangements for the Cult of the Dead in Ugarit and Samaria. Pp. 59-65 in *Memorial Lagrange*. Paris.

Tadmor, H.

1979 The Decline of Empires in Western Asia ca. 1200 B.C.E. Pp. 1-14 in Frank Moore Cross, ed. *Symposia Celebrating the Seventy-fifth Anniversary of the American Schools of Oriental Research (1900-1975)*. Cambridge, MA.

Thureau-Dangin, F.

1907 *Die Sumerischen und Akkadischen Königsinschriften*. Vorderasiatische Bibliothek I, 1. Leipzig.

1934 Un comptoir de laine pourpre à Ugarit, d'après une tablette de Ras-Shamra. *Syria* 15: 137-46.

1935 Une lettre assyrienne à Ras-Shamra. *Syria* 16: 188-93.

Toueir, K.
1975 Découverte d'une tombe Myceniènne à Ras ibn Hani prè d'Ugarit-Ras Shamra. *Archéologia* 88: 67-70.

Toynbee, J. M. C.
1971 *Death and Burial in the Roman World.* London.

Tromp, N.
1969 *Primitive Conceptions of Death and the Netherworld.* Biblica et Orientalia 21. Rome.

Tsumura, D. T.
1974 A Ugaritic God, *MT-W-ŠR,* and His Two Weapons (*Ugaritic Textbook* 52: 8-11). *Ugarit-Forschungen* 6: 407-13.

Turner, V.
1975 *Revelation and Divination in Ndembu Ritual.* Ithaca and London.

Ullendorff, E.
1962 Ugaritic Marginalia, II. *Journal of Semitic Studies* 8: 339-51.

Vallogia, M.
1976 *Recherche sur les "Messagers" (WPWTYW) dans les Sources Egyptiennes Profanes.* Geneva.

Van Selms
1954 *Marriage and Family Life in Ugaritic Literature.* London.
1970 Yammu's Dethronement by Baal: An Attempt to Reconstruct Texts UT 129, 137 and 68. *Ugarit-Forschungen* 2: 251-68.

Van Zijl, P. J.
1972 *Baal: A Study of Texts in Connexion with Baal in the Ugaritic Epic.* Alter Orient und Altes Testament 10. Neukirchen-Vluyn.

Vattioni, F.
1969 I Sigilli Ebraici. *Bibilica* 50: 375-88.

Ventris, M., and Chadwick, J.
1959 *Documents in Mycenaean Greek.* Cambridge.

Virolleaud, C.
1933 La naissance des dieux gracieux et beaux: Poème phénicien de Ras Shamra. *Syria* 14: 128-51.
1936 *La Légende de Keret, Roi des Sidoniens.* Mission de Ras Shamra 2. Paris.
1954 Les nouveaux textes alphabétiques de Ras-Shamra (XVIIe campagne 1953). *Comptes rendus de l'Académie des inscriptions et belles-lettres* 1954: 255-59.
1957 *Le Palais royal d'Ugarit,* 2. Mission de Ras Shamra 7. Paris.
1968 Le dieu *Rpu,* roi du monde, et son entourage. Pp. 551-57 in Nougayrol, *et al. Ugaritica* 5.

Ward, W. A.
1961 Egypt and the East Mediterranean in the Early Second Millennium B.C. *Orientalia* 30: 22-45, 129-55.

Watson, W. G. E.
1976a The Pivot Pattern in Hebrew, Ugaritic and Akkadian Poetry. *Zeitschrift für die Alttestamentliche Wissenschaft* 88: 239-53.

1976b Ugarit and the OT: Further Parallels. *Orientalia* 45: 434-42.

1977a The Falcon Episode in the Aqhat Tale. *Journal of Northwest Semitic Languages* 5: 69-75.

1977b The Research Team "Ugarit-Forschung." *Newsletter for Ugaritic Studies* 13: 10.

Watters, W. R.

1976 *Formula Criticism and the Poetry of the Old Testament.* Beihefte zur Zeitschrift für die Alttestamentliche Wissenschaft 138. Berlin.

Weidner, E. F.

1923 *Politische Dokumente aus Kleinasien: Die Staatsverträge in Akkadischer Sprache aus dem Archiv von Boghazköi.* Boghazköi Studien 8-9. Leipzig.

1932-33 Der Vertrag Asarhaddons mit Ba^{c}al von Tyrus. *Archiv für Orientforschung* 8: 29-34.

1959 *Die Inschriften Tukulti-Ninurtas I. und Seiner Nachfolger.* Archiv für Orientforschung Beiheft 12. Graz.

Weippert, M.

1975 Über den Asiatischen Hintergrund der Göttin '^{c}Asiti.'" *Orientalia* 44: 12-21.

Welch, J. W.

1974 Chiasmus in Ugaritic. *Ugarit-Forschungen* 6: 421-34.

Wekkel, R., and Warren, A.

1942 *Theory of Literature.* New York.

Wilson, J. A.

1941 The Egyptian Middle Kingdom at Megiddo. *American Journal of Semitic Languages and Literature* 58: 225-31.

Woolley, L.

1953 *A Forgotten Kingdom: Being a Record of the Results Obtained from the Excavations of Two Mounds Atchana and Al Mina, in the Turkish Hatay.* Baltimore.

1955 *Alalakh.* Oxford.

Worden, T.

1953 The Literary Influence of the Fertility Myth in the Old Testament. *Vetus Testamentum* 3: 273-97.

Xella, P.

1978 *Problemi del Mito nel Vicino Orient Antico.* Rome.

Yamashita, T.

1975 Professions. In *Ras Shamra Parallels,* II, 41-68.

Yaron, R.

1969 Foreign Merchants at Ugarit. *Israel Law Review* 4: 70-79.

al-Yasin, I.

1952 *The Lexical Relation between Ugaritic and Arabic.* Shelton Semitic Series I. Ringwood Borough, NJ.

Yeivin, S.

1966 Review of Helck (1962) in *Bibliotheca Orientalis* 23: 18-27.

1967 Amenophis II's Asianic Campaigns. *Journal of the American Research Center in Egypt* 6: 119-28.

Young, D. W.
1977 With Snakes and Dates: A Sacred Marriage Drama at Ugarit. *Ugarit-Forschungen* 9: 291-314.

Young, G.
1928 *An English Prosody on Inductive Lines.* Cambridge.

Young, G. D.
1950 Ugaritic Prosody. *Journal of Near Eastern Studies* 9: 124-33.

Zaccagini, C.
1973 *Lo Scambio dei doni nel Vicino Oriente durante i secoli XV-XIII.* Rome.

Zlotnick, D.
1966 *The Tractate "Mourning."* Yale Judaica Series, 18. New Haven.

INDEXES

GENERAL INDEX

GEOGRAPHICAL NAMES INDEX

ANCIENT PERSONAL NAMES INDEX

UGARITIC WORDS AND PHRASES INDEX

Words and phrases are alphabetized as in Gordon, *Ugaritic Textbook*; the varied methods of transliterating the three *aleph*'s used by the different authors are preserved.

UGARITIC TEXTS CITED

SCRIPTURE INDEX

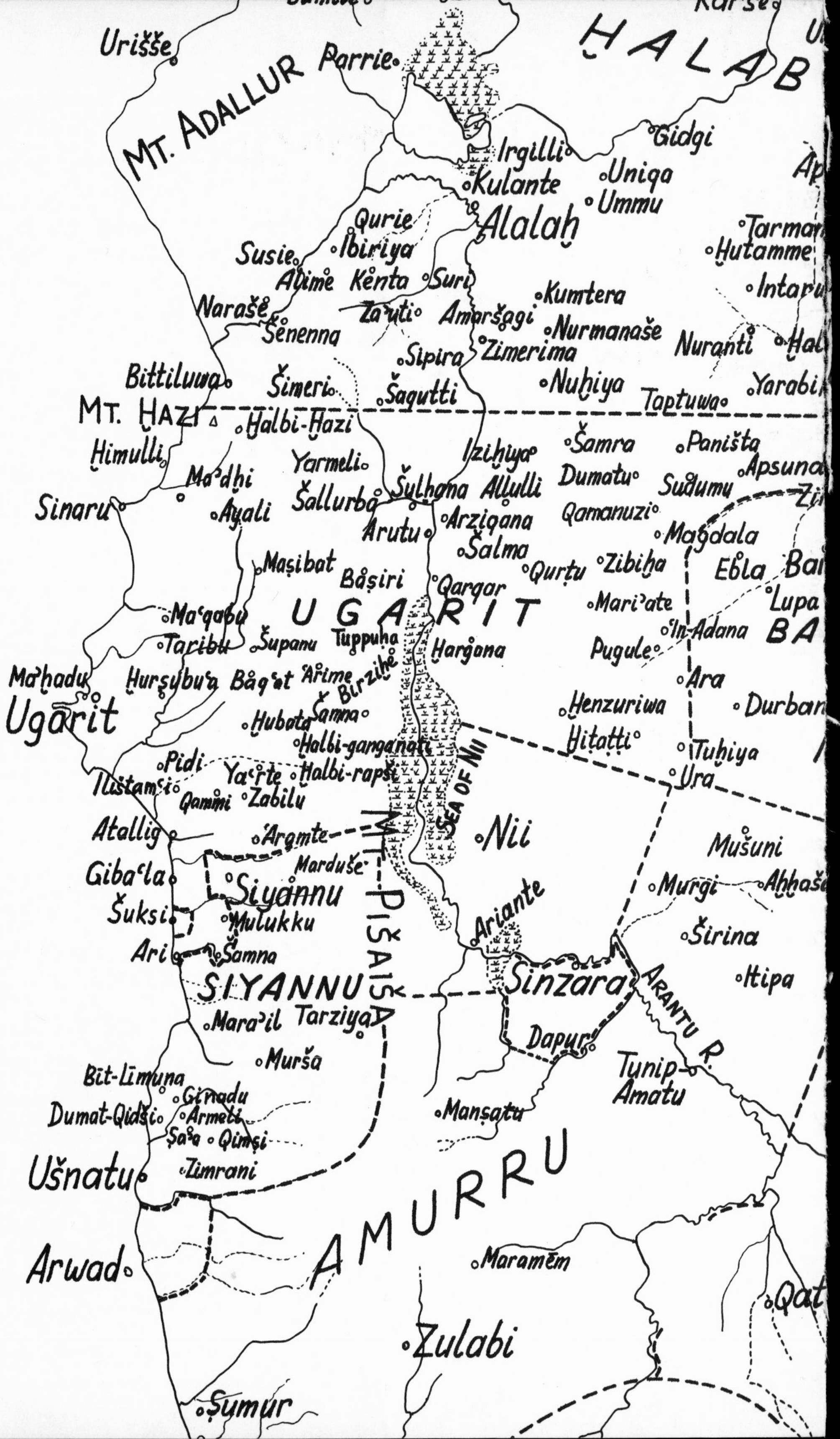

Urišše
HALAB
Mt. Adallur
Parrie
Gidgi
Irgilli
Kulante
Uniqa
Ummu
Alalaḫ
Qurie
Ibiriya
Susie
Alime
Kenta
Suri
Hutamme
Kumtera
Naraše
Za'uti
Amaršagi
Nurmanaše
Šenenna
Zimerima
Nuranti
Sipira
Bittiluwa
Šimeri
Šaqutti
Nuḫiya
Taptuwa
Yarabi
Mt. Ḫazi
Halbi-Ḫazi
Ḫimulli
Yarmeli
Iziḫiya
Šamra
Paništa
Apsuna
Ma'dḫi
Šallurba
Šulḫana
Allulli
Dumatu
Sudumu
Sinaru
Ayali
Arzigana
Qamanuzi
Arutu
Magdala
Šalma
Maṣibat
Qurṭu
Zibiḫa
Ebla
Bâṣiri
Qarqar
UGARIT
Mari'ate
Lupa
Ma'qabu
In-Adana
Taribu
Šupanu
Tuppuḫa
Hargana
Pugule
Ma'ḫadu
Ḫurṣubu'a
Bâq'at
Arime
Birziḫe
Ara
Ugarit
Henzuriwa
Durban
Šamna
Hubata
Halbi-gangan̈ati
Ḫitatti
Tuḫiya
Pidi
Ya'rte
Halbi-rapši
Ura
Ilištamʾi
Qammi
Zabilu
SEA OF NII
Atallig
'Aramte
Nii
Mušuni
Gibaʿla
Marduše
Siyannu
Murgi
Aḫḫaše
Šuksi
Mulukku
Ariante
Šamna
Širina
Ari
SIYANNU
Mt. Pišaiša
Sinzara
Itipa
Arantu R.
Mara'il
Tarziya
Dapur
Murša
Tunip-Amatu
Bit-Līmuna
Ginadu
Dumat-Qidši
Armeli
Mansatu
Ṣa'a
Qimṣi
Ušnatu
Zimrani
AMURRU
Arwad
Maramēm
Zulabi
Ṣumur